Total World Sport

Publisher and Creative Director: Nick Wells
Project Editor: Cat Emslie
Picture Research: Gemma Walters, Rosanna Singler
Art Director: Mike Spender
Layout Design: Vanessa Green
Digital Design and Production: Chris Herbert
Copy Editor: Sonya Newland
Proofreader: Dawn Laker
Indexer: Sue Farr

Special thanks to: James Pinniger, Ian Cruise and everyone at Hayters;
Chelsea Edwards, Sarah Sherman, Sophie Bray and Julie Pallot.

For author and contributor credits see page 524.

07 09 11 10 08
1 3 5 7 9 10 8 6 4 2

This edition first published in 2007 by
FLAME TREE PUBLISHING
Crabtree Hall, Crabtree Lane
Fulham, London, SW6 6TY
United Kingdom
www.flametreepublishing.com

Flame Tree Publishing is part of
The Foundry Creative Media Co. Ltd.

Picture Credits

Topham Picturepoint: 5 (tcl, tcr, bcl, br), 6, 7 (tr, tcr, bl, bcr, br), 10–13, 14 (l), 15, 17–67, 71– 75, 127, 155, 161–71, 181, 187,
191–95, 203, 207, 227, 231, 237–41, 245–47, 251–65, 271–73, 277, 281–83, 287–93, 296 (r), 299–305, 311–25, 329–39,
343–45, 357–59, 368–81, 385–421, 427–33, 437, 443, 447–51, 455–65, 469, 473, 477, 481–85, 489, 493, 497–99, 501–05,
509–17, 521–23.

Corbis: 4 (cr), 107–09, 117, 121, 133, 209, 217–19, 235, 307, 475, 479, 487

Empics: 1–2, 4 (l, cl), 5 (tl, tr, bl, bcr), 7 (tr, bcl), 8, 69, 77–105, 111–115, 119, 123–25, 129, 135–53, 157–59, 173–79, 183–85,
189, 197–99, 201, 205, 211–215, 221–25, 229, 233, 243, 249, 267–69, 275, 279, 285, 295, 296 (l), 297, 309, 327, 333, 341,
347–55, 361—67, 383, 423–25, 435, 439, 445, 453, 467, 471, 491, 507, 519

Getty Images: 4 (r), 7 (cr), 131, 495

Jung-Hwang, Ahn 70
Juventus 50

K
Kaiser's Cup (sailing) 510
Kansas City Chiefs *112*
Khorkina, Svetlana 364
Kipketer, Wilson 348
Klaasen, Jelle 294
Klammer, Franz 488
Kono, Tommy 478
Korbut, Olga 356
Korea (football) 70
Kratochvilova, Jarmila 332
Kukoc, Toni *158*

L
Laker, Jim 166
Langer, Bernhard 220
Lara, Brian 186
Lauda, Niki 392
Lautenschlager, Christian 372
Laver, Rod 238
Le Mans disaster (1955) 378
LeMond, Greg 436
Leonard, Sugar Ray 464
Levassor, Émile 370
Levegh, Pierre 378
Lewis, Carl 334
Lexcen, Ben *516*
Lipton, Thomas 508
Liston, Sonny 452
Liverpool 50, 54, 74
Lomu, Jonah 94
Long, Michael 132
Louganis, Greg 504
Louis, Joe 446
Louis, Spyridon 298
Lowe, John 288

M
MacArthur, Ellen 522

Manchester United 30, 38, 64
Mandela, Nelson *102*
Mansell, Nigel 396
Maradona, Diego 52
Marciano, Rocky 450
Marino, Dan 118
Matthews, Stanley 28
McEnroe, John 244
McNeill, Billy *36*
Meninga, Mal 92
Mennea, Pietro 326
Miami Dolphins *110*
'Mille Miglia' (motor racing) 376
Miller, Johnny 208
Mize, Larry 216
Moitessier, Bernard 514
Montgomerie, Colin *230*
Morris, Tom 194
Moss, Stirling 376
motor racing
    19th century 370
    1910s 372
    1930s 374
    1950s 376–83
    1960s 382–83, 386–91
    1970s 386–93
    1980s 394–97
    1990s 396–405
    2000s 400–407
motorcycle racing 384–85
Munich air disaster (1958) 30

N
Namath, Joe 114
Nash, Bob 'Nasty' 106
Navratilova, Martina 252
Nelson, Byron 196
Nemov, Aleksei 362
Never Say Die (racehorse) 414
New York Giants *108*

New York Jets 114
New Zealand (All Blacks, rugby union) 76, 88, 90, 94, 102
Nicholls, 'Gwyn' 76
Nicklaus, Jack 204
Noah, Yannick 246
Norman, Greg 222
Nurmi, Paavo 302
Nuvolari, Tazio 374

O
Olympic Games (athletics)
    1896 298
    1910s 300
    1920s 302
    1930s 304
    1940s 308
    1960s 314–17
    1970s 324
    1980s 328, 334
    1990s 338–41, 346, 362
    2000s 352–55
Olympic Games (basketball) 150
Olympic Games (diving) 504
Olympic Games (gymnastics) 356–59
Olympic Games (hockey) 232
Olympic Games (swimming) 502
Olympic Games (weightlifting) 478
Olympic Games (wrestling) 476
O'Sullivan, Ronnie 280
Ovett, Steve 328
Owen, Michael *68*
Owens, Jesse 304

P
Palmer, Arnold 200

Pasarell, Charlie 240
Patterson, Floyd 452
Pearce, Stuart 60
Pelé 40
Peters, Jim 310
Pienaar, Francois *102*
Piggott, Lester 414, 428
Pinza (racehorse) 412
Platini, Michel 48
Player, Gary 202
Ponting, Ricky 188
Pro-Bowl (American football) 108
Prost, Alain 394
Puskás, Ferenc 22

R
Reardon, Ray 266
Red Rum (racehorse) 420
Reed, Willis 148
Retton, Mary Lou 360
Rice, Jerry 124
Richards, Gordon 412
Risman, Augustus John 'Gus' 80
Robinson, Sugar Ray 448
Rollo, David *84*
Ronaldo 62
Rossi, Paolo 46
Rudolph, Wilma 316
rugby league 80, 82, 92, 100
rugby union
    1900s 76
    1920s 78
    1960s 84–87
    1970s 88–91
    1990s 94–99, 102–5
Rugers College football team *106*
Russia (basketball) 150
Russia (football) 32
Russia (ice hockey) 486
    see also USSR

Ruth, George 'Babe' 138, 140
Ryder Cup (golf) 206, 218, 230

S
sailing 508–23
Sampras, Pete 254
Sanchez-Vicario, Arantxa 250
Sandow, Eugen 474
Schmeling, Max 446
Schumacher, Michael 404
Schwarzenegger, Arnold 480
Scotland (rugby union) 84
Scotland (sailing) 508
Seles, Monica 258
Senna, Ayrton 398
Shergar (racehorse) 426
Simpson, O.J. 116
Simpson, Tom 434
skating see figure skating
skiing 488–89
    see also cross-country skiing
Slater, Andrew 282
Sloan, James Forman 'Tod' 408
Snead, Sam 226
Snell, Peter 318
snooker
    1920s 264
    1970s 266
    1980s 268–75
    1990s 276–81
    2000s 282–85
Sobers, Garfield 170
South Africa (Springboks, rugby union) 86, 102
Southgate, Gareth 60
Spillane, Pat 134
Spitz, Mark 502
St Helens 82

Stepney, Alex 38
Stewart, Jackie 386, 388
streakers 282
Super Bowl (American football) 112, 114
Surtees, John 384
swimming 500–503, 506–7

T
Taylor, Dennis 274
Taylor, Phil 290
Tendulkar, Sachin 182
tennis
    1960s 238–41
    1970s 242
    1980s 244–51
    1990s 252–59
    2000s 260–63
Test matches (cricket) 164, 168, 178
    see also Ashes
Test matches (rugby league) 100
Thompson, Daley 330
Thorburn, Cliff 272
Thorpe, Ian 506
Thorpe, Jim 300
Torvill, Jane (Torvill and Dean) 492
le Tour de France (cycling) 434–39
Tretiak, Vladislav 490
Tri-Nations Tournaments (rugby league) 100
Triple Crown (horse racing) 422
Turpin, Randolph 448
Tweddle, Beth 366
'24 Hours of Le Mans' (motor racing) 378
Tyrell, Ken 386
Tyson, Mike 468, 472

U
Uruguay (football) 20
US Masters (golf) 216, 220–25, 228
US Open (golf) 198, 206, 208–13
US Open (tennis) 254, 260
USA (football) 18
    see also American football
USA (hockey) 234
USA (ice hockey) 490
USA (sailing) 516, 518
USSR (ice hockey) 490

V
van Barneveld, Raymond 292
Van Vollenhoven, Tom 82
Viktor, Ivo 40
Villeneuve, Jacques 402

W
Waddle, Chris 60
Wade, Virginia 242
Wakefield, Wavell 78
Walcott, Jersey Joe 450
Wales (rugby union) 76
Walsh, Courtney 184
Walter, Fritz 26
Warne, Shane 192
Watson, Michael 470
Watson, Tom 212
weightlifting 478–79
Wembley Stadium 16
West Germany (football) 26, 34, 58
West Germany (hockey) 232
West Ham United 16
West Indies (cricket) 184, 186
White, Jimmy 270

Willard, Jess 442
Williams, Venus and Serena 262
Wimbledon (tennis) 240–45, 248, 252, 260
Winter Olympics 484, 488–97
Woods, Tiger 224, 228
World Championships (athletics) 330, 332, 344
World Championships (darts) 292, 294
World Championships (ice hockey) 486
World Championships (snooker) 264, 272–75, 280–83
World Cup (football)
    1950s 18, 20, 26
    1960s 34, 40
    1980s 46
    1990s 56, 60, 66
    2000s 66, 68, 70
World Cup (rugby union) 96, 102, 104
World League of American Football (WLAF) 122
World Matchplay Championships (darts) 288
World Series (baseball) 140
wrestling 476–77

Y
Yashin, Lev 32

Z
Zaharias, Mildred 'Babe' 306
Zidane, Zinedine 66

Total World Sport

Mark Ryan, James Pinniger, Chris Hatherall, Tony Stevens, Andrew Sleight,
Toby Skinner, Sam Peters, Ben Hunt, Neil Martin, Simon Vincent, Alan Wilson,
Nick Callow, Marc Isaacs, Clive Hetherington, Jonathan McKeith

Foreword: Sir Trevor Brooking

**FLAME TREE
PUBLISHING**

Contents

How To Use This Book 8

Foreword 10

Introduction 12

Rugby and Football..**14**

Football 16

Rugby 76

American Football...106

Australian Rules Football 126

Gaelic Football 134

Ball Games and Target Sports **136**

Baseball 138

Basketball 146

Cricket 160

Golf 194

Hockey 232

Tennis 238

Snooker 264

Darts 286

Athletics and Gymnastics **296**

Athletics 298

Gymnastics 356

Racing and Speed Sports **368**

Motor Racing 370

Horse Racing 408

Cycling..434

Boxing and Strength Sports..**440**

Boxing 442

Other Strength Sports..474

Winter Sports **482**

Swimming and Sailing **498**

Swimming 500

Sailing 508

Authors and Contributors 524

Index 525

How To Use This Book

You are encouraged to use this book in a variety of ways, each of which caters for a range of interests, knowledge and uses.

- The book is organized by the main types of sport, and within those sections it is broken down into specific sports, each entry in chronological order.
- The entries relate to the best (and worst) or most memorable moments and figures throughout popular sporting history.
- The thematic and chronological format provides the reader with a fascinating journey through time and space, to savour the triumphs of your favourite sports and discover amazing achievements in others you know less well.
- The comprehensive index enables the reader to find specific names quickly and easily.

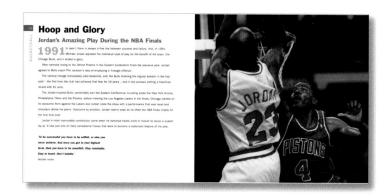

Hoop and Glory

Jordan's Amazing Play During the NBA Finals

1991 In sport, there is always a fine line between success and failure. And, in 1991, Michael Jordan adjusted his individual style of play for the benefit of his team, the Chicago Bulls, and it ended in glory.

After narrowly losing to the Detroit Pistons in the Eastern Conference finals the previous year, Jordan agreed to Bulls coach Phil Jackson's idea of employing a 'triangle offence'.

The tactical change immediately paid dividends, with the Bulls finishing the regular season in the top spot – the first time the club had achieved that feat for 16 years – and in the process setting a franchise record with 61 wins.

The Jordan-inspired Bulls comfortably won the Eastern Conference, brushing aside the New York Knicks, Philadelphia 76ers and the Pistons, before meeting the Los Angeles Lakers in the finals. Chicago carried on its awesome form against the Lakers and Jordan stole the show with a performance that was head and shoulders above his peers. Overcome by emotion, Jordan openly wept as he lifted the NBA finals trophy for the first time ever.

Jordan's most memorable contribution came when he switched hands while in mid-air to score a superb lay-up. It was just one of many sensational moves that were to become a trademark feature of his play.

'To be successful you have to be selfish, or else you never achieve. And once you get to your highest level, then you have to be unselfish. Stay reachable. Stay in touch. Don't isolate.'

Michael Jordan

1. Entry title

2. Subtitle gives extra information about the subject of the entry.

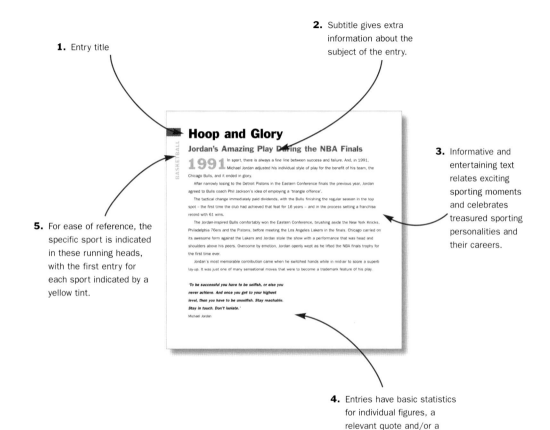

3. Informative and entertaining text relates exciting sporting moments and celebrates treasured sporting personalities and their careers.

5. For ease of reference, the specific sport is indicated in these running heads, with the first entry for each sport indicated by a yellow tint.

4. Entries have basic statistics for individual figures, a relevant quote and/or a caption where the picture merits further explanation.

Foreword

'Sport' is defined in the dictionary as 'an athletic activity requiring skill or physical prowess, often of a competitive nature'. However, it is much, much more than that, whichever discipline one chooses to take part in or watch. Indeed, snooker and darts, for example, may not require the 'physical prowess' of other sports but few will deny the skill needed, and competitive sporting fervour inspired, when they are played at the top of their game.

Passion is probably the key factor in what makes sport so special. Crowds cannot help but get caught up in the excitement whenever top athletes display that deep-rooted will to win. The battle between individuals or teams at the peak of their talent captures the imagination of the public like nothing else.

Those contests also inspire all who view them. Generations of youngsters have grown up dreaming of emulating the heroes and heroines they have seen, either in the flesh or on their television screens, and that is as true today as it has always been.

This book aspires to capture the essence of the drama that is often as compelling as any theatre production, and in many cases more so. How many times have sports commentators stated that the action unfolding in front of them could simply not have been scripted? And many times this is completely correct – and true at one time or another for all of the sports covered in this comprehensive book.

The fervour is not just confined to popular games such as football, rugby and cricket, which dominate the television airwaves. For example, sailing is a sport which, although extremely popular, is rarely seen on mainstream TV. However, when Dame Ellen MacArthur was chasing the record for circumnavigating the globe single-handedly,

people who had never even been in a sailing boat were gripped by her quest as news bulletins updated her progress on an hourly basis.

Similarly, when the Jamaican Olympic team entered the bobsleigh event at the Winter Games in 1988, millions tuned in to watch a sport they may previously have known nothing about. That wonderful tale of battling against the odds also highlighted another key factor in why people love sport so much: it is not always about winning. Glorious failure is often much more absorbing then straightforward success, while the most riveting stories of all are the so-called 'David versus Goliath' battles when the underdog comes out on top.

But even putting aside the winners and losers, sport can also be described as art. Who could fail to be moved by the grace and beauty of gymnasts like Nadia Comaneci and Olga Korbut? Or the agility of those who compete on the ice, such as Torvill and Dean?

Overall, though, perhaps the most important aspect of sport is the way it can unite people from totally different cultures and countries. This is most succinctly summed up in the famous Olympic spirit that urges 'mutual understanding with a spirit of friendship, solidarity and fair play'.

Whatever the reason, the stories are endless, so the task of selecting which performances and events made it into this book must have been a tricky one. Enjoy!

Sir Trevor Brooking, former West Ham and England player (47 caps) and Chairman of Sport England (1999–2002).

Introduction

There is a rather cruel saying in journalistic circles that those who can't play end up writing and talking about sport instead. But hopefully by reading this book you'll come to realize that everyone is talking about it these days – and it is twice as interesting when you know a lot more about it!

In fact, what makes sport such a integral part of our lives is not only the enjoyment and excitement it provides during the heat of battle but also the way it continues to weave its magic long after. So, even in these days of high-tech computer games, 3D graphics and robots that all but tie your shoelaces for you, nothing grips the nation like a sporting debate.

Where would football be without the pundits who pore over every dramatic goal, every controversial decision and every transfer for instance? And what about the boxing aficionados who talk long into the night about whether Muhammad Ali really was the greatest? Or the tennis fans who want to know whether Roger Federer's Wimbledon victory matches the great finals of Borg and McEnroe?

There can't be many sporting addicts who haven't sat in a group at some stage of their lives and discussed their all-time highlights. And we have done exactly the same in putting this book together.

Some of the most memorable pieces of sporting action ever are here for you to enjoy – from Babe Ruth's home run against the Chicago Cubs in the 1932 World Series to Red Rum's Grand National hat-trick in 1977.

You will notice that I chose the word 'some' rather than 'all' to describe our listings and that was deliberate, because sport remains such a subjective affair. There may well be readers who believe passionately that some of the events listed here do not deserve their place on these pages – and that other, greater achievements have been erroneously left out. But that's okay, because if we all agreed on which players and which teams inspired us most then pubs and living rooms across the world would be deathly quiet on a Saturday afternoon!

It is also worth explaining that we have not set out to produce an exhaustive history of any one sport, but rather to sum up the greatest players, events, stories and controversies across a whole spectrum of disciplines. England's 1966 World Cup triumph is included, of course, but so is Franz Klammer's thrilling Winter Olympic victory over Bernhard Russi in the 1976 downhill ski final.

Not all of the entries are events, either. You will find detailed and informed profiles of sportsmen and women, and also some of the most memorable news stories they inspired, ranging from scandals to tragedies. It would be difficult to sum up what football meant to the world, for instance, without mentioning the Munich Air Crash or referring to the terrible events of Hillsborough and Heysel.

But it's not all doom and gloom, because history has also provided us with some amazing moments when the power of sport has overcome huge odds – and intense political pressure – to provide fairytale endings. No one in what was once Czechoslovakia, for example, will ever forget the way their ice-hockey team scored two memorable victories over Russia in the World Championships of 1969, sparking riotous scenes in Prague.

And Jesse Owens' sprint double at the 1936 Olympics in Germany, at the height of the Nazi regime, still ranks as possibly the most inspiring and courageous achievement in athletics history.

You may not agree, of course. Perhaps you prefer the achievements of basketball's Magic Johnson, the goals of Pelé, the flamboyancy of George Best, the perfect score of Nadia Comaneci. It's all in here, ready for you to explore, ready for you to enjoy. Just dip in and be inspired to talk about sport – it's what conversation should be all about!

FOOTBALL & RUGBY

Football and rugby are two of the most popular team sports around the world. The modern game of football was established in England in the late nineteenth century, but the ancient Chinese are said to have played a similar game called Cuju, or 'playing a ball with the foot', roughly 1,800 years earlier. There is also evidence to show that ball games in Egypt, involving large numbers of people, were linked to religious ceremonies.

Records indicate that these games were sometimes used to till the soil in local villages. Many believe that rugby was born in 1823 when William Webb Ellis first took the ball in his arms and ran with it, thus originating the distinctive feature of the game. Whatever the true origins of the two games, they are now watched and played by millions of people each week. Variations of the two games are played around the world, most notably in America, where American Football, or gridiron as it is often referred to, reigns supreme. Its influence can also be seen in its aggressive cousins, Aussie rules and Gaelic football.

The White Horse Final

Wembley's First Double-Act

1923 Had the horse been any other colour, he probably would not have passed into FA Cup legend. But Billie was white – or 'grey' in equine parlance – and the effect was historic.

Perhaps it was the striking beauty of the mighty animal that caused the crowds to part and obey; or maybe it was the no-nonsense way that the policeman riding him, George Scorey, went about his business. What is certain is that Billie and Scorey made a formidable team at the FA Cup final of 1923, the first at the new national stadium in Wembley; so formidable, in fact, that the sight of horse and rider clearing thousands of fans from the pitch is remembered far more vividly than the final itself, between West Ham and Bolton Wanderers.

An estimated 200,000 supporters had crammed into the 127,000-capacity Wembley, and so it was inevitable that they would spill out on to the turf sooner or later. For a while the situation seemed out of control, and might even have led to a postponement, had it not been for Billie the horse. With a winning blend of majesty and menace, Wembley's first double-act cleared the pitch in less than an hour, and the crisis was over.

The match went ahead only 45 minutes late, and Bolton beat the Hammers 2-0. But it was Billie's final – The White Horse Final – and a footbridge would be named after the hero of 1923 when the stadium finally reopened in 2007.

Opposite: Mounted police, including George Scorey on the legendary white horse, ride in to part the overflowing crowd so that the 1923 FA Cup Final can commence.

The 'Miracle on Grass'

England Humiliated by the United States

1950 In what became known as the 'Miracle on Grass', England suffered one of the greatest footballing shocks of all time at the World Cup in Brazil. They were among the favourites to win, while the USA were 500-1 outsiders, having lost their last seven matches. England had just beaten Chile without Stanley Matthews, and left him on the bench that fateful day. But they still had the great Tom Finney, Stanley Mortensen, Billy Wright and Alf Ramsey. The result should have been a formality.

However, England were not adapting well to conditions in Brazil, and seemed unnerved by the crowd in Belo Horizonte's compact Estádio Independência. Although only 10,000 watched the match, they reacted wildly to what they saw in a way that British players were completely unused to back home.

And there was plenty for the Brazilians to shout about, especially when Joe Gaetjens deflected Walter Bahr's effort past England's goalkeeper Bert Williams, who was on his hands and knees when the ball crossed the line in the 37th minute.

English attempts rained down on the American goalkeeper Frank Borghi's goal, as the giants of the game tried to avert defeat. Somehow American luck held, thanks to a mixture of stunning saves and shots hitting the woodwork or flying just wide. The USA won 1-0, and – partly because of this upset – England failed to qualify for the knockout stage.

'At the time, I didn't realize how big a victory it really was...We weren't that familiar with the World Cup. As the years went by, the significance of that victory has become more important.'

American Half-Back Walter Bahr on America's remarkable victory.

The 'Maracanazo'

Uruguay Beat Brazil to Win the Cup

1950 The decisive match in that 1950 World Cup became known as the 'Maracanazo' – or 'Maracana blow'. Rather than a final, it was a round-robin match that Brazil needed to draw and Uruguay had to win in order to lift the trophy. Rio de Janeiro's monumental stadium, the Maracana, was packed with 100,854 screaming Brazilians, and it was a match the home nation simply had to win, with coins already made in the team's honour and a triumphant song ready to be released on record.

But Uruguay was ready too. Their captain, Obdulio Varela, countermanded the pre-match instructions of the coach, Juan Lopez, and ordered his team to attack rather than wait for their seemingly inevitable fate. At first it did not work, and Brazil went ahead just after half-time, to thunderous reactions from the volatile crowd.

Uruguay held its nerve, and Alberto Schiaffino temporarily silenced spectators with his 66th-minute equalizer. Just as the fans were starting to herald the draw that Brazil needed, Alcides Edgardo Ghiggia struck Uruguay's winner, 11 minutes from time. Apart from within the underdogs' small but ecstatic circle, a sickening silence descended upon the Maracana, and some fans even committed suicide soon afterwards. Despite the widespread disbelief, Uruguay were world champions by 2-1.

'I went to the dressing rooms a few minutes before the end. Walking along the corridors the infernal row ceased. Emerging from the tunnel, a stunned silence reigned in the stadium. No national anthem, no guard of honour, no speeches.'

FIFA President Jules Rimet on the extraordinary upset.

Ferenc Puskás

'The Galloping Major'

1950s Ferenc Puskás did not look like a world-class footballer – until they gave him a ball. Short and increasingly chubby as his long career progressed, he nevertheless commanded huge respect because of his amazing range of skills and the teams he inspired.

What the 'Magical Magyars' did to England in 1953 will never be forgotten. Fielding the likes of Stanley Matthews, Stan Mortensen and captain Billy Wright, the English were considered a formidable force in world football, and their defeat to the USA three years earlier was believed to have been no more than a blip. But Puskás engineered a 6-3 trouncing at Wembley Stadium, and left Wright flying in the wrong direction as he pulled the ball back towards him and blasted what he later described as his favourite goal. England went to Budapest the following May looking for revenge. This time they were thrashed 7-1.

Puskás scored a remarkable 85 goals in 84 internationals for Hungary, finishing with four games for Spain after his switch to Real Madrid.

In 1960, the 'Galloping Major' – he had been an army officer back home – scored three goals in the European Cup final in Glasgow to help Real beat Eintracht Frankfurt 7-3. He scored another hat-trick in the 1962 showpiece, but Madrid lost 5-3 to Benfica.

He was once asked whether these performances were his best ever. 'No, I played better against a team called Turku in Finland,' he replied with a smile. 'We won 17-0.'

Puskás died in 2006, but he will never be forgotten.

Ferenc Puskás

Born: 2 April 1927   **Died:** 17 November 2006

Place of Birth: Budapest, Hungary

Position: Forward

Teams: Kispest AC/Honvéd, Real Madrid, Hungary, Spain

Alfredo di Stefano

'Don Alfredo'

1950s Hard and aloof, Alfredo di Stefano was not the most popular player who ever lived, but he was certainly one of the very best. His wonderful range of passing was matched only by his ability to be in the right place at the right time to score so many goals. Driving through midfield to spearhead attack, di Stefano was Real Madrid's most important player in their golden era, upstaging even the great Ferenc Puskás. When the Hungarian scored three goals in the 1960 European Cup final win over Eintracht Frankfurt, the Argentinian master fired four.

From 1953 to 1964, di Stefano won no fewer than five European Cup medals, one World Club championship, eight Spanish League medals and one Spanish Cup. He scored 428 goals in 510 games – a record unimaginable in the modern era – and 49 of those came in 58 European Cup games. Twice he was voted European Footballer of the Year. All that was missing from the revered Don Alfredo's trophy cabinet was a World Cup winners medal, but it never came, partly because so many top players had left Argentina by the time of the 1958 and 1962 tournaments. He played seven times for his native country, and won 31 caps for his beloved Spain after switching loyalties. His 23 goals for his adopted country were a record at the time, but not even the great di Stefano could inspire Spain to World Cup glory. Later he went into management, and won league titles with Boca Juniors in Argentina and Valencia in Spain. Don Alfredo was a true great.

Alfredo di Stefano

Born: 4 July 1926

Place of Birth: Buenos Aires, Argentina

Position: Centre Forward

Teams: River Plate, Huracán, Millonarios, Real Madrid, RCD Espanyol, Argentina, Spain

The Miracle of Bern

West Germany Beat Hungary

1954 When a team which has not lost for 31 games and four years finally succumbs in the most important match of all, it can be called a miracle or a great sadness. What made West Germany's 3-2 victory in the final of the 1954 World Cup in Switzerland particularly astonishing was the fact that Hungary had given them an 8-3 drubbing earlier in that very tournament. But if you look deeper into the story, Hungary's fall at the final hurdle is not just a celebration of the renowned German ability to bounce back, it is also a cautionary tale about what can happen to great teams in the fierce intensity of any given tournament.

Hungary had Ferenc Puskás, Jozsef Boszik, Sándor Koscsis and many other legends. On their march to the final, scoring nine against the Koreans and eight against Germany, there were casualties, however. In the latter thrashing, Puskás took a kick on the ankle that affected his mobility when Germany came looking for revenge in the showpiece. There was a 4-2 victory over Brazil in Bern, but it was a battle, with several players injured and three sent off.

Fatigue eventually caught up with Hungary in the final, but not before they went two goals ahead thanks to Puskás and Zoltán Czibor. The Germans, who had put seven past Turkey in their last group game, hit back against the firm favourites with two goals in 10 minutes from Max Morlock and Helmut Rahn.

In the second half, Rahn checked his stride before shooting; Hungary's keeper, Gyula Grosics, was wrong-footed and slipped, and West Germany were ahead. A tiring Puskás thought he had equalized in the last minute but was ruled offside, to his great fury. The Magical Magyars were beaten. West Germany had their first world title.

Opposite: German Captain, Fritz Walter holding the World Cup Trophy after West Germany's triumph over competition favourites Hungary.

Stanley Matthews

'The Wizard of the Dribble'

1950s The Peter Pan of football, his teasing, unreadable skills on the wing led Stanley Matthews to be nicknamed 'The Wizard of the Dribble'.

He was still tormenting defences at an age when many men have already accepted the limitations of middle age. Matthews won the FA Cup in his third final at the age of 38, played his last game for England at 42, and scored a promotion-clinching goal for Stoke City aged 48.

Spanning three decades, Matthews' 54-match international career began against Wales in 1934 and finished in Scotland in 1957 – a mind-boggling time frame by modern standards. He was an inspiration in the team that beat Germany 6-3 in Berlin in 1938, and he made five goals in England's 7-2 thrashing of Scotland in 1955.

What Matthews is most famous for, however, is the FA Cup final of 1953. With his Blackpool team 3-1 down to Bolton, he told teammates he could not go home again without the cup, having failed twice before. Suddenly he began to launch raid after mesmerizing raid down the right, and led the unlikeliest of comebacks. Blackpool finished 4-3 winners and the star of the show was chaired round Wembley. The occasion was for ever known as the 'Matthews Final'. Its hero was knighted for services to football in 1965. He left memories for generations to savour.

Stanley Matthews

Born: 1 February 1915   **Died:** 23 February 2000

Place of Birth: Stoke-on-Trent, England

Position: Right Wing, Midfielder

Teams: Stoke City, Blackpool

The Munich Air Disaster

The Death of Busby's Babes

1958 By mid-afternoon on 6 February 1958, Manchester United's returning players were growing nervous at Munich's Riem airport. They had just beaten Red Star Belgrade in the European Cup and had stopped in Germany to refuel. It should have been a happy journey.

People were saying this could be the year for the Busby Babes, so-called because the average age of Matt Busby's team was only 24. They had reached the European Cup semi-finals the previous year and were only knocked out by the mighty Real Madrid. But young stars like Duncan Edwards, who was still only 21, despite his 18 England caps, were learning fast. Edwards, a half-back, was starting to show signs of true greatness, and had already played 175 times for United.

Now it was 3.04 p.m., and the pilot of British European Airways Flight 609 was making his third take-off attempt after previous problems with an engine. But a blizzard was blowing and slush on the runway prevented the plane from taking off. At the end of those terrifying moments it overshot the runway, hit buildings and burst into flames.

Seven Busby Babes were killed that day and there were 15 other fatalities. The manager, Busby, needed blood transfusions to survive. Bobby Charlton sustained head injuries. Fifteen days later Duncan Edwards lost his fight for life, and the game of football lost one of its most precious jewels.

'People still haven't forgotten. Strangers come up and tell me: "He were a good 'un".'
Anne Edwards, mother of Duncan, 1993

Opposite: One of the 'lucky' ones – Matt Busby lies in hospital after the crash.

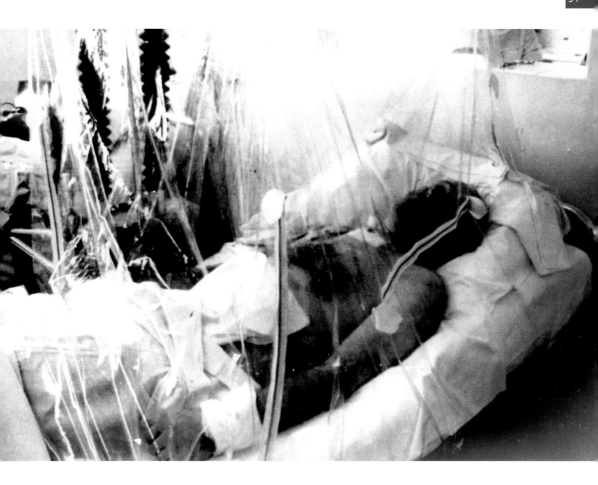

Lev Yashin

The KGB Panther

1960s Strangely, for one of the most masterful exponents of goalkeeping the world has ever seen, Lev Yashin would have preferred to do just about anything other than stand between the posts.

The legendary Russian later admitted: 'I ran, did the high jump, boxed, wrestled, played ice hockey and water polo. When I played football as a fourteen-year-old I wanted to score goals, but I got moved further and further back until I was left in goal.'

Accepting his fate at last, Yashin set out to become the best goalkeeper in the world. His first great honour was to win a gold medal with the Soviet team at the 1956 Olympics in Melbourne, Australia. At club level, meanwhile, he played for Dynamo Moscow, linked to the Russian secret service, and was even paid as a KGB Sergeant.

Despite the Cold War, football fans worldwide took Yashin to their hearts. When Russia won the European Nations Cup in 1960, Yashin was the star of the show. The English fans christened him 'The Panther', because of his distinctive all-black goalkeeping kit and feline agility.

Yashin was European Footballer of the Year in 1963, the first goalkeeper ever to win the award. In 1966 Russia reached the semi-finals of the World Cup in England thanks to his acrobatics. Yashin, already a legend, had boosted his reputation further still, and went on to win 78 caps for his country.

Lev Yashin

Born: 22 October 1929   **Died:** 20 March 1990

Place of Birth: Moscow, Russia

Position: Goalkeeper

Teams: Moscow Dynamo, Russia

England Win the World Cup

The Day Football Came Home

1966 Alf Ramsey, England's manager in 1966, had predicted that his team would win the World Cup long before the tournament started. When the players thought they had fulfilled that prophecy, only to be denied by a last-gasp German equalizer in normal time, Ramsey gathered his exhausted men around him and told them to go out and win it again.

The willpower of the manager should not be underestimated. He had physically prevented players from swapping shirts with a dirty Argentina team earlier in the tournament, and resisted the clamour to reinstate the injured but fast-recovering star striker, Jimmy Greaves, in time for the final. Ramsey preferred a big lump of a centre-forward called Geoff Hurst, and many thought the manager was mad.

England were in the final against West Germany because Bobby Charlton had scored twice in the semi in a 2-1 win over Portugal. But now they had begun slowly and the Germans scored first. Hurst seemed to justify his place when he equalized, and then Martin Peters nudged England ahead. Now it was all square again and extra time was about to begin.

Hurst responded to Ramsey's rallying cry with a thumping shot that hit the crossbar and bounced down on to the goal-line. The Russian linesman, Tofik Bharamov, gave a goal. Then in the last moments of extra time Hurst broke away, hit the ball as hard as he could and secured the first hat-tick in a World Cup final. England had won 4-2, and Bobby Moore lifted their only major international trophy to date.

'Some people are on the pitch. They think it's all over' (Hurst scores) 'it is now!'

The immortal words of BBC commentator Kenneth Wolstenholme.

The Lisbon Lions

Celtic Become First British Side to Win European Cup

1967 Liverpool won it five times and kept it. Manchester United won it twice, and so did Nottingham Forest. The list goes on, but the very first British side to win the European Cup was not English. In fact, Jock Stein's Lisbon Lions were about as Scottish as they come. The entire team hailed either from Glasgow itself or from the communities that surrounded it, no more than 30 miles away from the centre. That gave Celtic a stronger sense of identity than any of the British winners that followed in their footsteps in later years.

They would need all the passion and purpose they could muster against an elegant Inter Milan side that had won the European Cup two years earlier. But Celtic was not short of skill either, and had a ginger-haired winger called Jimmy Johnstone, who could leave the best defenders in his wake. He typified the confidence that flowed through the Scots, even after Inter's early penalty sent the Italians into the half-time break a goal ahead. Tommy Gemmill blasted a deserved equalizer with the game little more than an hour old, and now the Italians knew that negative tactics were not going to be enough.

It was Celtic who poured forward looking for the winner though, and got their reward six minutes from time. Stevie Chalmers turned a Bobby Murdoch drive past Giuliano Sarti in Inter's goal, Billy McNeill lifted the cup and Celtic were the envy of England's finest.

Opposite: Captain Billie McNeill raises the European Cup to fans, after beating opponents Inter Milan.

A Tribute to Munich

Manchester United Win the European Cup

1968 From the moment his 'Busby Babes' team perished on the ice at Munich airport in 1958, Matt Busby made it his personal responsibility to win Manchester United the European Cup, in order to honour the memory of those who had lost their lives.

Ten years later at Wembley, only Benfica and Eusébio, their world-famous talisman, stood in Busby's way.

The tough Scotsman was not about to feel intimidated by the opposition, however. He had a new superstar of his own – young Georgie Best – and in Bobby Charlton, a survivor of the Munich tragedy, he had an ally who understood perfectly why this had to be United's night.

Charlton opened the scoring and Eusébio hit back. But Best dribbled round the keeper to put his side ahead again, and even a teenager called Brian Kid got in on the act with a classy goal. Charlton's second settled it at 4-1, and provided the right conclusion to a moving story. The European Cup was destined for Old Trafford, and there was an inescapable feeling that it was meant to be.

For Busby and Charlton, who had carried a decade of weight on their shoulders as they sought to make the dream a reality, the realization that they had finally done it was almost too much. They hugged tearfully, knowing that their colleagues and close friends of 1958 had been remembered and honoured in the best way that was left to those who had survived.

Opposite: Goalkeeper Alex Stepney shows off the European trophy during Manchester United's lap of honour.

Pelé

The King of Football

1970s

Pelé is widely regarded as the greatest footballer of all time. He won the World Cup as a skinny 17-year-old, scoring two goals in the final against hosts Sweden in 1958. He appeared to show no nerves as he brought his amazing array of skills to the world stage for the first time, only tears of disbelief when he realized what he had achieved so soon.

Pelé was part of Brazil's squad for their 1962 World Cup triumph as well, but was injured early in the tournament. He won his third World Cup in Mexico in 1970, and by then had the physical power to go with his grace and imagination. Apart from an outrageous amount of ability, what set him apart from the rest was his realization that there was absolutely nothing he could not do. Brazil's magician attempted to beat Czechoslovakia's keeper, Ivo Viktor, from inside his own half at that World Cup – something that had never been attempted before on a top stage. The startled Viktor tried to scramble back in a panic, but the ball sailed a yard wide of the post.

Another memorable moment from the 1970 tournament – arguably the best ever – was the audacious dummy Pelé sold to Uruguay's goalkeeper, Ladislao Mazurkiewicz, as he left his adversary in no-man's-land and reached the ball in time to turn his shot just past the upright again.

When near-misses are remembered for decades, you know the player concerned was extra special. But it should not be forgotten that he scored when it really mattered, including in the 1970 final against Italy, with a towering header to help clinch Brazil's 4-1 triumph. Pelé's personal tally by the time he retired was more than 1,200 goals, including 77 for Brazil. Diego Maradona only scored 34 for Argentina. Enough said.

Pelé (Edson Arantes do Nascimento)

Born: 23 October 1940

Place of Birth: Três Corações, Brazil

Position: Forward

Teams: Bauru, Santos, New York Cosmos, Brazil

The Total Football Triple

Ajax Become Triple European Cup Winners

1971–73

Total Football was the concept that won Ajax of Amsterdam an amazing three European Cups in a row in the early 1970s. When Ajax first triumphed in 1971, their coach was Rinus Michels, one of the founding fathers of Total Football. The idea was that each individual player should have the intelligence, fitness and skill to play in any position on the pitch. Therefore there was to be no clear distinction between defenders, midfielders and strikers; the team should move as one at all times, with players slotting in where they were most needed at any given time.

If it sounded impressive in theory, it was even more devastating when put into practice, with Johan Cruyff and Johan Neeskens showing the way.

In 1971 Ajax beat Celtic and Atletico Madrid on the way to the final against Panathinaikos, who had the legendary Ferenc Puskás as their coach. Michels was not worried and neither was Ge Van Dijk, who scored after just five minutes in a 2-0 victory.

A Romanian coach called Stefan Kovacs took charge for the next European campaign, and took Total Football to a new level. There were wins over Arsenal and Benfica on the way to a European Cup final against Inter Milan in Rotterdam. Cruyff was the master, with two second-half goals to seal a treble, because Ajax had won their domestic league and cup too.

When Ajax went all the way for a third year running, knocking out Bayern Munich and Real Madrid before Johnny Rep's winner against Juventus in Belgrade, everyone knew that the Dutch team would go down in history as the most fluent, adaptable and tactically astute club side the world had ever seen.

Opposite: Johann Cruyff demonstrating his talent against Bayern Munich in the European Cup.

Johan Cruyff

The Dutch Master

1970s Two words best sum up the Dutch Master, Johan Cruyff: elegance and balance. Few footballers have ever looked quite so graceful as the Ajax No. 14, who inspired the club to their hat-trick of European Cups from 1971–73 and almost led Holland to World Cup triumph in 1974. He was voted Player of the Tournament despite a 2-1 defeat to West Germany in the final. He helped the Dutch qualify for Argentina in 1978, but despised the Buenos Aires-based military 'junta' so much that he refused to play there, retiring instead. Holland may not have lost their second final in succession had his decision been different.

But Cruyff left many wonderful memories. His incredible ability to stay upright and poised while switching direction with a sudden drag of the heel led to the birth of the famous 'Cruyff Turn', a regular feature in football now but shocking when the Dutchman's partypiece pirouette first left a defender for dead.

His temperament sometimes let him down, though: he was sent off in his second international appearance, deposed as Ajax captain by a democratic vote, and is once alleged to have said: 'I don't think the day will come when someone says "Cruyff" and the other person doesn't understand.' It was all accepted as part of the package – the mark of a true genius.

Three times European Footballer of the Year, Cruyff went on to manage the Barcelona 'Dream Team' to four Spanish titles and the European Cup in 1992. He was voted European Player of the Twentieth Century ahead of West Germany's Franz Beckenbauer.

Johan Cruyff

Born: 25 April 1947

Place of Birth: Amsterdam, Netherlands

Position: Midfielder

Teams: Ajax, Barcelona, Los Angeles Aztecs, Washington Diplomats, Levants, Feyenoord, Holland

Rossi's Magic Moment

Italy Wins a Third World Cup

1982 To understand the magical momentum behind Italy's march to unlikely glory in 1982, you have to consider the negativity that surrounded the team through the group stages of the World Cup in Spain. The coach, Enzo Bearzot, was criticized for pinning his hopes on a young striker called Paolo Rossi, who had just come back from a ban for his alleged part in a match-fixing scandal. The doubts intensified when Italy failed to win a single match in their group and Rossi fired blanks. They scraped through to the second group stage but there were calls in Italy for the team to come home, to spare the nation more misery.

Then something extraordinary happened. The Italians suddenly sprang to life and beat Diego Maradona's Argentina 2-1, albeit largely thanks to some cynical defending. Now they needed to beat the mighty Brazil, who had only to draw in order to reach the semi-finals. This was Rossi's finest hour, as he scored a clinical hat-trick to help the underdogs to a dramatic 3-2 victory – a result that sent the shell-shocked Samba Boys back to South America.

Once he started, Rossi could not stop scoring, and netted two more in the semi-final win over Poland. He got another in the final, where Italy beat the Germans 3-1, though the enduring image is Marco Tardelli's wonderfully emotional reaction to his own sizzling strike.

In Rome an all-night street party saw ecstatic fans climb on top of their cars, wave flags and beat drums until dawn. The team was no longer a disgrace, Rossi was no longer a flop. He had won the Golden Boot with six goals in the last three matches, and Italy had secured their third World Cup triumph against the odds after a 44-year wait.

Opposite: Italy's captain holds aloft the World Cup trophy after Rossi's invaluable scoring contribution.

Michel Platini

France's Hat-Trick Hero

1980s One of the greatest creative midfielders of all time, the best and worst of Michel Platini was seen in less than 12 months during the mid-1980s.

All his artistry, authority and goal-scoring prowess was on show at the 1984 European Championship. He scored France's winner against Denmark, hat tricks against Belgium and Yugoslavia, and the winner in a 3-2 nail-biter against Portugal in the Marseilles semi-final. Crucially, he fired France's opener in the final triumph against Spain, when his tricky free kick crept under Luis Arconada. Nine strikes in five games made Platini top scorer, Player of the Tournament, champion on home soil and the most celebrated European player in the business. In many ways this represented the highlight of his career, because World Cup adventures in 1982 and 1986 ended in semi-final heartbreak despite his magic.

In May, 1985, Platini went in search of a European Cup winners' medal at Heysel, Brussels, where Liverpool were the opposition. Rioting broke out, disaster struck and 39 people were crushed to death before the match even kicked off. Many complained afterwards that the game should not have been played at all under such tragic circumstances, but the authorities were frightened that more deaths would follow if it was called off.

Juventus were awarded a dubious penalty, perhaps to appease its furious supporters. Platini scored from the spot but instead of showing restraint, he celebrated self-indulgently. His reactions were criticized later, though he won new respect as a football administrator when he retired. He had scored 41 goals in 72 international appearances, and 68 goals in 147 league games for Juventus. The talent, at least, was unquestionable.

Michel Platini

Born: 21 June 1955

Place of Birth: Joeuf, France

Position: Midfielder

Teams: AS Joeuf, Nancy, St Etienne, Juventus, France

The Heysel Stadium Disaster

A Black Day in Brussels

1985 Like most disasters, the Heysel tragedy could have been avoided. It was even predicted by a Brussels newspaper *Le Soir*, which warned its readers on the morning of the match to watch out for the 'apocalypse'.

The Brussels Fire Chief, Alan Gibson, was excluded from a vital pre-match security meeting, a pitiful chicken-wire fence was erected to separate Liverpool supporters from Italian families at one end of the ground, and a woefully inadequate police presence gave mayhem the green light.

Liverpool thugs, angry at the beating some of their own had suffered in Rome before the previous year's European Cup final, began to throw missiles then charged through the flimsy barrier.

The myth that a collapsing wall caused the deaths has endured, when the reality was that the crush occurred because there was no way out of that corner of the stadium in the crucial, fatal moments before the wall in question finally collapsed. More lives would probably have been lost had the wall not given way. Bodies were piled one upon another in the fight for breath, and 39 football-lovers lost their lives. Incredibly, the match went ahead after mounted police had battled to prevent a potentially lethal counter-charge by Juventus hooligans from the other end of the stadium.

English clubs were banned from European competition for five years as a result of what happened, but that was no consolation for the Italian families who had lost their loved ones.

'If I had known about the fatalities I wouldn't have wanted to play. You go along to watch a game.'
Kenny Dalglish

Diego Maradona

Argentina's Flawed Genius

1980s Many followers of football believe that Diego Maradona was even better than Pelé. His sudden bursts of acceleration more than matched those of the Brazilian, and he was more dynamic in his approach to the game. But whether Maradona matched Pelé's easy grace and innovative magic is another matter entirely.

For a start, Maradona lacked a little of the height he needed to be truly perfect as a footballer. In 1986, however, he found a way to make up for it as he challenged England's goalkeeper, Peter Shilton, for a ball in their World Cup quarter-final in Mexico. Maradona punched his goal into the net and turned away in triumph, thus convincing the referee that he had done nothing wrong. Later he called it the 'Hand of God'.

What salvaged his reputation was the sheer quality of his rampaging second goal, when he skipped and swerved past half the England team before beating Shilton again. That incredible strike was voted Goal of the Century on the FIFA website in 2002. It was all too much for the English, who went home 2-1 losers, while Maradona continued to find the back of the net. His two goals also saw off Belgium in the semi-final; and in a dramatic 3-2 victory over the Germans in the final, it was Maradona's pass that set up Jorge Burruchaga for the last-gasp winner, after the Europeans had somehow clawed their way back into it from two down.

Maradona had won Argentina their second World Cup in eight years. There would be heartbreak ahead for the little genius, though, as the Germans took their revenge in the final of Italia '90, and Maradona was thrown out of the 1994 tournament for drug-taking. But he will for ever be defined by what happened against England in 1986.

Diego Maradona

Born: 30 October 1960

Place of birth: Lanus, Argentina

Position: Attacking Midfielder

Teams: Barcelona, Napoli, Seville, Argentina

The Hillsborough Disaster

Liverpool's Second Tragedy

1989 It was a dreadful coincidence that Liverpool fans were also involved in the next great tragedy of the 1980s after Heysel – the Hillsborough disaster of 1989.

Their team were playing Nottingham Forest in an FA Cup semi-final at Sheffield Wednesday's ground. Traffic problems had led to the late arrival of thousands of Liverpool supporters at the Leppings Lane end just before kick-off. In order to allow them entry to the small area of terracing behind the goal, the police opened exit gates that did not have turnstiles. To distribute the latecomers safely, stewards or police needed to direct them in even numbers into pens along the entire terrace. But no one did, and the vast majority headed for the nearest pens: three and four. This resulted in disaster.

Police and security staff were slow to take any action to relieve the crush that was building. They were reluctant to allow fans on to the pitch in case a fight broke out with opposing supporters, and the situation was allowed to deteriorate until it became fatal.

English football launched an enquiry, and the Taylor Report recommended that stadiums become all-seater. This suggestion was implemented, and such a terrible tragedy should never happen again in Britain.

Ninety-six people died from the injuries they sustained that day, however. They are commemorated both at Hillsborough and at Anfield, home to Liverpool and its supporters.

'The only safe stadium in my view is an empty one.'

South Yorkshire coroner Stefan Popper, at the inquest.

Gazza's Tears Grip a Nation

England's Exit from Italia '90

1990 Paul Gascoigne was the new, refreshing face in the England team at Italia '90. Already known inside the football world for his crazy pranks, 'Gazza' had been branded 'daft as a brush' by his own international manager, Bobby Robson. But Gascoigne looked anything but stupid as his dazzling skills and bubbly presence helped England to negotiate tough knockout ties against Belgium in Bologna and Cameroon in Naples on the way to a World Cup semi-final against Germany in Turin.

The problem was that he had picked up a yellow card on that path to the last four, and one more caution would prevent him from playing in the World Cup final should England win through.

In a tense match against the Germans, Gary Lineker had put England back in the hunt after Franz Beckenbauer's side had drawn first blood. With the match in the balance, a careless tackle earned Gazza that dreaded yellow card, and he suddenly realized the consequences.

The tears poured down his cheeks and for a moment he looked too distraught to carry on. Gary Lineker asked his manager to 'have a word'. To his credit, Gascoigne pulled himself together for the sake of his team, and England were only denied in a cruel penalty shoot-out.

As the disappointed Geordie returned home, he could not have imagined that his tears had propelled him to superstardom. Even people who did not like football loved Gazza for the little-boy-lost way he had worn his heart on his sleeve. Life would never be the same again for Paul Gascoigne.

Opposite: Paul Gascoigne cries as he leaves the pitch
following England's World Cup defeat by Germany.

Franz Beckenbauer

Der Kaiser

1990 When Andreas Brehme's eighty-fifth-minute penalty sealed World Cup glory for the Germans at Italia '90, Franz Beckenbauer became part of a very select duo. Until that moment, only Mario Zagallo of Brazil had won the trophy as a player and a manager. Now Der Kaiser had done it too – and he did not stop there. Today it is hard to see how anyone else in football has been more influential or more successful. For Beckenbauer helped win Germany the right to stage World Cup 2006, and organized the highly successful tournament on a number of levels. 'You only get one chance to do that in your lifetime,' he said later. He should know. He has done it all and won it all.

Beckenbauer was made captain of West Germany in 1971, five years after finishing on the losing side against England in the World Cup final at Wembley. He was a supremely elegant defender who made surging runs into attack, a tactic previously unseen in football. He led his country to the 1972 European Championship, inspiring his team to a 3-0 victory over the Soviet Union, and was named European Footballer of the Year.

In 1974 Beckenbauer won the European Cup with Bayern Munich and captained West Germany to World Cup glory over Johan Cruyff's Holland in the Olympic Stadium in his native Munich. Not content with that, he followed up his perfect year with more European Cups in 1975 and 1976.

Management later came equally easily to Beckenbauer, even though he had not been given much training in the role. He almost won the World Cup for West Germany in 1986, reaching the final, but made no mistake at the next tournament with the revenge victory over Diego Maradona's Argentina. Der Kaiser is football's Mr Perfect.

Franz Beckenbauer

Born: 11 September 1945

Place of birth: Munich, Germany

Position: Sweeper

Teams: Bayern Munich, Hamburg, New York Cosmos, West Germany

England's Penalty Heartache

A Decade of Spot-Kick Disasters

1990s By the early twenty-first century, England supporters expected their team to make a mess of penalty shoot-outs. They knew their star players would lose their nerve, that it would not have occurred to the overpaid coach that a sports psychologist might be useful to help prepare for the most stressful sporting showdown of all.

Back in the 1990s, however, England fans thought differently. They believed in the ability of their heroes to come good when it really mattered – like in a World Cup semi-final penalty shoot-out against the Germans. They even tried to believe in Stuart Pearce when he stepped up to take a penalty. A rugged defender but no subtle expert, he was always likely to hit and hope. He did – and missed. When Chris Waddle almost ballooned his own spot-kick out of the ground, England were out. A glorious adventure was over.

Fast-forward six years to Wembley, and Euro '96. Football was coming home – or so the song went – and when England enjoyed spectacular wins over Holland and Scotland, the entire country started to believe. There was a penalty shoot-out against Spain, and the gutsy Pearce took another penalty. He scored, and his defiant, contorted features are frozen in history.

Perhaps it was not so crazy to hand crude defenders the ultimate responsibility of deceiving a goalkeeper in a shoot-out after all. Terry Venables, Robson's successor, clearly had no objections. After another hard-fought draw in the semi-final against arch-rivals Germany, Gareth Southgate stepped up to take his turn in the penalty drama. A wonderfully colourful and noisy Wembley held its breath. He failed. The party was over. More heartbreak, more disbelief. We're used to it now. But we weren't then.

Opposite: Goalkeeper Tim Flowers consoles a heartbroken Gareth Southgate after his penalty miss.

Ronaldo

'The Phenomenon'

1990s The funny thing about Ronaldo is that when you expect him to conquer the world he falls to pieces, and when you think he will fall to pieces he conquers the world.

In 1998, Ronaldo was the world's greatest footballer. He was already a World Cup winner, having been part of Brazil's victorious squad at World Cup '94. Bobby Robson, his manager at PSV Eindhoven, said he could be better than Pelé, and Ronaldo responded with 54 goals in 57 games for the Dutch club.

Now it was time for The Phenomenon's coronation in a World Cup final in France in 1998. But rumours began to circulate that he was not going to play. He had suffered a sudden convulsive fit. He came out anyway for the final, in body but not in mind. Ronaldo did next to nothing and France won 3-0.

Jump forward four years to the 2002 final, and Brazil are up against Germany. That Ronaldo had been involved at all came as something of a shock, given his weight and injury problems. Yet he had already scored six goals in as many games, including the semi-final clincher against Turkey. In the World Cup final he confounded his critics by scoring two more goals to hand Brazil the trophy yet again. Ronaldo has even equalled Pelé's tally of 12 World Cup goals and has won FIFA World Player of the Year three times. Not bad for a guy who was accused of not being able to handle the pressure of expectation.

Ronaldo Luis Nazário de Lima

Born: 22 September 1976

Place of birth: Rio de Janeiro, Brazil

Position: Striker

Teams: Cruzeiro, PSV Eindhoven, Barcelona, Inter Milan, Real Madrid, Brazil

Never Say Die...

Manchester United Seal the Treble

1999 The night Manchester United won the treble in Barcelona, it looked as though the success of their domestic season had caught up with Alex Ferguson's men. In the space of a couple of weeks, they had secured the Premiership title against Spurs, and won the FA Cup final by beating Newcastle. Now, however, they were being comprehensively outplayed by Bayern Munich.

Lucky to be only 1-0 down, United had just watched the Germans hit the woodwork twice. Bayern stars were smiling condescendingly at their United counterparts, taunting them, acting as though they had won already. They almost had. Even the Champions League trophy itself was already decorated in their colours.

Teddy Sheringham's injury-time equalizer changed all that. The Germans suddenly looked crushed and desperate; they waited for the final whistle of normal time so they could regroup for the extra period. There was not going to be one.

United won a corner, David Beckham swung in a beauty, Sheringham headed back across goal and Ole Gunnar Solskjaer stabbed home the killer blow. The Germans were now weeping openly. Within seconds the final whistle blew and their misery was complete.

United had more than a treble. The 31-year wait for a second European Cup was over. And even football fans who disliked United allowed themselves the briefest smile in admiration for the crazy, Never Say Die way in which they had won it.

'History is made, Manchester United are the Champions of Europe again and nobody will ever win a European Cup final more dramatically than this.'

Commentator Clive Tyldesley

France Wins the Double

Zidane Rules France's Glory Days

2000 France were not among the favourites for the 1998 World Cup, which had not been won by the host nation for 20 years. They did not have a prolific goalscorer – a young Thierry Henry only managed three in the tournament – and the French public did not seem to care about their football in the way the English, Italians and Spanish did. But for all the doubts and initial apathy, France did have two key factors in their favour: a brilliant midfielder called Zinédine Zidane, and a healthy dose of good fortune.

The captain, Laurent Blanc, scored a Golden Goal to beat Paraguay, and the French scraped through again in the quarter-finals, thanks to a penalty shoot-out victory over Italy. Blanc kissed the bald head of goalkeeper Fabien Barthez before every match, and this lucky gesture worked. The hosts were gaining momentum, and Zidane was putting in some imperious performances in the centre of the park.

A double from defender Lilian Thuram in the semi-final saw off Croatia, and then it was time for the showpiece against Brazil. Ronaldo was hopeless, instead it was Zidane who ruled, scoring with two headers in a 3-0 triumph. Paris celebrated all night; the team was mixed race just like the city that united around it. Zidane was voted World Player of the Year.

It would happen again two years later.

Roger Lemerre had taken over from World Cup-winning coach Aime Jacquet, but Zidane was still king at Euro 2000. His free-kick stunned Spain, and his Golden Goal sent Portugal crashing in the semi-final. But Italy seemed to have won the final until Sylvain Wiltord's last-gasp equalizer. Then David Trezeguet sealed a famous comeback with a Golden Goal of his own. France had done it. Things changed at World Cup 2006, but in those days Zidane was simply untouchable.

Opposite: The French side celebrate winning the European Championships, and therefore completing the double.

Germany 1 England 5

The Miracle of Munich

2001 One of the happiest shocks in English footballing history, the Miracle of Munich nevertheless had a sting in its tail – it ensured Sven-Göran Eriksson's long and fruitless reign as England coach.

By the end of that memorable night in Munich, Eriksson had become a god in the eyes of England fans, and Michael Owen had blasted his way into the record books. Whatever difficulties arose in later years, the Swede retained his credibility because of this single dream result.

Victory did not look likely when Carsten Jancker put the Germans ahead after just six minutes. They had lost only one qualifier in the last 60, and had not been beaten in the Olympic Stadium since 1973. Germany had even won the last match at the old Wembley to put themselves firmly in control of the qualifying group.

But Owen equalized with a volley past Oliver Khan, and Steven Gerrard drilled a beauty from outside the area to put Sven's men ahead by half-time.

The second half saw Germany collapse at the feet of Owen, who fired England's third and then skipped away to score yet another from Gerrard's through ball. That glorious hat-trick made Owen the first England striker to achieve the feat against the Germans since Geoff Hurst in 1966. Emile Heskey made it five, and the England fans among 63,000 spectators went wild. Though the result helped them qualify outright for World Cup 2002, Eriksson's England would never hit such heights again.

Opposite: Michael Owen powers forward to score his third goal of the game and help England to their 5-1 victory.

Golden Goal Stuns Italy

Ahn Jung-Hwang Scores for the Red Devils of Korea

2002 The Korean Republic's World Cup fairytale took on a scarcely believable scale of romance in the Daejeon Stadium, when they knocked out the mighty Italians with a dramatic Golden Goal. The relief and joy shown by Ahn Jung-Hwang, the Koreans' best striker, was almost indescribable after he outjumped the legendary Paolo Maldini to head home Lee Young Po's cross in the 117th minute. For it was Ahn who had missed a penalty after just four minutes, allowing Christian Vieri the chance to score an opener to hand the initiative to the Italians. Now he had consigned his error to distant memory, left the Italians no chance of reply, and caused an eruption among South Korea's 'Red Devil' fans to compare with any celebration seen since World Cups began.

The Korean stadia had been flooded in a sea of crimson since the start of the tournament, and the noise was deafening when Seol Ki-Hyeon pounced upon Christian Vieri's error to throw the Koreans a lifeline and send the match against Italy into extra time. There were only 38,588 packed into the Daejeon Stadium, but they sounded like a hundred thousand as the extra-time victory was secured, and celebrations spread to central Seoul and throughout the country.

Guus Hiddink, the brilliant Dutch coach who had masterminded the success, claimed: 'What the Korean players have done is unique.' They went on to beat Spain in a shoot-out before falling to Germany in the semi-final. Ahn was ecstatic until told that his club, Perugia, didn't want him back because he had knocked Italy out.

Opposite: Korean Republic's Ahn Jung-Hwang leaps to head in their golden goal, consequently knocking Italy out of the World Cup.

Greece Win Euro 2004

The Underdogs Emerge Victorious in Portugal

2004 Sometimes a team with no stars and precious little flair can work wonders by finding a unity of purpose under a coach with a genius for organization. Such a phenomenon occurred at Euro 2004 in Portugal, where a team that had never won a match in a major final – and began as 100 1 outsiders took the tournament by storm.

Greece, whose coach was a cantankerous German called Otto Rehhagel, started as they finished – by humbling mighty Portugal and their superstar, Luis Figo. Then Angelos Charisteas shot through the legs of Iker Casillas to bag a draw against Spain, and a goal from Zisis Vryzas in a 2-1 defeat by Russia saved the Greeks from elimination.

They were still not rated, but they were getting good in the air. Charisteas headed his country's sixty-fifth minute winner to knock out France in the quarter-finals, Traianos Dellas put out the Czechs the same way in the semi-final, and then the head of Charisteas proved decisive again in the fifty-seventh minute of the showpiece against Portugal. No one could quite believe what was happening, least of all the Portuguese team and their fans, who had come to crown Figo, the Real Madrid star, king of Europe at last. But Greece held on to complete the impossible dream, and Rehhagel safely predicted: 'This story will go around the world.'

Greece captain Theo Zagorakis won Player of the Tournament, and the heroic Charisteas announced: 'This is the biggest moment in Greek football history.' On the international stage, it was the only moment in Greek football history. And neutrals loved the romance of it.

'I made certain decisions. These decisions have been followed by the players. I only advise the players and we have great results.'

Greece coach, Otto Rehhagel, makes World Cup victory sound simple.

Opposite: A triumphant captain, Theodoros Zagorakis lifts the trophy.

The Reds Defeat the Romans

Liverpool Win the Champions League

2005 Around 40,000 fanatical Liverpool supporters had come a long way and were determined to make themselves heard, even though their team had been humiliated in a nightmare first half.

It was the Champions League final in Istanbul, and AC Milan were already three goals ahead, through Paolo Maldini and a double from Hernan Crespo. As they walked back to the dressing room at half-time, some Italian players even reached out to feel the cup, which was sitting on a podium by the touchline.

'You'll Never Walk Alone' rang around the Ataturk Stadium, and some of the Milan backroom staff shook their heads in disbelief. They were impressed by the defiance, but did these crazy English supporters not realize the game was already over?

The rest, as they say, is history. Liverpool's captain, Steven Gerrard, began the fight back with a well-aimed header, and gestured to the fans to turn up the volume further still. Seven minutes later they had good reason, because Vladimir Smicer and Xabi Alonso had maintained the charge to bring it level at 3-3.

Jerzy Dudek saved impossibly from Andriy Shevchenko, and soon it was all down to a penalty shoot-out. Jamie Carragher urged Dudek to play a rubber-legged clown, the persona first created by Bruce Grobbelaar to defeat the Romans under similar circumstances in 1984. Dudek revived the role to perfection, Andrea Pirlo and Shevchenko fluffed their penalties and Liverpool's amazing fight back had won them their fifth European Cup. They even got to keep it, so the Italians would never touch it again.

'Lifting the trophy has to be the best feeling ever.'

Steven Gerrard after Liverpool's amazing Champion's League victory.

Wales Halt Rampant All Blacks

Gwyn's Win

1905 The size of Wales's achievement on 16 December 1905 can only be measured by what happened on the rest of the All Blacks' groundbreaking tour of Britain and France. Dave Gallaher's Originals, as the New Zealanders became known, won every other match on tour so easily that they rarely conceded a point. By the time they arrived at the National Stadium in Cardiff, they had just beaten Ireland and England, both victories comfortable at 15-0. Their only close match had been their first Test against Scotland, but that had also been won 12-7. On New Year's Day they would go on to annihilate France 38-8. Away from the Test arena, all 20 of the other tour matches were won at a stroll.

But stubborn Wales refused to give the awesome All Blacks a clean sweep. Captained by Erith Gwynne Nicholls – known simply as 'Gwyn' – there was to be an upset and much controversy at Cardiff. Edward 'Teddy' Morgan, a pacey winger from Aberdare, was the hero of the day, running in the only try of the match in a frenetic first half.

The Welsh complained that some of the All Black tactics in the loose were beyond the boundaries of acceptable aggression. Some went as far as to say that Gallaher's team were dirty. But the All Blacks were more infuriated by the refereeing of the Scottish official, John Dallas, whom they felt had disallowed a perfectly good try that would have protected their unbeaten record.

The historic Welsh triumph left Gallaher bitter about the local reaction to his team's uncompromising style. New Zealand's captain said: 'I must confess that the unfair criticism to which I have been subjected, while in Wales especially, has annoyed me.' It sounded like sour grapes to the proud victors.

Opposite: Gwyn's Welsh squad that overcame questionable New Zealand tactics in order to claim a well-earned victory.

The Rise of the Tricolors

France Take on the Might of the Home Nations

1927 French rugby finally took off in the 1920s, culminating in their first win against England in 1927, followed by their maiden victory over Wales in 1928.

On examining their early Test record, the only wonder is that the French were still bothering to play the game at all by the time the 1920s arrived. And given the fabulously flamboyant way in which rugby was to develop there, it is surprising that they managed just one victory in 31 Test matches between 1906 and 1920. Perhaps that nail-biting 16-15 win over Scotland in 1911 gave the French just enough hope that they could one day compete on equal terms with the teams from over the Channel.

A 15-7 win over Ireland at Lansdowne Road in 1920 was followed by victories against the USA at home and Scotland away. They drew with England and Scotland in 1922, but there had never been wins against the English or Welsh going into the 1927 season.

On 2 April that year, at the Stade Colombes in Paris, a 30-year-old winger called Edmond Vellat made his historic dash for the try-line, and England were sunk for the first time. The following year, France beat Wales 8-3 with two tries from a younger winger by the name of Robert Houdet. At last France had victories against all the Home Nations. Troubled times lay ahead in the 1930s, including temporary expulsion from the Five Nations amid allegations of professionalism, but no one could take away their hard-earned achievements of the 1920s.

Opposite: England player Wavell Wakefield tries to prevent the onslaught of a French attack.

Augustus John 'Gus' Risman

An All-Time Rugby League Great

1930s Most rugby players become legends if they score 1,000 points and last more than a decade. Gus Risman scored 4,052 points and played for more than a quarter of a century. And he would have scored a lot more had his career not been interrupted by the Second World War.

He was 41 when he lifted the Challenge Cup at Wembley in 1952, after Warrington Town had beaten Featherstone Rovers 18-10. Captaining his side from full-back, he kicked a penalty in the first minute and converted two tries later on.

Cardiff-born of Latvian parents, Risman had been through the same glorious process before the war, when Salford beat Barrow in the 1938 final. On that occasion he was carried shoulder-high by his team-mates, who were all pictured smoking a celebratory cigarette as they did so. Ahead of his time, Risman was the only one not smoking, and that self-discipline partly explains why he was able to go on for so long.

In a career lasting from 1929 to 1954, he played 873 matches, kicked 1,678 goals and scored 232 tries. He was capped 17 times for Great Britain in three different positions, and was captain of Great Britain for the 1946 'Indomitables' (named after the warship in which they sailed) tour Down Under, the first big tour undertaken by any sport after the war. Risman is still a legend among legends.

John Risman

Born: *c.* 21 March 1911   **Died:** 17 October 1994

Place of birth: Cardiff, Wales

Caps: 36

Teams: Salford, Workington, Batley

Van Vollenhoven's First of Three

St Helens v Hunslet, Challenge Cup Final

1959 Former Springbok rugby union star Tom Van Vollenhoven had such blistering pace to go with his unreadable sidestep and deceiving swerve that it was inevitable that he would leave a masterpiece or two from his wonderful career with St Helens. Those who were there insist that the first of his three tries in the 1959 final against Hunslet was quite simply one of the greatest scored in the entire history of rugby league.

Before Van Vollenhoven moved into overdrive, it was the underdogs of Hunslet who looked capable of shocking the favourites. They were winning 12-4 after 25 minutes, and growing in confidence by the second. Then something happened to shatter their self-belief, and a run so special that it would probably have shattered the composure of any team in the world.

Van Vollenhoven had been spotted scoring a hat-trick for the Springboks against the British Lions in 1955, and had been playing rugby league in England since 1957. He scored an amazing 62 tries in the 1959 season, but nothing quite like this. Picking up speed from deep inside his own half, he beat five Hunslet defenders with his trademark body-swerve and searing pace. His 75 metre run down the touchline ended when he veered inside to touch down under the posts, but he looked as though he could have gone on for ever.

'Vol' scored two more tries that day, despite pulling his hamstring, and was out of this world. Union's loss was league's gain.

Tom Van Vollenhoven

Born: 29 April 1935

Place of birth: Bethlehem, South Africa

Caps: 7

Teams: Northern Transvaal, St Helens, South Africa

England v Scotland, Five Nations

Hancock's Mud-Drenched Try

1965 Once in a while, something truly memorable will emerge from the mire of a match played between poor teams in terrible conditions. So it was at Twickenham in 1965, and the crowd had to wait an awfully long time to see some magic. When it finally arrived, however, the moment was so powerful that it made them forget all the mediocrity they had witnessed beforehand.

The match was between England and Scotland, who were both failing to distinguish themselves in that year's Five Nations Championship. The Scots saw the chance to redeem themselves when David Chisholm, their fly-half, dropped a second-half goal.

The English were pinned in their own half in the dying moments, when their 26-year-old winger Andy Hancock took hold of the ball and set off. It was only his second international match, and few would have had the confidence to attempt what he did. Evading the first tackle with a typical swerve, he managed to find a surprisingly rapid rhythm as he skipped across the gluey surface. Mud-drenched as they all were, other players were finding it hard to get to him. A gateway to glory opened up along the touchline, and Hancock ran the length of the pitch to score one of the most memorable tries in England's illustrious rugby history. Though Scotland were denied victory, they shared the spoils at 3-3 under the points system in operation at the time. Low-scoring stuff – but what an ending.

Opposite: Scottish player David Rollo in training, prior to the mud-soaked match.

A Political Victory

England's Closely Guarded Win Over South Africa

1969 A few days before Christmas 1969, there was anything but peace and goodwill at Twickenham. Massive anti-apartheid protests had hounded the Springboks wherever they went, and now it took a huge police presence just to make sure the game went ahead. There were demonstrators inside as well as outside the stadium, and they were in conflict with spectators who had just come to see a game of rugby. Some were there that day to see a skilful player touch down under the posts. Others wanted to break through the wall of police and chain themselves to those same posts, in the hope that they could prevent the match from taking place at all.

In this troubled atmosphere, the game was eventually played, and England gained their first victory over the Springboks by coming back from 8-0 down to win 11-8. Piet Grayling, the powerful Springbok forward, breached England's defence to score the first try, and Piet Visagie, the tourists' elegant fly-half, kicked the rest of their points. But Bob Hiller's side gained a foothold when Peter Larter ran in a try shortly before the break, and John Pullin bulldozed his way over the line for the decisive second-half score.

Hiller was on target with a couple of kicks and England secured their historic win. But it was a bitter-sweet day at Twickenham, and left everyone wondering how long a South Africa divided by the evil of apartheid would be able to participate in international sport.

Opposite: England player David Duckham dives to secure a try ahead of his South African opponent.

The Lions Roar in New Zealand

Britain's Pride Against the All Blacks

1971 With a mixture of magic at half-back and true grit up front, the British Lions secured their first series triumph in New Zealand. It was all the tastier because it came against a legendary All Blacks vintage, with the home side led by the fearsome Colin Meads.

Ian 'Mighty Mouse' McLoughlin scavenged a priceless first-Test try from a charge down in Dunedin, and the Lions clung on grimly to win 9-3. But the backlash came in the form of a heavy second-Test defeat, and the Lions captain, John Dawes, and coach Carwyn James, needed to show all their leadership skills to steady the ship.

But they had two Welshmen at half-back who did not need anyone to boost their confidence in the run-up to the penultimate Test in Wellington. Legend has it that the fly-half Barry John said: 'Just give me the ball and I'll win it for you. It's only the All Blacks.' His deceptively powerful partner, scrum-half Gareth Edwards, did just that after holding off several would-be tacklers, and John kept his promise to dive over. Gerald Davies had already done the same on the wing, and the Lions won by a comfortable-sounding 13-3.

In the all-important final Test, the lead changed hands several times before J.P.R. Williams pulled the trigger on a massive drop-goal and waved at the crowd like a pop star when it sailed over. The Lions got a pop star's welcome when they arrived home, too. Fans immediately grasped the immensity of the achievement.

Opposite: The victorious British Lions team returning home as stars. In front are captain John Dawes (left), manager Dr Doug Smith (centre) and Barry John (right).

Edwards' Try for the Barbarians

Taking Up Arms at Cardiff Against the All Blacks

1973 It was, quite simply, the try of the twentieth century. It is a measure of its thrilling quality that the title was never seriously disputed, even in a sport that produces so many spectacular scores. To go over against any All Blacks side takes teamwork and guile. But what the Barbarians did at Cardiff Arms Park on 27 January 1973 was so audacious, so fluent and so miraculously successful that it will be celebrated for as long as the game of rugby union exists.

The move began with no fewer than three stunning sidesteps from Phil Bennett. Seemingly trapped near his own try-line, yet steadfastly refusing to kick, the Welsh fly-half brought roars from the crowd with his matador skills and offloaded to J.P.R. Williams. Anyone who thinks the All Blacks were a willing support act in what followed should remember that, at this perilous point in the move, one of their players, Bryan Williams, almost took Williams's head off with a wild high tackle. But down the left flank the Barbarians surged nevertheless, the momentum maintained by some superb combinations between John Dawes, Tom David and Derek Quinnell.

Finally, from nowhere, Gareth Edwards appeared with an electrifying dash to the try-line. His spectacular dive rounded off the stuff of dreams. Was Quinnell's final pass forward? Who cares?

Gareth Edwards

Born: 12 July 1947

Place of birth: Gwaen-ace-Gurwen, Wales

Caps: 63

Teams: Barbarians, Wales, British Lions

Mal Meninga

Danger From Down Under

1980s A giant of a centre and a colossus as captain, Mal Meninga goes down in history as one of the greatest players ever to have graced a rugby league pitch. In a 13-year Test career he set a world record by scoring 270 points, went on an unprecedented four Kangaroos tours and became the only man to have captained them on two of those trips – 1990 and 1994. To have achieved such a record while bouncing back from no fewer than four arm breaks leaves him up there with the most revered hard men and rugby legends.

Meninga's most memorable moment came at Old Trafford, with the second Test in the balance at 10-10. Deep in his own half, Ricky Stuart drew opponents and Meninga burst on to his well-timed pass. It was the start of an awesome 80 metre dash to clinch the match, and Great Britain's Garry Schofield was left sprawling in his wake as he flew over the line.

Meninga featured in 43 Tests for Australia and led his country 23 times. He was the man Great Britain most feared over the years, and they rarely got the better of him in all that time. It was the same story in Australia, where among his many honours Meninga won five NRL Grand Finals. His power and athleticism, matched with excellent handling skills, solid defence and superb awareness of what was happening around him, made Meninga the complete player.

Mal Meninga

Born: 8 July 1960

Place of birth: Queensland, Australia

Caps: 45

Teams: Queensland, Brisbane, Canberra, Australia

Jonah Lomu

Kiwi Bulldozer

1990s Imagine having to tackle a man who stands six feet five inches tall, weighs nearly 20 stone and can do the 100 metres in 10.8 seconds. Journalists who asked to try – so they could experience the fear of coming up against Lomu during the 1995 Rugby World Cup – were told it was too dangerous. England's rugby players were supposed to be able to handle the challenge, but in truth they just bounced off him or found themselves being run over.

Lomu scored four tries against England in that World Cup semi-final, a one-man demolition job in a 45-29 rout. He left South Africa with seven tries for the tournament and a runners-up medal in his pocket. Soon afterwards, he powered over for touchdowns in each decisive Bledisloe Cup match; and he broke Australian hearts again in 2000, when a world-record crowd of 109,874 watched him score a last-gasp winning try after the Wallabies had led 35-34.

Lomu ran in eight tries at the 1999 World Cup, and looked to have repeated his semi-final heroics of the previous tournament when he swatted away French defenders for a devastating early double. But France stormed back for an unforgettable 43-31 victory, and the giant wing was never destined to lift the Webb Ellis trophy. Even so, his personal tally of 15 tries in two global tournaments is a world record he thoroughly deserves.

Despite battling a serious kidney complaint called nephrotic syndrome, Lomu still managed 73 caps and 215 points for the All Blacks. He was simply unique.

Jonah Lomu

Born: 12 May 1975

Place of birth: Auckland, New Zealand

Caps: 63

Teams: Counties Manukau, Wellington, Cardiff Blues, North Harbour, Hurricanes, Chiefs, Blues, New Zealand

Psychological Warfare

England v Australia, Rugby World Cup Final

1991 Some put Australia's triumph down to the running power of David Campese, Tim Horan and even a Wallabies forward called Willie Ofahengaue; others pointed to rock-solid defence and the tactical acumen of the half-back pairing, Nick Farr-Jones and Michael Lynagh.

But those who worked closely with Australia and England in the build-up to that final will always be convinced that the biggest single factor behind the Wallabies' victory was Campese's mouth. When the controversial three-quarter was not embarrassing all comers with his sublime skills, he spent his time insulting the England rugby team. He attacked the host country's lack of expansive ambition, asking why they bored the world rigid with a forward-led game when they had jewels like Jeremy Guscott and Rory Underwood outside.

Will Carling's team had reached the final with a winning formula, but instead of sticking to it, they fell for Campese's psychological warfare and tried to spin the ball out wide during the showpiece at Twickenham. It did not quite work. There was a moment at 12-3 down when Rory Underwood was about to go clear in the corner, but Campese appeared to knock on deliberately in order to destroy the position. No penalty try was awarded, and Tony Daly's earlier effort for Australia – created by a storming surge from Ofahengaue – remained the only score that did not come from the boots of the goal-kickers, Michael Lynagh or Jonathan Webb. Australia had won 12-6 and England had paid the price for listening to the provocative 'Campo'.

'I knew that '91 was the final throw of the dice for me, which meant a lot of pressure and a lot of build-up and speculation.'

Nick Farr-Jones (pictured opposite kicking the ball from the scrum)

England's Back-to-Back Grand Slams

Carling's Team Achieve the Improbable

1991 & '92 Given their World Cup failures in 1991 and 1995, it is easy to forget that Will Carling's England achieved something very special in 1991 and 1992, albeit on a rather more localized stage. Back-to-back Grand Slams are so hard to achieve that an England team had not managed the feat since 1923 and 1924.

The rugby was not always pretty, but Carling's England did have supreme entertainers in the form of the elegant Jeremy Guscott at centre and the prolific Rory Underwood on the wing. Up front, they had hard men such as Brian Moore and Dean Richards, who would give their heart and soul to ensure an England victory when the fate of a match was in the balance. And there were nervous moments during that unbeaten, two-year reign – none more tricky than the breakaway try France scored at Twickenham, when Philippe Saint-André completed a scintillating move that swept the length of the pitch. Carling's men kept their heads and still came out 21-19 winners that day. They always won during those memorable domestic squabbles, whether they looked the better side or not.

Jason Leonard, England's veteran prop, summed up what they had done quite nicely when he revealed later: 'It wasn't until we fell short during the following two Five Nations tournaments that I realized just how hard it had been to achieve what we did in 1991 and 1992.'

While it was not beautiful, it remains historic, and captain Carling deserved his moments of glory.

'Murrayfield was the big turning point for me as a captain. I realized we had to be more ruthless and professional in our approach to these games.'

Will Carling

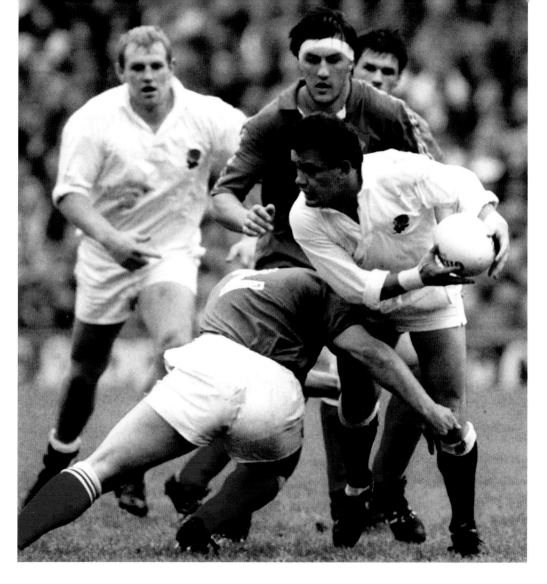

Australia 10 Great Britain 33

Shock Result at Second Test, Melbourne (LEAGUE)

1992 There was no indication from the first Test in Sydney that Great Britain were about to pull off one of their biggest shocks against the seemingly unassailable Australia. They had crashed 22-6 in that opener, and shown so little form that most people thought the Ashes would already be decided by the end of the next contest.

A crowd of 30,000 had come to Melbourne to see a rout, and they duly got one. Incredibly, however, it was the British who ran in five tries and played like a team that did not know what defeat meant. Garry Schofield was an immense leader of the destruction, while the British power base came from a pack entirely composed of Wigan players. The sense of unity was infectious, and quickly spread through the whole British team. Australia, not used to such confidence from their rivals, simply folded in the face of it. They knew it was not their night when Martin Offiah ran on to a forward pass and was allowed to carry on with typical searing pace to the try-line.

The margin of victory equalled Great Britain's biggest ever against the Australians, and set up a mouth-watering third Test in Brisbane. This time, however, the Kangaroos did not underestimate their opponents, and showed just enough grit to emerge 16-10 series winners. Even so, the Melbourne victory went down in history as one of the best British performances of all time against Australia. It had to, because they did not win there again until 2006, losing eight consecutive Tests against Australia and New Zealand in the interim.

Melbourne 1992 remains a wonderful mystery, when everything simply clicked.

Opposite: After 1992, succes in Australia did not come until fourteen years later – here Lee Gilmour aids Great Britain in victory over the Aussies in the Tri-Nations Tournament 2006.

Triumph of the Rainbow Nation

South Africa v New Zealand, World Cup Final

1995 The final itself was a war of attrition, as South Africa somehow contained the awesome power of Jonah Lomu and clinched victory with a late drop-goal from their polished fly-half Joel Stransky. But it was the backdrop to the event that turned the occasion into one of the most intriguing and important since international sport was first played. The scene after the victory remains among the most dramatic and historic that a crowd will ever witness.

The All Blacks went down with food poisoning shortly before the final, and coach Laurie Mains claimed later that their coffee had been spiked at a pre-match banquet. The allegation was never proven, but Jeff Wilson turned pale and had to rush off in front of watching millions; his teammates felt little better.

The need for South Africa to win was immense. It was, in effect, a new country that day, a 'Rainbow Nation' as Archbishop Desmond Tutu had christened it, where skin colour was no longer to be a cause for misery. Nelson Mandela went to the Ellis Park Stadium hoping for a win that would unite whites and blacks in celebration. He got it.

When Stransky's winning kick made it 15-12 and the final whistle blew, Springboks captain Francois Pienaar brought his players together in a tight circle, and they knelt as one to pray. Then a beaming Mandela appeared, wearing a copy of Pienaar's green No. 6 shirt, to present the trophy.

'Thank you for what you have done for South Africa,' Mandela said.

'You have done so much more,' replied Pienaar respectfully.

Apartheid really was history. As the crowd left the stadium, one British journalist said: 'I think I'll just go back to my room and smile for a while.' That was how everyone felt – unless they were a New Zealander.

'South Africa owes you a lot today.'

Nelson Mandela congratulating Francois Pienaar.

The Greatest Team in the World

England's Rugby World Cup Triumph

2003 The funny thing about England in the 2003 World Cup was that they had been far and away the best team on the planet all year long; and now, when it really mattered, there were signs that Clive Woodward's team were starting to run out of steam. There was a series of tired performances on the way to a dour semi-final victory over France, helped by heavy rain and an extraordinary lack of resolve among the Gallic opposition. Everyone knew it would be different against Australia in the final, though at least half the Sydney stadium was decked out in white as England fans travelled halfway round the world to see if the dream would finally come true. In broad sporting terms, the country had been frustrated since the football triumph of 1966.

England coach Clive Woodward loved his soccer and later went to work in the rival game. Martin Johnson liked it too, and both were aware that they stood on the verge of achieving something almost as big as the prize Alf Ramsey and Bobby Moore had given the nation 37 years earlier.

But Australia scored the first try of the final, through Lote Tuqiri. Jason Robinson, who had been out-jumped for the opener, used his searing pace to bring about England's swift reply. Ben Kay fumbled on the line when he might have pressed home England's increasing dominance, and although Johnson's men were 14-5 ahead at half-time, Elton Flatley's nagging goal-kicks kept clawing it back all the way into extra time. Just 21 seconds before the end of that period, Matt Dawson's last charge set up Jonny Wilkinson's decisive drop-goal, and some England fans almost fainted in the excitement. Those close to Martin Johnson said he had never looked so primitively triumphant as the moment when he raised the Webb Ellis trophy above his head for the country that had founded the game. Back home, close to a million people greeted the players at an unforgettable victory parade through London's West End. Not even the boys of '66 had received such acclaim.

'A hot chocolate please…'

Wilkinson ordering room service at the team hotel after the win, while
the rest of his teammates drowned themselves in Champagne.

Buffalo Gets Nasty

American Football's First Transfer

1920 Bob Nash became the first ever player to be transferred between two NFL (National Football League) teams in December 1920. Nicknamed 'Nasty', Nash played his college football for Rutgers – one of the teams which had participated in the first college match back in 1869. When the professional game took off in Ohio 51 years later, with the formation of the American Professional Football Association (APFA), Nash was playing for the Akron Pros. They were one of the original four teams from Ohio to form the American Professional Football Conference (APFC) in 1920 when spiralling wages were causing dysfunction and uniformity was widely called for.

Teams from other states joined to form the APFA later that year, and a league of some description was underway. However, by late 1920, many of the APFA teams were disbanding and hopes of a bona fide championship were fading. Akron was one of four teams – along with Buffalo All-Americans, Canton Bulldogs and Decatur Staleys – still harbouring championship aspirations.

The four teams played a series of matches against one another in December 1920, after which Akron remained undefeated. It was during one of these games that Nash was sold to Buffalo for $300 and five per cent of the gate receipts.

Five years later, he had gone on to become the first ever captain of the New York Giants and enjoyed a successful 10-year career in the game.

Opposite: Rutgers, Bob Nash's college team today,
running out on to the field led by head coach
Greg Schiano.

Pro-Bowl Begins

The Post-Season All-Star Game Kicks Off

1939 The Pro-Bowl began as an annual end-of-season All-Star game between the National Football League champions and a team of top professionals. It first became part of the NFL schedule in January 1939 and took place at Wrigley Field, Los Angeles, California.

The New York Giants were the reigning NFL champions and they hammered a team made up of players from other league teams and two independent sides – Los Angeles Bulldogs and Hollywood Stars. But, for the next four seasons, the All-Star team was made up solely of NFL players, until the event was cancelled following the last game of the 1942 season. When the Pro-Bowl resumed in 1951, the format had changed to a game between All-Stars of two different conferences.

The event has usually been contested between the American and National conference; although between 1954 and 1971 the Eastern and Western conferences competed. Players are traditionally voted into the All-Star teams by fellow professionals and coaches, although fans have also voted since 1995. The Most Valuable Player award has been presented at the match since 1951, and between 1957 and 1971 there were two awards, one for best offensive back and one for best defensive linesman.

Opposite: Pro-Bowl today: NFC New York Giants and AFC Denver Broncos clash in the Pro-Bowl 2006.

Texan Triumph

Cowboys Come Out Fighting

1960 The NFL took the decision to award the city of Dallas, Texas, a franchise in 1960, with oil magnate Clint Murchison Jr and Bedford Wynne obtaining the licence. The franchise was originally named the Steers and then the Rangers, before settling on Dallas Cowboys for the 1960 season. Tex Schramm, previously of the Los Angeles Rams, was hired as general manager and former New York Giants defensive back Tom Landry was appointed head coach.

They were made to play as a 'swing' team in their first year in which they faced up to every team once. On 24 September, the Cowboys played the first game at their Cotton Bowl home – and lost 35-24 to the Pittsburgh Steelers.

They failed to pick up a win for the rest of that season, but they did earn a tie away to New York in their penultimate game, finishing the year with a 0-11-1 record. But Dallas did not have to wait much longer for their first victory. They scraped a win against Pittsburgh 27-24 at the Cotton Bowl on the first day of the 1961 season.

Within five years, they had claimed their first Eastern Division Championship. The Cowboys won their first Super Bowl in 1972 against Miami Dolphins and went on to win four more, although their most recent success was more than a decade ago, in 1995.

Opposite: The Dallas Cowboys defending a field goal kick against the Miami Dolphins during Superbowl VI, 1972.

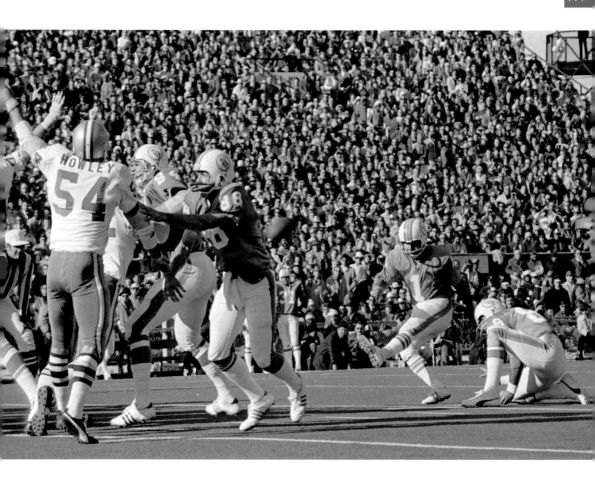

The Birth of Super Bowl

Green Bay Get it All Started

1967 The Super Bowl was created in 1967 when two rival leagues, the National Football League (NFL) and the American Football League (AFL), decided to merge.

The AFL had become the NFL's first serious competitor for 40 years when it began in 1960, and within six years merger talks had started. It was decided during these talks that the winners of the respective leagues should meet on an annual basis to determine the world champion of American Football. This match would be known as the Super Bowl. The NFL originally wanted this clash of giants to be known as The Big One, but AFL founder Lamar Hunt came up with the name Super Bowl after seeing his daughter play with a toy called Super Ball. The name did not become official for another two years, though, as owners originally labelled the contest with the less-than-inspiring title of AFL-NFL World Championship game.

Super Bowl I, which took place in 1967, was contested between the Green Bay Packers of the NFL and the Kansas City Chiefs of the AFL. The game was played in Los Angeles. Over 61,000 fans watched Bart Starr lead the Packers to a 35-10 victory, throwing two touchdowns and picking up the first Super Bowl Most Valuable Player award.

The Packers went on to win the Super Bowl again a year later, and the AFL had to wait until 1969 before the New York Jets became their first winners. By this time the titanic match was already an American institution.

Opposite: Quarterback for the Kansas City Chiefs, Len Dawson, searches for an opening to pass during Superbowl I against the Green Bay Packers.

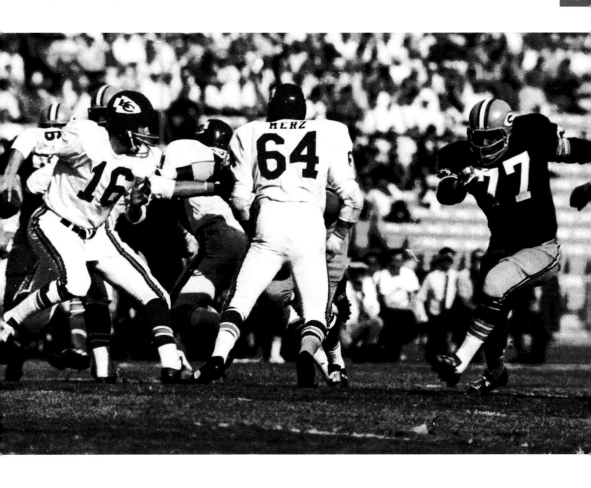

Joe Jets In

Namath Leads the Underdogs to a Famous Victory

1969 Joe Namath helped cause one of the biggest upsets in Super Bowl history as he starred in the New York Jets' 16-7 win over the Baltimore Colts in 1969.

The Colts, of the NFL, were widely regarded as one of the best teams in history at the time, and the Jets, from the AFL, were given little hope. The only two previous Super Bowls had been easily won by NFL giants the Green Bay Packers, and there were many who believed that the AFL was not yet strong enough to compete with its towering opposition.

When quarterback Namath had been drafted out of college football just over four years earlier, he was selected by teams from both leagues; but he opted for the Jets on the advice of club owner Sonny Werblin, who signed him for $400,000. Namath went on to become an AFL All-Star in three of the next four seasons, and it was he who responded to the league's critics prior to the Super Bowl, proclaiming: 'The Jets will win on Sunday; I guarantee it.'

He backed his famous statement up by putting in an MVP (Most Valuable Player) performance on the day, completing 17 of 28 passes for an incredible 206 yards in a historic victory. Namath instantly became an icon for the AFL and boosted the league's legitimacy ahead of its impending merger with the NFL.

Opposite: Quarterback Joe Namath manages to make his pass prior to being taken out by the Colts defence.

Sensational Simpson

O.J.'s Historic 2,000 Yard Rush

1973 O.J. Simpson became the first ever player to rush over 2,000 yards in a season when he posted 2,003 yards in 1973.

He was playing for the Buffalo Bills at the time, and although he had averaged only 622 yards per season before 1972, he had managed 12 touchdowns, and was finding his way into the public consciousness.

Simpson had been drafted out of college by the NFL in 1969, and joined the struggling Bills – who had first pick after their dismal 1-12-1 record the previous season. The truth was, though, that on a weak side, the running back was finding it tough to make an impact – until 1972, that is, when he finally broke the 1,000 yard mark in a season.

After his record-breaking campaign the following year, Simpson rushed over 1,000 yards every year for the next three seasons and became renowned as one of the greatest running backs of all time. He gained 11,236 yards in total throughout his career, which finished with an unsuccessful spell with the San Francisco 49ers in 1979. The tally placed him fourteenth on the NFL's all-time rushing list, and he was inducted into the Hall of Fame in 1985. Simpson also picked up the NFL Player of the Year award two years running – 1972 and 1973 – and played in six Pro Bowls.

O.J. Simpson

Born: 9 July 1947

Place of birth: California, USA

Position: Running Back

NFL Draft: Pick 1/Round 1/1969

Dan the Man

Marino Breaks Record for Touchdown Passes

1984 Dan Marino broke a host of NFL records throughout the 1984 season, including throwing the highest number of touchdown passes in the space of a year.

Playing for the Miami Dolphins, quarterback Marino took only eight games of the season before breaking Bob Griese's record for single-team touchdown passes, and also beat the same man's record for most passing yards in one season. He broke two other NFL records that year, with 362 pass completions and 5,084 yards gained, as well as his 48 touchdown passes in a season as the Dolphins reached the Super Bowl.

The Dolphins met the San Francisco 49ers in a match that pitched Marino against the NFL's other great quarterback of the time – Joe Montana. Marino had a decent game, in which he completed 29 of his 50 passes for 318 yards and one touchdown – but two of these passes were intercepted and he also fumbled a ball for the game's only handling error. The result was that the 49ers won 38-16 and this was sadly Marino's only Super Bowl appearance.

He had only broken into the professional game the previous year, but he went on to complete more pass attempts and more completions than anyone else in the history of the game, and whatever happened later in his career, the legendary quarterback's achievements that season cannot be taken away from him.

Dan Marino

Born: 15 September 1961
Place of birth: Pennsylvania, USA
Position: Quarterback
NFL Draft: Pick 27/Round 1/1983

Quarterback Quality

John Elway Masterminds 'The Drive'

1987 John Elway crafted a 15 play, 98 yard offensive drive in the 1986–87 AFC Championship game, and the feat turned him into an NFL legend.

In this historic game, Elway's team, Denver Broncos, were seven points down to the Cleveland Browns with six minutes to play. Quarterback Elway found himself and his teammates pushed back to their own two-yard line after a long Browns punt; but what happened next will go down in NFL history.

Elway orchestrated a series of unstoppable downs all the way to the other end of the field, which culminated in a five yard touchdown pass to Mark Jackson. The play became known simply as 'The Drive'. Having tied the scores, the game was taken into overtime. But Elway was not finished yet. He constructed a 60 yard drive that ended in the game's winning field-goal, scored by Rich Karlis. The final score was 23-20 to the Broncos – a team led back from the dead by the innovative play of their quarterback.

The season did not end perfectly for Elway and the Broncos, as they were defeated by the New York Giants at the Super Bowl two weeks later – but the now-legendary quarterback earned his first call-up to the Pro Bowl nonetheless.

John Elway

Born: 28 June 1960

Place of birth: Washington, USA

Position: Quarterback

NFL Draft: Pick 1/Round 1/1983

A Global Game

Founding of the World League of American Football

1991 The World League of American Football was founded in 1991 as competition for the long-established NFL.

The United States Football League had started in a similar fashion five years earlier, but this ill-fated league lasted less than 12 months. However, the WLAF was different in the sense that it was an NFL-backed concept that would act more as a feeder league and carry the game to a global market.

When it began, it was made up of six teams from the USA, one from Canada and three from Europe. US cities like Birmingham, Alabama and San Antonio, Texas had not had football teams since the demise of the USFL. But apart from the places it was played, the WLAF never took off throughout the rest of the USA and eventually collapsed. Its lack of superstars made it seem like a minor league rather than a serious competitor for the NFL. This was also backed up by NFL teams loaning their fringe players out to the WLAF to gain them some experience.

The league did receive television coverage through the USA Network and ABC, but in 1992 the NFL pulled the plug on it. However, in 1995 the NFL once again attempted to launch the game outside the USA, and formed an entirely European-based NFL Europe. This more successful plan, away from the elite pros of the USA, still exists today, and has largely done what the WLAF was meant to do – brought American football to the attention of countries outside the Americas.

Opposite: NFL Europe: Frankfurt Galaxy's offence drives through the Amsterdam Admirals' defence during the World Bowl in 2006.

Rice The Record-Breaker

Jerry Rice's 127th Touchdown

1994 Jerry Rice helped the San Francisco 49ers reach the Super Bowl in 1994 while moving into first place in the NFL's all-time list for career touchdowns, with 127.

Wide-receiver Rice, who had starred for home town college team Mississippi Valley during the 1984 season, was drafted into the NFL with the 49ers in 1985. In his rookie season he recorded 49 catches for 927 yards and followed that up with 86 catches, 1,570 yards and 15 touchdowns in 1986. For the next six years he would lead the NFL for receiving and touchdown receptions, and he was named the league's Player of the Year in 1987.

But the following season was arguably his crowning year, as the 49ers reached the Super Bowl. During the season he had caught 64 passes for 1,306 yards and nine touchdowns, and in the big match alone he recorded five catches for 215 yards and one touchdown, as the 49ers beat the Cincinnati Bengals 20-16. He was rightly handed the MVP award.

The 49ers retained the Super Bowl in 1989 with Rice again influential, but it was not until 1994 that he would go back there again. That season got off to the perfect start, as Rice broke the all-time touchdown record in the opening game against the Los Angeles Raiders. The 49ers beat the San Diego Chargers in that year's Super Bowl.

Jerry Rice

Born: 13 October 1962

Place of birth: Mississippi, USA

Position: Wide Receiver

NFL Draft: Pick 16/Round 1/1985

Graham Farmer

Uniting a City

1950s Commuters in Perth, Western Australia, travel along the Graham Farmer Freeway every day, which includes the 'Polly Pipe', the tunnel linking East Perth to West Perth. It is a fitting tribute to Graham 'Polly' Farmer, who played for bitter rivals East Perth and West Perth in the 1950s and 1960s, and united them in respect for a man who many say revolutionized the sport with his prodigiously long and accurate handballs.

The Aboriginal Farmer played for East Perth between 1953 and 1961, winning an incredible seven Fairest and Best awards in his nine seasons at the club, and gaining call-ups to the All-Australian team in 1956, 1958 and 1961.

Farmer moved to Geelong in 1961 for the unprecedented fee of $4,000. He took the team to a Premiership in 1963, captained the side for three seasons and won two successive Fairest and Best awards. In 1967, he returned to Western Australia but he surprised many by not reuniting with East Perth, instead signing for their rivals. There he helped them to two Premierships in four seasons, both times by beating East Perth. It is typical of this modest man – who was inducted into the Australian Football Hall of Fame as a 'Legend' in 1996 – that there is no ill-will towards him on either side of the city.

Opposite: The Perth Skyline; the city that Graham Farmer was able to unite through his impartial play.

The Greatest Comeback of All

Carlton Crush Collingwood in a Classic

1970 The question still being asked in the bars of Melbourne is, 'Were you there at the 1970 Grand Final between Carlton and Collingwood?' There are many who have the privilege of saying 'yes' – a record crowd of 121,696 crammed into the Melbourne Cricket Ground to watch one of the great comebacks in Australian Rules history, when Carlton overturned a 44-point half-time deficit to win by 10 points.

The clash between white-collar Carlton and blue-collar Collingwood was always going to be fiery – the two teams are close neighbours and have the longest-standing and most intense rivalry in the sport. Collingwood were strong favourites, having already beaten Carlton three times in a dominant season, once by a massive 77 points. So there was not much surprise when Collingwood turned the screw in the first half, with free-scoring forward Peter McKenna collecting five goals as his team went in 73-29 ahead. During the half-time break, Carlton coach Ron Barassi issued a famous injunction to his players to 'handball, handball, handball', encouraging a fluid style of play in the second half that many say changed Australian Rules Football forever.

Inspired by Blues legend Alex Jesaulenko, Carlton seemed possessed during the second half. It culminated in a hopeful Jesaulenko punt that seemed to stop and then, as if being sucked by destiny, rolled gently through the posts to complete a 111-101 win.

Opposite: The Melbourne Cricket Ground where the battle was fought between Carlton and Collingwood.

Gary Ablett

God-Given Talent

1980s Despite never being far from controversy, Gary Ablett is widely regarded as one of the greatest players of the modern era. His career featured spectacular peaks and troughs, but he rarely let his off-field travails affect his outstanding contribution on it.

Ablett came from a sound family sporting tradition. His mother was a talented track and field athlete, his father a champion horse trainer, while four of his brothers went on to play professional football. Though his early career did not go to plan – he played only six games for Hawthorn FC in his debut season – a move to Geelong in 1984 galvanized him. As a result of playing 15 games and kicking 31 goals he was awarded the Best and Fairest award (the highest club-based award in Australian Rules Football) at Geelong that same year.

For the next 12 years Ablett was one of the flagship stars of what was to become the Australian Football League. He was nicknamed 'God' by his adoring fans, a label that was to irk him after he became a born-again Christian in 1986.

Ablett announced his retirement in 1991, but his insatiable appetite for the game meant he returned halfway through that season. In total, by the time he hung up his boots in 1997, he had played 242 games for Geelong, kicked 1,021 goals for the team and had been voted into the AFL and Geelong teams of the century.

Gary Ablett

Born: 1 October 1961
Place of birth: Victoria, Australia
Goal total: 1,030 (inlcuding for Hawthorn)
Teams: Hawthorn, Geelong

Michael Long

Aboriginal Hero

1993 Michael Long is known not only as an Australian Rules great, but also as a campaigner against racism and an ambassador for Australian Aborigines. A superstar for Essendon for over a decade, Long is perhaps most famous for his incredible performance against Carlton in the 1993 Grand Final. Long ran amok in the game, amassing 20 kicks and 13 handballs to win the Norm Smith medal for the best player on the ground. That year was also International Year for the World's Indigenous People, and it was symbolic that Graham Farmer, another indigenous great, presented Long with his award.

Long made his Essendon debut in 1989 and retired in 2001, when injury forced him to pull out of the Grand Final the night before the game. He is also well known for accusing Collingwood ruckman Damien Monkhorst of racially taunting him during the 1995 season, which had a major effect in combatting racism in the game.

Since retiring, he has been busy campaigning for Aboriginal rights in Australia. In 2004, he walked from Melbourne to Canberra in 'The Long Walk' to speak to the prime minister, John Howard, who he had famously called 'cold-hearted' after Howard refused to apologize for the country's historical treatment of its indigenous people.

Michael Long (shown opposite, second from right)

Born: 1 October 1961

Place of birth: Darwin, Australia

Teams: Evagnago, West Torrens, St. Mary's, Essendon

NaNNaNNaN

Pat Spillane

Gaelic Great

1980s Of all the stars of Gaelic football, none has shone brighter than Pat Spillane, who played for the dominant Kerry team in the 1970s and 1980s. The left half-forward was named in the Gaelic Athletic Association's Gaelic Football Team of the Millennium.

He was born in 1955 near Kenmare in Co. Kerry, and won eight All-Ireland Senior Football Championship medals, the first as a 19-year-old in 1975, the last in 1986. He has received nine GAA All Star Awards, more than any other player in Gaelic football history.

Spillane is considered one of the most imaginative and entertaining players in the history of the game, and his quotes were often as colourful as his performances on the pitch. He famously coined the phrase 'puke football' in reference to the blitz style of play that was pioneered by Ulster teams of the era.

He made an amazing comeback from a ruptured cruciate in 1981, playing through the pain barrier the following year until he had an operation. 'No one came back playing football in Ireland having ruptured their cruciate in the eighties,' he said in an interview. 'I came back a much harder individual.'

He retired in 1991, having lost to Down in an All-Ireland semi-final.

Pat Spillane

Born: 1 December 1955

Place of birth: Kerry, Ireland

Position: Half-forward

Teams: Kerry, Munster

Opposite: Kerry v Dublin in the replay of the All-Ireland final in 1976.

BALL GAMES & TARGET SPORTS

America leads the way in many of the world's most popular ball games, notably basketball and baseball – two of the most popular pastimes in the USA. Sports that involve a bat as well as a ball rely as much on concentration, mental strength and timing, as on power and aggression. Nowhere is that more evident than in arguably the most popular sport in the world, golf.

Team games involving the bat and ball, meanwhile, regularly pit an individual against an entire team. For instance, in sports such as baseball and cricket, the batsmen are continually asked questions by the pitchers and bowlers respectively and must come up with the answers with split-second timing. Tennis and hockey are also explored in this section as we get to grips with some of the best-loved ball games and target sports.

Babe Sox it to 'Em

Babe Ruth Joins the Yankees for a Record Fee

1919 Without any doubt, the most important move in the history of baseball took place in December 1919, when the dominant force in the game, the Boston Red Sox, decided to offload one of their star players.

The Sox had won the World Series in 1903, 1912, 1915, 1916 and 1918 before choosing to reshuffle their roster – with catastrophic consequences. Boston Red Sox's new owner, Harry Frazee, sold a promising ball player called George Ruth to bitter rivals, the New York Yankees. The price was $100,000 and there was also a $350,000 loan used to finance Frazee's girlfriend's Broadway play, but the deal became known as the 'Curse of the Bambino' – in reference to Ruth's nickname 'Babe'.

Over the next century, the Yankees, who had never previously won anything, would go on to scoop 26 World Series titles while the Red Sox suffered disaster after disaster, which translated into a barren 84 year run until they won the World Series in 2004.

Babe Ruth

Born: 6 February 1895   **Died:** 16 August 1948

Place of birth: Maryland, USA

Career home runs: 714

Teams: Baltimore Orioles, Boston Red Sox, New York Yankees

'Where Do You Want It?'

Babe Ruth and the World Series Final

1932 Born in Baltimore, Maryland, George Herman 'Babe' Ruth revolutionized the game of baseball with an awesome batting technique, which earned him the nickname the 'Sultan of Swat'. In 1927, Ruth hit an almighty 60 home runs in 154 games and set the standard for big hitters in the big league. His hulking frame enabled him to generate phenomenal power at the plate, making his swing seem almost effortless.

Ruth's crowning glory, however, arrived in the 1932 World Series in game three against the Chicago Cubs. With the pressure mounting, Ruth had already faced two balls and two strikes in the fifth innings. But with Cubs' pitcher Charlie Root on the mound, Ruth nonchalantly pointed to the bleachers at centre-field before launching the longest home run ever recorded at Wrigley Field – to exactly where he had signalled.

The Yankees went on to win the World Series – the club's third title in four years – and Ruth's audacious exhibition of skill became ingrained into the fabric of the game.

'To understand him you had to understand this: he wasn't human.'

Joe Dugan

Opposite: Babe Ruth crosses the plate after hitting a home run in the first innings of the 1932 game.

Go Joe, Go

Joltin' Joe Becomes Baseball's Top Earner

1949 On 7 February 1949, Joe DiMaggio signed a contract for $100,000 ($70,000 plus bonuses) to make him baseball's wealthiest player. That huge deal was fully justified, however, because DiMaggio – the son of Sicilian immigrants – had made groundbreaking strides in the game since joining the New York Yankees from the San Francisco Seals in 1936. Even as a rookie, the quietly spoken DiMaggio made a huge impact, winning the championship in each of his first four seasons – an unprecedented achievement in any American sport.

A sporting icon, DiMaggio was worshipped by the American public and became arguably one of the most popular players to have ever picked up a bat. His most impressive achievement was undoubtedly a hot streak between May and July 1941, in which he managed to record a hit in 56 consecutive games. That phenomenal run included a total of 15 home runs and 55 runs batted in. The American public was gripped with excitement by the feat.

DiMaggio retired from the game in 1951 after amassing 361 home runs. He averaged 118 runs batted in (RBI) per season and compiled a .325 lifetime batting average. Nicknamed the 'Yankee Clipper' and 'Joltin' Joe', DiMaggio left an indelible mark on the game he loved and was an immaculate ambassador for baseball.

Joe DiMaggio

Born: 25 November 1914　　**Died:** 8 March 1999

Place of birth: California, USA

Career home runs: 361

Teams: New York Yankees

'I'd like to thank the good Lord for making me a Yankee.'

Joe DiMaggio

Premium Bonds

Bonds Breaks McGwire's Home-Run Record

2001 A thoroughbred baseball player, Barry Bonds – son of former major-league baseball Most Valuable Player Bobby Bonds – wrote himself into the record books by hitting 73 home runs in a single season in 2001.

California-born Bonds started out with the Pittsburgh Pirates and developed a reputation as a big hitter at the plate – striking 16 home runs in his rookie year. In 1990, he was named Major League Baseball's (MLB's) MVP and hit 33 home runs while boasting an enviable batting average. But it was only when he joined the San Francisco Giants in 1993 that Bonds started making significant strides towards Babe Ruth's legendary total.

In 1996, he joined an elite group of ball players that formed the 300 homer/300 stolen-base club, alongside some familiar names, including André Dawson, Willie Mays – his godfather – and his own father, Bobby.

After a hugely productive 2000, Bonds stepped up a gear the following year and – by his team's opening 50 games – he had struck 28 home runs. By the All-Star break in the season, he had struck 39 and boasted a .863 hitting percentage – a ratio not seen in the game since the days of the legendary Mickey Mantle. When the season finally came to an end, he had reached the 73 mark, surpassing Mark McGwire's tally of 70 in 1998, and written his name into the record books – at the age of 36.

Sadly, his towering achievements have been dogged by rumours of alleged steroid abuse which has taken the shine off his phenomenal achievement.

Barry Bonds

Born: 24 July 1964
Place of birth: California, USA
Career home runs: 734
Teams: Pittsburgh Pirates, San Francisco Giants

Wilt's Ton of Joy

Wilt Chamberlain Scores 100

1962 Nicknamed 'Wilt the Stilt' and the 'Big Dipper', Wilt Chamberlain revolutionized the game of basketball with a series of record-breaking feats in his illustrious career. But perhaps his most celebrated achievement came in March 1962, when he became the first player to score 100 points in a single game.

Playing for the Los Angeles Lakers, Chamberlain scored 59 points in the second half of his team's 169-147 win over the New York Knicks. Chamberlain sunk the century-making basket with just 45 seconds of the game remaining and was duly mobbed by fans. On the day, Chamberlain scored with 36 out of his 63 attempts, but afterwards he said he was actually embarrassed with his ratio of successful shots.

Chamberlain also boasted the second-best individual tally of 78 until that record was broken by Lakers star Kobe Bryant in January 2006, when he accumulated 81.

One of Chamberlain's most revered achievements was his unique quadruple double-double – the name given to a player recording 40 points, and 40 rebounds or 40 assists in one game. He achieved the feat on 21 January 1960, when he scored 58 points and grabbed 42 rebounds against the Detroit Pistons.

Chamberlain, a 7 foot 1 inch giant, made an indelible mark on the game of basketball and was duly inducted into the NBA's (National Basketball Association's) Hall of Fame in 1978, after breaking dozens of records during his illustrious career.

Wilt Chamberlain

Born: 21 August 1936   **Died:** 12 October 1999

Place of birth: Pennsylvania, USA

Height: 7 ft 1 in

Draft: 1959, Philadelphia Warriors

Reed 'Em and Weep

Willis Reed Inspires a Maiden Knicks Victory

1970 A one-club man, New York Knicks favourite Willis Reed's finest hour in his trophy-laden career came on 8 May 1970, in game seven of the NBA finals against the Los Angeles Lakers.

In front of an expectant Madison Square Garden crowd, Reed – then 27 – shrugged off a troublesome thigh injury and seized control of the game. He was nothing short of inspirational as the Knicks won the game 113-99 to take the NBA title to the 'Big Apple' for the first time ever.

After winning the NBA Rookie of the Year award in his debut year (1964), Reed provided tremendous service to the Knicks before injury forced him to retire in 1974. In his glorious career, he played in seven All-Star games and in the 650 appearances he made for New York, he averaged 18.7 points and 12.9 rebounds per game.

He was inducted into Basketball's Hall of Fame in 1982 and is widely considered to be one of the greatest ever players to have worn the Knicks' colours. Accordingly, they retired his No. 19 shirt as a fitting tribute to his achievements for the club.

Willis Reed

Born: 25 June 1942
Place of birth: Louisiana, USA
Height: 6'9"
Draft: 1964, New York Knicks

'Go for the moon. If you don't get it, you'll still be heading for a star.'

Willis Reed

Shorn From the USA

The USA is Cheated Out of Gold

1972 Controversy reigned in Munich when the USA lost its first basketball contest at Olympic level – the USSR stealing the title by a single point in the final. The shock result ended the USA's 63-game winning streak and broke an uninterrupted run of seven consecutive Olympic gold medals.

All the pundits expected to see an American win, but the Soviet team was a well-drilled and proficient unit, and the contest evolved into an absolute classic. After visibly rattling the red-hot favourites, the Soviets began to pull away before the USA reduced the deficit to just one point – making it 49-48 with only 40 seconds remaining.

The Soviets tried to kill the game off but, with time almost up, Doug Collins led a breakaway and was fouled en route to the basket. There were still three seconds on the clock as Collins kept his nerve and sank both free throws to put the USA in front 50-49, but the horn to signal full-time was incorrectly sounded during his second attempt. The players became completely confused and after the referee had reset the clock to three seconds, the USA held on and celebrated on the court.

However, R. William Jones, secretary-general of FIBA (*Fédération Internationale de Basketball* or, simply, the International Basketball Federation), stepped in and ordered the clock to be reset for a second time at three seconds – and the USSR grabbed the opportunity with both hands as Aleksander Belov scored to claim a hugely contentious victory.

In disgust, the USA appealed against the decision, ultimately unsuccessfully, and then refused to accept their silver medals.

Opposite: Aleksandr Belov tips the balance in favour of the Soviet team as he scores the winning basket.

Now That's Magic

Earvin Johnson Plays Every Position on Court

1980 As a 21-year-old rookie, Earvin Johnson justified his nickname 'Magic' with a spellbinding display to help the Los Angeles Lakers record an NBA finals win over the Philadelphia 76ers.

Point guard Johnson was the missing piece in the Lakers' jigsaw and, alongside highly-rated centre Kareem Abdul-Jabbar, he captivated fans with his mixture of steely determination and showmanship. But it was Johnson's versatility in that season's finals against Philadelphia that really endeared him to the nation. With Abdul-Jabbar injured, Johnson started at centre in game six of the series in Philadelphia, but subsequently played in every position on the court while giving the performance of his life.

Johnson scored 42 points, clocked up 15 rebounds and recorded seven assists. As a result, the Lakers won the decisive match to clinch the series 4-2 and lift the NBA Championship. Accordingly, Johnson was named the finals' Most Valuable Player and, even though he went on to experience further highs in his career, that single game was arguably his finest moment.

Earvin Johnson retired from the game in 1992, but the 'Magic' of that night still lingers on in the hearts of basketball fans across the world.

Earvin Johnson

Born: 14 August 1959

Place of birth: Michigan, USA

Height: 6 ft 9 in

Draft: 1979, Los Angeles Lakers

'All kids need is a little help, a little hope and somebody who believes in them.'

Magic Johnson

Ruler of the Court

Michael Jordan's Golden Decade

1990s In the 1990s, Michael Jordan was the most famous sportsman in the world and, for a decade, his achievements on the basketball court were unparalleled. After establishing himself as one of the most potent forces in the NBA, the Chicago Bulls guard touched greatness during the 1990-91 season and managed to sustain a phenomenal level of form during the seasons that followed.

Brooklyn-born Jordan won six NBA championships (1991, 1992, 1993, 1996, 1997 and 1998) and was named the NBA's Most Valuable Player five times (1988, 1991, 1992, 1996 and 1998). In addition, on two occasions he won the accolade of triple MVP – picking up the top honour for being the greatest performer in the regular season, the finals and the All-Star game.

Jordan's fame rose to such an extent that even those who were not basketball fans had heard of his prowess as a sportsman. His athleticism and professionalism set a benchmark for the sport and greatly enhanced the game's worldwide popularity.

Jordan shocked his fans when he retired in 1993, but he rekindled his love for the game in 1995 and continued to play until his second and final retirement in January 1999, leaving behind some breathtaking memories and groundbreaking achievements.

Michael Jordan

Born: 17 January 1963
Place of birth: New York, USA
Height: 6 ft 6 in
Draft: 1984, Chicago Bulls

Hoop and Glory

Jordan's Amazing Play During the NBA Finals

1991 In sport, there is always a fine line between success and failure. And, in 1991, Michael Jordan adjusted his individual style of play for the benefit of his team, the Chicago Bulls, and it ended in glory.

After narrowly losing to the Detroit Pistons in the Eastern Conference finals the previous year, Jordan agreed to Bulls coach Phil Jackson's idea of employing a 'triangle offence'.

The tactical change immediately paid dividends, with the Bulls finishing the regular season in the top spot – the first time the club had achieved that feat for 16 years – and in the process setting a franchise record with 61 wins.

The Jordan-inspired Bulls comfortably won the Eastern Conference, brushing aside the New York Knicks, Philadelphia 76ers and the Pistons, before meeting the Los Angeles Lakers in the finals. Chicago carried on its awesome form against the Lakers and Jordan stole the show with a performance that was head and shoulders above his peers. Overcome by emotion, Jordan openly wept as he lifted the NBA finals trophy for the first time ever.

Jordan's most memorable contribution came when he switched hands while in mid-air to score a superb lay-up. It was just one of many sensational moves that were to become a trademark feature of his play.

'To be successful you have to be selfish, or else you never achieve. And once you get to your highest level, then you have to be unselfish. Stay reachable. Stay in touch. Don't isolate.'

Michael Jordan

No Bull – Chicago are the Best

Chicago Bulls Make History with Their 70th Win

1995–96 Records are there to be broken and, with a genuine air of invincibility, the Chicago Bulls reached a milestone during the 1995–96 season by ending the regular season with a 72-10 record.

The Bulls' roster oozed quality from the starting line up to the bench, and it translated into the best single season improvement – moving from the previous season's record of 47-35. Every single player who wore the Bulls' uniform during that regular season performed at the zenith of their powers, ranging from Michael Jordan scooping his eighth scoring title to Dennis Rodman picking up his fifth straight gong for rebounds. Meanwhile, Steve Kerr was the NBA's leading three-point specialist. Just one glance at the Bulls' starting five reads like a Who's Who of NBA legends – Jordan, Rodman, Scott Pippen, Ron Harper and Luc Longley.

The 72 wins total chalked up that year remains the best regular-season record of all time, and the Bulls effortlessly made the impossible look relatively straightforward. Unsurprisingly, Chicago defeated Seattle in the finals and Bulls coach Phil Jackson was deservedly named coach of the year, while Toni Kukoc was the Sixth Man of the year (a 'sixth man' being a regularly playing substitute).

All in all, an *annus mirabilis* for the celebrated basketball team from the Windy City.

Opposite: Bulls' Toni Kukoc leaps to shoot over the head of SuperSonics opponent Gary Payton.

Bradman Takes on the English

A Magnificent Year

1930 No player in the history of cricket has captured the public's imagination more than Don Bradman did on the tour of England in 1930. Bradman was just 21 years old when he began his first international tour, and he went on to score 2,960 runs at an average of 98.66, including 10 centuries. He scored a double hundred in his first innings of the tour against Worcestershire and then 185 not out in his second against Leicestershire. English crowds flocked to watch the new batting phenomenon and the Test series was dubbed 'Bradman versus England'.

In the third Test at Leeds he became only the third player to score a hundred before lunch in England, and was 309 not out at close of play on the first day. He was out for 334 on the second morning – at the time a world record for Test cricket. Bradman finished the Test series – which Australia won 2-1 – with 974 runs at an average of just under 140, including two doubles and a triple hundred.

Bradman's prodigious batting inspired Douglas Jardine to come up with the 'bodyline' tactics that marred the following Ashes series.

Don Bradman

Born: 27 August 1908   **Died:** 25 February 2001

Place of birth: New South Wales, Australia

Batting average: 99.94

Teams: New South Wales, Australia

Sir Len Lets Loose

Hutton's 364 Against the Aussies

1938 England went into the final Test of the 1938 Ashes at the Oval 1-0 down, before Len Hutton proceeded to play one of the most remarkable innings in Test history. The young Yorkshireman surpassed Don Bradman's then-world-record Test score of 334 as England posted a mammoth first-innings total of 903 for seven.

As a boy of 14, Hutton had watched Bradman's mammoth innings and marvelled at the Australian's strokeplay. Eight years later he was to surpass his hero's achievement. England captain Wally Hammond wanted 1,000 on the board to be certain of victory and Hutton, adapting his game perfectly to the needs of the occasion, obliged by staying at the crease for 13 hours and 17 minutes. At the time, Hutton's innings was the longest ever played in first-class cricket. He gave only one chance, and that a stumping, as he hit 35 fours, 15 threes, 18 twos and 143 singles.

Denis Compton, who was out for one in the same innings, later said of Hutton's knock: 'Apart from his endurance, his concentration and dedication were fantastic, he was just never out of tempo. I have never seen anyone who looked less likely to get out.'

Len Hutton

Born: 23 June 1916   **Died:** 6 September 1990

Place of birth: Yorkshire, England

Batting average: 56.67

Teams: Yorkshire, England

A Glorious Summer

Compton and Edrich Take Centre Stage

1947 The 1947 English cricket season will forever be remembered for the scintillating batting of Middlesex and England pair Denis Compton and Bill Edrich. The opening partnership created batting records that may never be beaten, and lit up a country desperate for optimism in the dark days following the Second World War.

The pair were integral to England beating South Africa 3-0 in the five-match Test series, with four of Compton's record 18 hundreds in the season coming in Tests. Compton topped the first-class averages with 3,816 runs at 90.85, while Edrich ended the season with 3,539 at 80.43. Remarkably, Edrich also captured 67 wickets in the season as the pair helped Middlesex to the County Championship title.

The only cloud in that perfect summer came in the very last county match at Lord's when Compton was forced to retire to the pavilion because of knee trouble. He came out to make a second-innings century, another against the South Africans, and a further 246 – the knee strapped – for Middlesex against The Rest at The Oval. As a batsman, though, he was never quite the same again, and the injured knee eventually forced his retirement nine years later.

Opposite: Denis Compton following through on another fantastic shot to aid England's win over South Africa.

Perfect Ten

Jim Laker Claims the Australian Team

1956 It is impossible to utter the name Jim Laker without thinking of the 19 wickets he took in what became known as 'Laker's Test' against Australia at Old Trafford in 1956.

Laker, arguably the finest off-spinner in history, took nine for 37 in the first innings and followed it up with all 10 for just 53 in the second, as England claimed a memorable victory. Laker finished with match figures of 19 for 90, and to this day they remain the best figures in a first-class match.

Remarkably, Laker had also taken all 10 wickets in an innings for Surrey against the same Australian tourists earlier in the season. Australian wickets had at this time become so unresponsive to finger spin that sides became almost entirely reliant on pace and wrist spin. On a dry turner, this could explain their susceptibility to Laker, but it should be remembered that Tony Lock – an equal of Laker as a finger spinner – was bowling at the other end and collected just one wicket in the match.

Laker's achievement of taking 10 wickets in an innings has been repeated only once in Tests, by Anil Kumble in 1999.

Jim Laker

Born: 9 February 1922   **Died:** 23 April 1986

Place of birth: Yorkshire, England

Batting average: 14.08

Teams: Yorkshire, Surrey, Auckland, Essex, England

The Basil d'Oliveira Affair

Storm in South Africa

1968 Born and raised in Cape Town, Basil d'Oliveira was classified as a 'Cape Coloured', and therefore grew up as a second-class citizen in South Africa's apartheid era. Quite clearly one of the finest cricketers in his country, 'Dolly' was nevertheless banned from first-class cricket. Despite this, all-rounder d'Oliveira dominated the SACBOC (South African Cricket Board of Control – the first non-racial cricket organization in South Africa) league for more than a decade on primitive tracks that clearly favoured the bowlers.

He arrived in the north of England in 1960, after West Indian fast bowler Wes Hall pulled out of a contract with Middleton in the Central Lancashire League. D'Oliveira's impressive form for Middleton led to a career in county cricket with Worcestershire. His fine technique, honed by years playing on bad wickets, saw him selected for an England Test debut in 1966.

Coming into Test cricket aged 34, d'Oliveira was a natural. His strength and timing enabled him to score freely off any bowler, and was at his best cutting, driving and pulling off the back foot. When the squad for the 1968 tour to South Africa was announced and d'Oliveira's name was missing, the public were outraged, thinking that the omission of the 1967 Cricketer of the Year was for political reasons.

Dolly eventually replaced the injured seam bowler Tom Cartwright, but South Africa refused entry to the England party, who then cancelled the tour. Sporting exile followed for the apartheid nation, but d'Oliveira went on to play many more Tests for England.

Basil d'Oliveira

Born: 4 October 1931

Place of birth: Cape Town, South Africa

Batting average: 40.06

Teams: Middleton, Worcestershire, England

Sir Garfield Smashes Nash

Sobers Hits Six Sixes in an Over

1968 On 31 August 1968, Sir Garfield Sobers' place in cricket's hall of fame was cemented, when he became the first player in history to hit six sixes in an over.

The West Indian all-rounder was playing for his county Nottinghamshire, and Glamorgan's Malcolm Nash was the unfortunate bowler on the receiving end of one of the most spectacular displays of clean hitting ever witnessed.

Nottinghamshire were chasing quick runs as they sought a declaration, and Sobers found himself up against Nash, normally a briskish, medium-pace bowler, experimenting as a slow left-armer. The experiment did not last long. Nash's first two deliveries disappeared into the stands of the Cricketer's Inn at Swansea, and it dawned on Sobers that he may be on to something special. The third flew straight into the pavilion enclosure and the fourth ball cleared the scoreboard. The fifth was hit long and straight, and although Roger Davis caught it, he fell over the boundary rope in the process, and another six was signalled.

Sobers pulled the sixth ball out of the ground and into St Helen's Avenue, confirming his place in history. The ball itself was not found until the following day.

Opposite: Sobers prepares to play a ball for his county team, Nottinghamshire, much to the dismay of the wicket-keeper.

Geoff Boycott's Historic Innings

A Hundred Hundreds

1977 Fairytales do not come much better than Geoffrey Boycott scoring his hundredth first-class hundred in an Ashes Test in front of a full house at Headingley.

A Yorkshireman to his very core, Boycott had returned to Test cricket two Tests previously, following a three-year self-imposed exile from the international arena. His return at Trent Bridge in 1977 had been marred by his running out local hero Derek Randall, although – typically – Boycott went on to score a hundred, his 99th.

In superb conditions for batting at the usually seamer-friendly Headingley, Boycott knew he had a chance to further etch his name in history when the fourth Test came round. When captain Mike Brearley won the toss and elected to bat, Boycott readied himself for his moment of destiny. He shrugged off the loss of Brearley for a duck and went on to produce a masterful knock against an attack containing Jeff Thomson, Len Pascoe and Max Walker. Boycott reached his hundred with a trademark on-drive off the bowling of Greg Chappell, and was engulfed by his adoring public.

He went on to score 191 as England won by an innings. Boycott said: 'If somebody had told me when I started out I'd score a hundred hundreds I wouldn't have believed them. But if they'd told me I'd score my hundredth hundred in front of a capacity Headingley crowd, against Australia, I'd have said "you're mad, you're crackers".'

Geoff Boycott

Born: 21 October 1940

Place of birth: Yorkshire, England

Batting average: 47.72

Teams: Yorkshire, England

Botham's Ashes

Beefy Bashes the Aussies

1981 Never has one player made such an individual impact on a series as Ian Botham did during the 1981 Ashes series. England were 1-0 down in the series at the start of the third Test, when Botham found the form of his life to save his side from a seemingly irretrievable position.

England looked to be stumbling to defeat at 135-7 in their second innings, still 95 runs behind Australia after following on. But Botham smashed a century in 87 balls to finish with 149 not out as England eventually posted a 129-run lead. Beefy then took the first Australian wicket with 56 runs on the board, before Bob Willis stunned the visitors with eight for 43 to leave them stranded 18 runs short, levelling the series.

At Edgbaston, in the following Test, Australia were again in a winning position, needing just 45 runs to win with five wickets in hand. Botham had other ideas, however, and skittled the remaining batsmen, conceding just one run in the process.

Fans thought Botham could do no wrong, so it was a major surprise when he found himself out first ball at Old Trafford in the first innings of the fourth Test. However, he bounced back with 118 in the second innings to help England to a 505-run lead that Australia never seriously threatened.

With the Ashes in the bag, a confident Botham claimed 10 wickets in the final drawn game at the Oval, completing a remarkable personal contribution.

Ian Botham

Born: 24 November 1955

Place of birth: Cheshire, England

Batting average: 33.54

Teams: Somerset, Worcestershire, Durham, Queensland, England

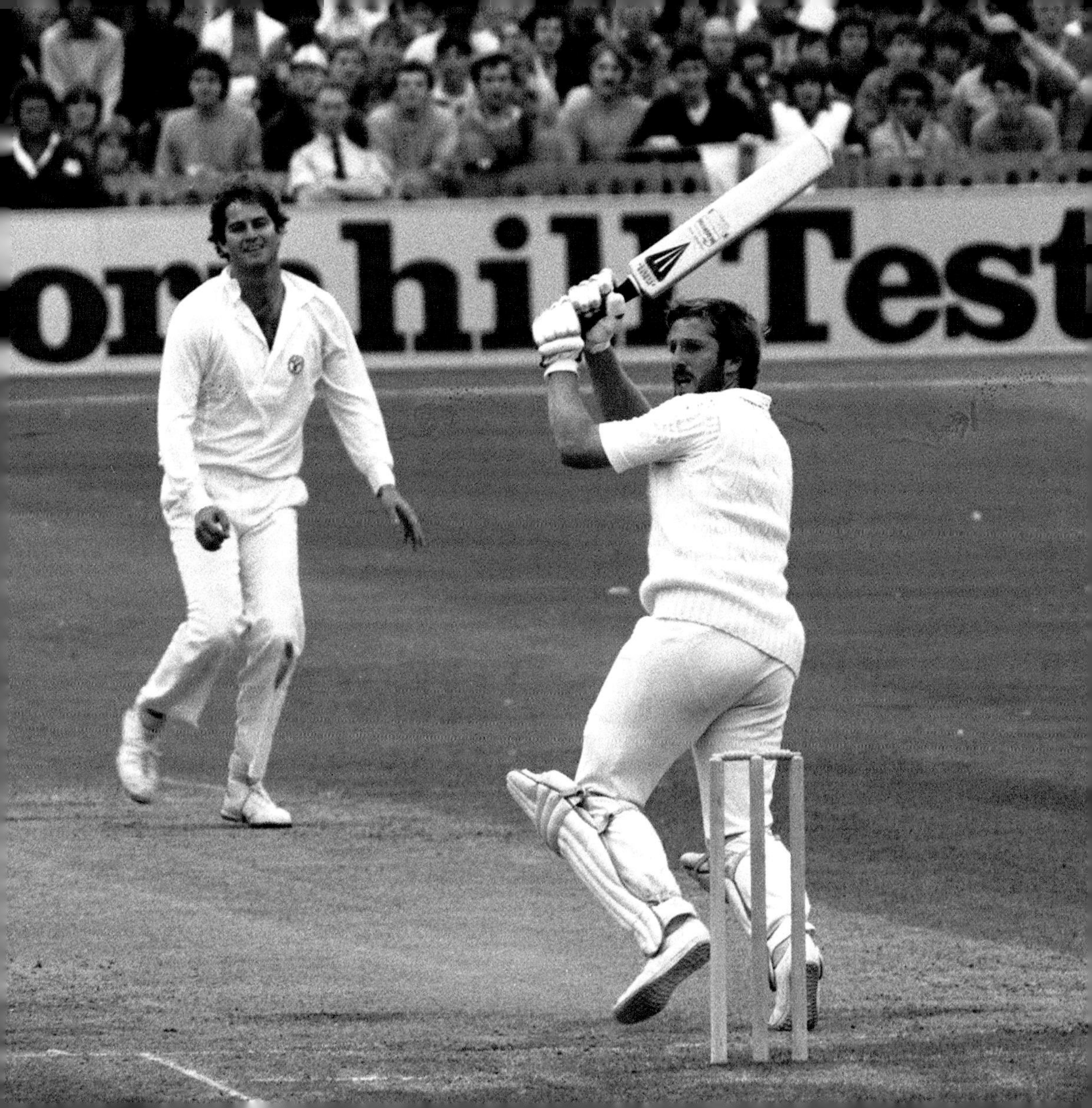

Golden Graeme

Hick Hits A Record-Breaking 405

1988 Graeme Hick never came close to fulfilling his abundant potential at Test level, and it was performances such as his record-breaking run at Taunton in 1988 that make his failures at the very top level such a mystery.

Playing for Worcestershire – the county side he represented throughout his entire career – Hick dismantled the Somerset attack on his way to an individual score of 405 not out. The Zimbabwean-born Hick's total was the highest innings recorded on the County Championship circuit since 1895, and was made all the more remarkable by the fact that, at one point, his side were in desperate trouble, at 132-5.

Speaking about his colleague's staggering innings, Ian Botham commented: 'I can't imagine you will see a greater innings than Graeme's today – he's certainly the best white batsman I've seen.'

Just as in Brian Lara's famous innings of 501 not out, Hick was given an early life when he avoided a big LBW shout on facing his first ball. He was later dropped on 148 but that blemish aside, Hick went on for 555 minutes of flawless batting, helping himself to 35 fours and 11 sixes – his last hundred coming off just 58 balls.

Graeme Hick

Born: 23 May 1966

Place of birth: Zimbabwe, Africa

Batting average: 31.32

Teams: Zimbabwe, Worcestershire, Queensland, England

Triple Nelson for England Star

Gooch Gets Going

1990 Graham Gooch's monumental innings of 333 at Lord's in 1990 understandably dominated the headlines, as England crushed India in the opening Test of the series. The long, hot summer had baked English pitches dry and Gooch had no hesitation in choosing to bat against an Indian bowling attack containing an ageing Kapil Dev, but little else in the way of threat.

Gooch batted for more than 10 hours, facing 485 balls and hitting 43 fours and three sixes, as England posted a mammoth first-innings total of 653 for four. Only Len Hutton and Wally Hammond have made higher individual scores for England in a Test.

India's response saw an audacious hundred from skipper Mohammad Azharuddin, but they looked dead and buried at 430 for nine on the fourth morning. Kapil had other ideas, and proceeded to smash Eddie Hemmings for four sixes in four balls to save the follow-on in the most audacious way imaginable.

Gooch was at it again in the second innings, scoring 123 to take the record for the highest individual batting aggregate in a single Test. India batted manfully in their fourth innings, but thanks to an inspired spell from Angus Fraser, England claimed a famous win. The final wicket saw a run-out from a direct hit – by that man Gooch.

Graham Gooch

Born: 23 July 1953

Place of birth: London, England

Batting average: 42.58

Teams: Essex, England

Michael Atherton Leads England

Captain Fantastic

1990s Captaining England was the fulfilment of destiny for Michael Atherton. Educated at Manchester Grammar School and Cambridge University, Atherton's teammates otched 'FEC' on to his coffin case in his first season at Lancashire. The initials stood for 'Future England Captain', and after making his Test debut in 1989 it was only a matter of time before the elevation came. Sure enough, in 1993, at the age of 25, Atherton was handed the reins when Graham Gooch resigned mid-series against Australia.

Atherton produced a typically gutsy 72 but he could not prevent England slipping to yet another defeat. That Test was to prove a microcosm of the record 54 games in which Atherton led his country, as his fellow batsmen were rarely able to match him for skill, guts and bloody-minded determination.

Atherton's pinnacle came against South Africa at Johannesburg in 1995–96, when he batted for almost 11 hours to score 185 not out, saving England from certain defeat. His nadir came at Lord's in 1994 with the 'dirt-in-the-pocket affair', when he was fined by the ICC for rubbing soil on the ball and subsequently hung out to dry by chairman of selectors Ray Illingworth.

Although England never came close to winning the Ashes under Atherton, his place in the hearts of the English cricketing public is assured.

Opposite: Michael Atherton launches the ball into the air for four, during the fourth Test against South Africa at Port Elizabeth, 1995.

Sachin Sets the Record

Tendulkar Hits the Most Test Cricket Centuries

1990s

Along with Brian Lara, Sachin Tendulkar is widely regarded as the greatest batsman of his generation. Sir Don Bradman once described him as the modern-day player most like him in his pomp.

Ever since he burst on to the international scene as a wide-eyed 16-year-old in 1989, Tendulkar was destined for greatness. He scored his maiden Test hundred against England in 1990 – a brilliant rearguard effort that saved the Test for India – and to date he has racked up a world record 35 Test-match centuries. The Little Master's 35th hundred took him past his guru Sunil Gavaskar on the all-time list and, at the age of 33, few would bet against him making it to 40. He is already the first player to score 50 international hundreds and a mark of the man's brilliance was that, in his prime, bookmakers would refuse to fix the odds of the game until Tendulkar was dismissed.

The only blip on Tendulkar's career was his inability to bring the best out of others as a captain. Like many geniuses before him, including Ian Botham, he was unable to relate to those less talented than him, and his best batting days came when in the ranks.

Sachin Tendulkar

Born: 24 April 1973
Place of birth: Mumbai, India
Batting average: 54.70
Teams: Bombay, India

Opposite: Tendulkar in the second Test aganst England in 1990.

West Indian Legends

Curtly Ambrose and Courtney Walsh

1990s Opening bowlers often work in tandem – think Trueman and Statham or Lillee and Thompson as examples from a bygone era. Few, however, operated with the same menace, accuracy and skill as the giant West Indian duo Courtney Walsh and Curtly Ambrose did over such an extended period of time.

Ambrose and Walsh worked together for a decade from 1988 onwards, terrorizing batsmen and winning the hearts of the cricketing public for their affable demeanour away from the field of play.

As the latest in a long line of fearsome pace men such as Malcolm Marshall, Michael Holding and Joel Garner, Ambrose and Walsh had much to live up to, the burden increasing with age as the West Indies side began to deteriorate at an alarming rate. Though Walsh ended up with the better record – he was the first bowler to take 500 Test wickets – Ambrose was the more frightening proposition. Certainly the English batsmen who trailed in his wake – as the big man took 6-24 as the tourists were skittled for 46 at Trinidad in 1993–94 – would testify to that.

As a partnership, the duo took 421 wickets in 49 Test matches and, although pace was their main weapon, they were also able to fashion wickets with intelligent spells of bowling. West Indies cricket is crying out for a new duo in the mould of Ambrose and Walsh, but as they are finding out, bowlers of their vintage do not come along very often.

Opposite: The West Indies' legendary partnership of Curtly Ambrose and Courtney Walsh.

Lara Lashes Out

West Indies Star's Glorious Season

1993–94 Not since the days of Sir Donald Bradman has a wicket been as coveted as that of Brian Lara's. With his distinctive high back-lift and exaggerated follow-through, there are few more captivating sights in world sport than the 'Prince of Trinidad' in full flow. Although he still plays to a level beyond the compass of most Test players, maintaining an average in excess of 50, his standards have understandably dipped from the ones he set during his prolific season of 1993–94.

Gary Sobers – the original West Indies cricketing icon – held the individual Test record of 365 runs for 36 years, before the Windies faced England on a docile St Johns wicket that was manna from heaven for Lara. By the time he pulled Chris Lewis to the square leg boundary to break the record, he was so exhausted that he sank to his knees and kissed the turf on which he would go on to break the record again a decade later.

Two months on Lara was tormenting English bowlers again, this time playing on the county circuit for Warwickshire against Durham. Lara was dropped by the Durham wicket-keeper Chris Scott when the diminutive genius had made just 18. Scott is reported to have sagely observed at the time: 'I suppose he'll go on to make a hundred now.' He wasn't wrong. Lara racked up an astonishing 501 not out, recording the largest individual first-class score of all time.

Brian Lara

Born: 2 May 1969

Place of birth: Santa Cruz, Trinidad and Tobago

Batting average: 52.88

Teams: Trinidad and Tobago, West Indies, Warwickshire

Ricky Ponting

Australian Action Man

2000s The pugnacious Tasmanian batsman is without question one of the most skilled and technically gifted willow wielders of his generation. Ponting made his limited overs debut for Australia in 1995, became part of the Test set-up later that year, at the age of 21, and was a permanent fixture in Steve Waugh's all-conquering side.

A savage hooker and puller of the ball who is equally adept at playing pace or spin, Ponting won the prestigious ICC (International Cricket Council) Test Player of the Year and Player of the Year awards in 2006. He has recently passed 9,000 Test runs and captained Australia to their successful World Cup defence in 2003.

It hasn't all been sweetness and light for Ponting, however. He publicly battled an alcohol addiction in the mid-1990s and was vilified in the Australian press in 2005 for becoming the first Aussie skipper to lose an Ashes series since 1987. However, in the face of adversity, Ponting is often at his best. He battled back from his drink problem to fend off competition from Adam Gilchrist and Shane Warne to claim the coveted captaincy of his country. Moreover, Ponting's Aussie side won 11 of their next 12 Tests in the wake of their 2005 defeat to England, while during the 2006–07 Ashes series, Ponting recorded his 33rd Test ton, becoming the most prolific Australian century-maker of all time.

Ricky Ponting

Born: 19 December 1974

Place of birth: Launceston, Tasmania

Batting average: 59.39

Teams: Tasmanian Tigers, Australia

Long-Awaited Ashes Triumph

Ecstasy for England

2005 England's last Ashes triumph had been in 1986–87, and despite an improving side there was only limited optimism from the public going into the 2005 series. English cricket fans are nothing if not loyal, however, and a full house at Lord's on the opening day created an electric atmosphere that remained for the entire series.

England lost at Lord's as Glenn McGrath took nine wickets in the match, but they had shown they had the stomach for the fight. With McGrath ruled out of the second Test at Edgbaston, England flew out of the blocks and, inspired by Andrew Flintoff, claimed one of the most remarkable victories in Test history, by just two runs. The image of Flintoff consoling Brett Lee in the aftermath has already gone down in Ashes folklore.

The momentum was with England and, despite the best efforts of Shane Warne, they claimed their second victory in the fourth Test at Trent Bridge after another nerve-jangling affair.

The scene was set for a momentous final Test, and no one was disappointed. Kevin Pietersen produced one of the finest innings in Ashes history to help England claim a draw – and to win the series. The irrepressible Flintoff, who scored 402 runs and took 24 wickets in the series, led the celebrations along with captain Michael Vaughan, and the whole of England basked in the glory of this long-awaited triumph.

Opposite: Ecstasy for England as they celebrate their
Ashes triumph at the Oval in 2005.

Wonderful Warne

The First Bowler to Take 700 Test Wickets

2006 Shane Warne has established himself as the finest leg-spinner ever to play cricket. Colourful and controversial, whatever people think of Warne as a person, there is no disputing he is a bowler of unparalleled brilliance. Few players have single-handedly won as many Test matches as Warne, who saves his very best for Australia's oldest adversaries, England.

Indeed his first ball in Ashes cricket, at Old Trafford in 1993, marked Warne out as a bowler of rare ability. The ball to former England captain Mike Gatting pitched six inches outside leg before ripping viciously across the bemused batsman and flicking the top of the stump. It set the tone for the rest of the series, and Warne went on to take eight wickets in the match and 34 in the series as Australia romped to victory.

His delivery and incredible control, allied to a ferocious will to win, has led to Warne being widely regarded as one of the best bowlers ever to grace the game. And during the Ashes series in 2006–07, he claimed his 700th Test victim, just days before announcing his retirement from international cricket. He finally finished his career with an amazing 708 Test wickets.

Shane Warne

Born: 13 September 1969

Place of birth: Victoria, Australia

Batting average: 17.32

Teams: Victoria, Australia, Hampshire

Tom Morris

Golf's First Superstar

1860s A pioneer of professional golf, Tom Morris was born in St Andrews, Fife, Scotland. He was taught by Allan Robertson, and is widely considered as the first pro golfer. Having first tackled the game at an early age, he played in the first Open in 1860, which he also helped to set up, but finished second to Willie Park. However, he won the Open the following year and then again in 1862, 1864 and 1867.

When he was not playing golf, Morris was a greenkeeper, club maker and course designer. He helped design courses such as Muirfield, Prestwick, Carnoustie and Rosapenna links in Ireland. The lasting influence he has had on the game is evidenced by the fact that it was Morris who stipulated that full courses should be 18 holes in length and encouraged the use of man-made hazards such as bunkers.

Morris is commemorated at the Home of Golf in St Andrews, which he returned to as greenkeeper in 1865, with the eighteenth hole named in his honour. He remained there until his death in 1908. Ironically, he died as a result of injuries sustained falling down a steep staircase inside the clubhouse. His legacy lived on through his son, Tom Morris Jr, who was an equally gifted golfer and won the Open five times.

Tom Morris

Born: 16 June 1821   **Died:** 24 May 1908

Place of birth: St Andrews, Scotland

Major championships: British Open: 1861, 1862, 1864, 1867

Awards and honours: Member, World Golf Hall of Fame

Brilliant Byron

Nelson Claims 11 on the Trot

1945 Byron Nelson set quite a phenomenal record when he triumphed at the Canadian Open in 1945 – he became the only person to win 11 golf tournaments in a row. This achievement bears out his reputation as one of the greatest golfers to have ever lived.

Born in 1912, Nelson turned professional in 1935 and won the first of his five majors in 1937, when he landed the Masters, before quitting his professional career in 1947. Although short, his time in the game saw him make 113 consecutive cuts, a record beaten only recently by Tiger Woods. But it was his performance in 1945 that cemented his place in the history books.

Having missed out on the call-up for national service because he was a haemophiliac, Nelson continued to play a full schedule on tour. His 11-tournament-winning run started at the Miami Four Ball in March and went through to the Canadian Open in August. It was a truly magnificent achievement – and it could have been even more. Nelson won another tournament in the middle of the streak, but because the purse was less than $3,000, it did not count as an official win.

Not only did Nelson win 11 tournaments on the bounce in 1945, he also managed another seven victories that year. In addition to this, he finished second in seven other events, which meant he was in the top two on 25 occasions – a record that is unlikely to be beaten.

'Byron Nelson accomplished things on the pro tour that never have been and never will be approached again.'

Arnold Palmer

Jack Fleck Wins the US Open

Hogan Shell-shocked

1955 Ben Hogan could have been forgiven for feeling confident when he reached the US Open play-off final in 1955 at the Olympic Club in San Francisco – for the four-time winner of the event only had an unknown called Jack Fleck standing in his way.

Fleck, who had started his golf career during the mid-1930s working as a caddie for a dentist in Iowa, decided to turn professional on his graduation from high school. Alongside his caddying duties, he worked as an assistant pro before joining the American Navy. While serving his country, he took part in the D-Day landings in Normandy. But his passion for golf never diminished, and two weeks after being discharged from the Navy he was a playing professional.

He hustled his way round the PGA (Professional Golfers' Association) Tour but his crowning glory came at the 1955 US Open, when he caused one of the greatest shocks in the history of the sport. Hogan was confident of success after the two players were tied over the previous four rounds. The title went to an 18-hole play-off, in which Fleck kept his nerve to win with a respectable score of 69, while Hogan could only manage a 72.

Perhaps the biggest shock was reserved for the American public watching at home on television. Broadcaster NBC had only allocated one hour's worth of air time, meaning they could not show the play-off. Foolishly, they announced Hogan as the winner before they went off air.

'I play with friends, but we don't play friendly games.'
Ben Hogan

Opposite: Jack Fleck warms up before his shock play-off win against Hogan.

Arnold Palmer

A Worldwide Wonder

1950s–60s Arnold Palmer is considered to be golf's first global superstar. Paving the way for later giants of the sport such as Tiger Woods, Palmer is said to have done for golf what Elvis did for rock and roll.

Turning professional in 1954 after winning the US amateur title, it took him only four years to win his first US Masters. His greatest sporting moment, however, came in 1960 when he won the US Open at Cherry Hills in June of that year. Chasing the leaders by six shots in the final round, the high-spirited and ever-confident Palmer held his nerve and birdied his last two holes, overtaking Jack Nicklaus and Ben Hogan to win the Open by a single stroke.

Palmer won 61 American titles, including the Open and four US Masters, plus 19 overseas titles. Many even credit him with instigating the rebirth of British golf, as several American golfers had shunned the British Open before Palmer, who actually went on to win the event in 1961 and 1962.

A victorious Ryder Cup captain in 1975, the American enjoyed huge popularity throughout his career, rising to a level of fame unseen in the game of golf before.

'Arnold is the reason golf enjoys the popularity it does today. He… made golf attractive to the television-viewing public. … there probably won't be another like him again.'

Jack Nicklaus

Opposite: Palmer rips of his sunshade after dropping the final putt that gave him the 1960 US Open.

Gary Player

The Man in Black

1960s Gary Player is probably one of the most dedicated golfers of all time and to this day lives one of the healthiest lifestyles. The 71-year-old still plays in seniors' competitions, posting scores in the mid-70s, and says his desire to compete is always there – and that is due to his strict fitness regime.

The South African won nine majors during his phenomenal career. His first came in the Open, at Muirfield, when he was just 23 years old. Two years later he picked up the Masters after beating Arnold Palmer in a play-off match.

His victory at Augusta was one of his greatest achievements. Palmer was going for his third win in the competition as the two went to sudden death. Both hit a greenside bunker, but while Player chipped out and putted in, Palmer lost his nerve and took a double bogey six to lose the match.

Player added the PGA Championship title to his collection in 1962 after winning at Aronimink in Pennsylvania. He then completed his full house by landing the US Open in 1965, beating Australian Kel Nagle.

Over his career, Player became known as one of the 'big three' belonging to the management company of Mark McCormack – the other two being Jack Nicklaus and Arnold Palmer.

Aside from playing golf, Player now spends his time designing courses, writing dietary books, raising funds for his own foundation to help children in Africa, and running a successful stud farm in his homeland.

'I've studied golf for almost 50 years now and know a
hell of a lot about nothing.'

Gary Player

Jack Nicklaus

Glorious Golden Bear

1960s–70s

Jack Nicklaus is regularly referred to as the greatest golfer of all time – and for good reason given his extraordinary total of 18 major titles. Nicklaus, affectionately known as the Golden Bear, modelled himself on the great Bobby Jones, earned his PGA Tour card at the tender age of 18, and secured his first US Open top 10 finish in 1961, when he was still an amateur. At the tournament a year later he defeated the great Arnold Palmer at Oakmont to land his first major and spark one of the sport's great rivalries – which also included the ferociously competitive South African Gary Player.

Nicklaus's career continued in the ascendancy and in 1965 he became the first man to win consecutive Masters titles. He followed this up with his first British Open success in 1965.

In the 1970s he won the British Open at St Andrews and, in adding the USA PGA title in 1971, he completed a mesmerizing double grand slam – winning every major title at least twice.

At the age of 46 he won his sixth and final Masters title, becoming the oldest winner of a golfing major, defeating Greg Norman by one shot with his son by his side as caddy. Although retired from the professional game, Nicklaus is still heavily involved in the sport – his company Golden Bear designs and builds golf courses all over the world.

'I never went into a tournament or round of golf thinking I had to beat a certain player. I had to beat the golf course. If I prepared myself for a major, went in focused, and then beat the golf course, the rest took care of itself.'

Jack Nicklaus

Jacklin Wins the US Open

Terrific Tony Topples America

1970 In 1970 Tony Jacklin dominated the US Open at the Hazeltine National Golf Club in Chaska, near Minneapolis. At 55 years old, the Englishman was widely considered past his peak, but he proved all his doubters wrong In spectacular fashion. Jacklin ate the course for breakfast and led the competition from start to finish, to eventually beat American Dave Hill by a phenomenal seven strokes.

What makes his achievement even more amazing is that the course was notoriously difficult that year and, since he reduced it to size, he was made an honorary member there. In beating Hill, Jacklin became the first European to win the US Open since Willie McFarlane took the title at the Worcester Country Club in Massachusetts in 1925. Significantly, no one from Europe has managed to repeat the feat since.

Although he stopped playing competitively in 1982, Jacklin captained the successful European Ryder Cup team in 1985, as they claimed their first win in 26 years. He then helped the team retain the trophy two years later in America. He now lives in America with his wife. He still has a hand in shaping the future of golf through his golf course design business. He also returns to Hazeltine every once in a while to play his favourite course.

Tony Jacklin

Born: 7 July 1944

Place of birth: Lincolnshire, England

Major championships: US Open: 1970; British Open: 1969

Awards and honours: Member, World Golf Hall of Fame; European Tour money leader: 1973; 7-time member, European Ryder Cup team; Captain, European Ryder Cup team: 1983, 1985, 1987, 1989; Order of the British Empire: 1970; Commander of the British Empire: 1990

Take a Stance On Me

Johnny Miller's Final Round Makes History

1973 Johnny Miller began the final day at the 1973 US Open six shots behind the leaders, after a disappointing 76 in the third round. By the end of his final round he had completed one of the most remarkable recoveries in history.

Trailing Julius Boros, Jerry Heard, Arnold Palmer and John Schlee as they prepared for the last round, Miller dutifully went to the range to strike a couple of balls. Having finished seventh in the competition the previous year, after a dismal final day's golf, he started toying with the idea of opening his playing stance a little. It was something few pros would consider – but it worked.

Miller blasted his way to an impressive 63 at the Oakmont Country Club in Pennsylvania to beat Schlee by a single stroke – setting a record low score for a round in the competition in the process – and he still considers the turning point to be the voice in his head provoking him to change his set-up. 'I had about fifteen balls left on the range and the thought occurred to me to open my stance way up, like an exaggerated Lee Trevino set-up,' recalled Miller. 'The thought wouldn't go away, so I figured, what the heck, I'll listen to the voice.'

Just as well he did. He went out in 32 and came back in 31 with birdies at holes 11, 12, 13 and 15, as he won his first major title.

Johnny Miller

Born: 29 April 1947

Place of birth: California, USA

Major Championships: US Open: 1973; British Open: 1976

Awards and honours: Member, World Golf Hall of Fame; PGA Tour money leader: 1974; PGA Tour Player of the Year: 1974; Member, two US Ryder Cup teams

Open Show of Defiance

Death Threat Fails to Deter Hubert Green

1977 The 1977 US Open final was the first tournament to be televised live from start to finish, but the real drama surrounded a sinister death threat that made it more of a soap opera than a sporting event.

Hubert Green teed his ball up at 2.05 p.m., ready to do battle with fellow American Lou Graham at Southern Hills Country Club in Tulsa, Oklahoma. Along with the added pressure of being in with a chance to win his first major in front of a live television audience, Green had just been informed that someone had threatened to kill him on the fifteenth hole. The night before, the Oklahoma City police station had received a call from an anonymous woman who claimed that her boyfriend and two other men were on their way to Tulsa armed with guns. She said they intended to shoot Green the next day on the course.

The police were put on red alert, although they suspected the call was a hoax from a punter who had put money on Green's defeat, hoping the threat would put him off his game. If that was the case it did not work, as the would-be assassins thankfully failed to materialize, while Green kept his nerve to post a final score of 70, which was just enough to clinch victory in front of a record number of spectators.

Hubert Green

Born: 28 December 1946

Place of birth: Alabama, USA

Major championships: US Open: 1977; PGA

Championship: 1985

Awards and honours: Member, US Ryder Cup team:

1977, 1979, 1985

Tom Watson's Miracle Shot

Thrills at the Beach

1982 Tom Watson played one of the greatest shots in US Open history at the Pebble Beach Resort in 1982, to achieve his only victory in the tournament.

The final day had come down to an intense battle between Watson and his rival Jack Nicklaus. Over 10 holes the two were embroiled in a close contest – but that all changed at the seventeenth. The Golden Bear had birdied 15 to move next to Watson on the leaderboard at four under par. But his smile was soon wiped away.

Nicklaus's tee shot was good and he promptly finished the hole and sat at the side to watch Watson – who had driven his two-iron tee shot into the rough between two bunkers – face the tough task of reaching the hourglass-shaped green. But Watson took a wedge and produced a deft chip to escape the heavy rough, before watching the ball roll into the hole to sneak an unthinkable birdie and, more importantly, put him into the lead.

Arriving at the eighteenth, Nicklaus was lost for words as Watson kept his nerve. His three-wood landed straight on the fairway and his seven-iron was within 6 m (20 ft). Nicklaus finished for par while Watson's putt curled into the hole to clinch the title and start a dance of celebration.

'I learned how to win by losing and not liking it.'

Tom Watson

Opposite: Watson hits from a trap on the second hole during the fourth round at Pebble Beach.

Super Seve

Ballesteros Wins the British Open at the 17th

1984 The 1984 British Open is remembered less for its golf than for the celebration of Spaniard Seve Ballesteros, who won his second Open title.

Going into the final round at St Andrews, defending champion Tom Watson had a share of the lead with Australian Ian Baker-Finch, with Ballesteros and Bernhard Langher a shot behind. After Baker-Finch hit the water early on, the final day came down to a battle between Ballesteros and Watson – who was going for his sixth Open victory. The day's play reached a climax when Watson reached the seventeenth while Ballesteros was playing the last. The American's second shot drifted wide of the green and landed on the road, ruining his chances of making par and keeping up with Ballesteros. Meanwhile, as Watson was finishing up on 17, Ballesteros holed a 4.6 m (15 ft) putt on the eighteenth to move clear into the lead. Watson needed to eagle the eighteenth and, after his second shot failed to get close to the hole, Ballesteros, the people's champion, was off celebrating.

The iconic image of the triumphant Ballasteros has been rubber-stamped in the competition's history and is still used today as Ballesteros's trademark for his clothing company.

'I look into their eyes, shake their hand, pat their back, and wish them luck, but I am thinking, 'I'm going to bury you.'

Seve Ballesteros

Mize is a Master

Sudden Death Triumph at Augusta

1987 Larry Mize enjoyed a largely successful career playing on the PGA Tour. However, he is mainly remembered for pulling off just one shot. It came in the play-off at the Masters in 1987 and earned him the famous green jacket ahead of Seve Ballesteros and Greg Norman.

Mize secured his place in the play-off after sinking a birdie at the last on the final day, to set himself up in a sudden death showdown with Ballesteros and Norman. The Spanish golfer put himself out of the running when he made bogey on the first extra hole, leaving Norman to go head-to-head with Mize.

Norman played a safe second shot on the second play-off hole – Augusta's par four, eleventh – but Mize's effort landed off the green and into the rough, yards away from the hole. Victory appeared to be all Norman's – on the fringe of the green and faced with a 15 m (50 ft) putt. But Mize took his sand wedge and sumptuously dug the ball out and on to the green. If that was not enough, the ball gathered pace before dropping into the hole a full 128 m (420 ft) away from where he was standing.

'It was the biggest golf thrill I've ever had,' said Mize later. 'You could tell by my reaction. I almost went into orbit.'

Larry Mize

Born: 23 September 1958

Place of birth: Georgia, USA

Major championships: Masters: 1987

Awards and honours: Danny Thomas Memphis Classic: 1983; Northern Telecom Open: 1993; Buick Open: 1993; Casio World Open (Japan Golf Tour): 1988; Dunlop Phoneix (Japan Golf Tour): 1989, 1990; Straight Down Fall Classic: 2000

Ryder Cup Scandal

War on the Shore

1991 With the war in Iraq raging, the US media used patriotic emotions to help their golf team recapture the Ryder Cup. The so-called 'War on the Shore' at Kiawah Island was littered with espionage, underhand tactics and sheer intense rivalry.

The Europeans had won the cup in 1985 and had successfully retained it in 1987. A draw at the Belfry followed in 1989, leaving the Americans in need of a real result on home soil to restore national pride.

The dirty tricks started when a local radio station launched a prank to make early morning telephone calls to the European team's hotel rooms. The espionage soon followed, as the Americans were caught tuning into the European's walkie-talkie frequency to discover their on-course tactics. But the rivalry was most evident in the bitter feud between Paul Azinger and Seve Ballesteros, after the American accused the Spaniard of coughing every time his partner, Chip Beck, went to hit the ball. The American had the last laugh, though, as the US triumphed to win back the trophy for the first time since 1983.

After the victory Azinger quipped: 'American pride is back. We went over there and thumped the Iraqis. Now we've taken the cup back. I'm proud to be an American.'

However, the contest left a sour taste in the mouth for many golf purists, and critics argued the American win was not achieved in the spirit of the game.

Opposite: Controversial Paul Azinger completes a shot during the 'War on the Shore'.

Bernhard Burns Up the Masters

Langer Back on Song

1993 Some would argue that the 1993 Masters at Augusta was simply a one-horse race – for German golfer Bernhard Langer was on fire. He kept his cool over the four days, to take his second Masters, eight years after winning his first.

Back in 1985, Langer made birdie on the par-four seventeenth to give him the security of being able to shoot a bogey on the eighteenth and win the green jacket. That is exactly what happened, and it was enough to take the title.

In 1993, he enjoyed a much more comfortable victory, although he did bogey the eighteenth again. Not that it mattered – for over the tournament Langer had been at his very best. He held the lead for the final 34 holes of the competition, boosting his confidence and giving him momentum. The defining moment this time came at the thirteenth hole, a tricky par-five. Langer holed a downhill putt to card an eagle, which moved him clear at the top of the leaderboard – ahead of Chip Beck. It was a solid display of accuracy, even though conditions at Augusta were so tough that play had to be suspended during the second round and finished on the Saturday.

Victory was especially sweet for Langer, because it proved his American doubters wrong. He had been harshly lampooned in the United States after he missed a short putt in the 1991 Ryder Cup, handing the Americans the trophy. By beating them in their own backyard, he had vindicated himself.

Bernhard Langer

Born: 27 August 1957

Place of birth: Anhausen, Germany

Major championships: Masters: 1985, 1993

Awards and honours: Member, World Golf Hall of Fame; European Tour money leader: 1981, 1984; European Tour player of the year: 1985, 1993; 10-time member, European Ryder Cup team; Captain, 2004 European Ryder Cup team

Faldo Fight-back Stuns Norman

Augusta Agony and Ecstasy

1996 Nick Faldo's victory at the 1996 Masters was simply spectacular – not just for his ability to claw back a six-stroke deficit, but also for Greg Norman's horrendous collapse.

The Englishman had begun the day trailing in the wake of the Great White Shark, who was sitting well clear at the top of the leaderboard. However, the six-shot lead Norman had built up over three days was reduced to nothing in the space of just 11 holes. Norman's demise continued, most notably when he hit the water at both the twelfth and sixteenth holes, to card two double bogeys. In stark contrast, Faldo played very well as the pressure piled upon Norman. Faldo moved into the lead, and when he holed a 6 m (20 ft) putt on the final green, it was enough to cement victory – and one of the most amazing comebacks ever seen. He finished with a round of 12 under par to win by five clear shots and take his sixth major. Norman recorded a nightmare 78 to finish runner-up, the eighth time he had been forced to accept second place in a major. Faldo's win heralded the glory days of British golf. His victory at Augusta meant that the Brits had won five of the last nine masters.

Nick Faldo (pictured opposite on the way to victory)

Born: 18 July 1957

Place of birth: Hertfordshire, England

Major championships: Masters: 1989, 1990, 1996;
British Open: 1987, 1990, 1992

Awards and honours: Member, World Golf Hall of Fame;
European Tour Order of Merit winner: 1983, 1992; European
Tour scoring leader, 1983, 1992; European Tour Player of
the Year: 1989, 1990, 1992; US PGA Tour player of the year,
1990; 11-time member, European Ryder Cup team

Tiger's Record-Breaking Masters

Woods Comes of Age

1997 When Tiger Woods won the Masters in 1997 he re-wrote the record books. At 21 years old he was not only the youngest winner of the tournament, but his winning margin of 12 strokes was also a new benchmark. Over the four days, Woods simply blew the field away with an emphatic performance. Come Sunday evening, he sat proudly at the top of the leaderboard with a total score of just 270, an incredible 18 under par – another record low.

Woods also became the first black player to win a major, a victory that golfing legend Gary Player said would open up the historically elitist sport to ethnic minorities. 'Tiger Woods has the opportunity to do something for the human race that no other golfer before him has,' said the three-time Masters champion. 'Imagine the black people in Africa – four hundred million watching Tiger Woods win the Masters. There has never been a world-champion golfer who is a black golfer.'

Although his victory was a landslide in the end, Woods' early challenge started slowly. However, by the time the second day drew to a close, he was already in front and by the third, his lead was up to nine shots. Colin Montgomerie, who was in second place at the time, had simply no chance of catching the youngster, who had turned professional just eight months previously.

'Every day on the golf course is about making little adjustments, taking what you've got on that day and finding the way to deal with it.'

Tiger Woods

Super Sam

Snead Wins PGA Lifetime Achievement Award

1998 There can be few worthier winners of the PGA Lifetime Achievement Award than the straight-talking American Sam Snead. He defied his critics to climb from poverty to the very pinnacle of the sport. He was helped along the way by his unique swing, which many have since tried to copy. In fact, Snead's swing was largely due to an out-of-line vertebrae, which allowed him to strike the ball further than his opponents.

His love of golf started when he hustled some cash working as a caddy at his local course in Virginia as a child, sometimes treading the fairways without any shoes because his father could not afford to pay for them. His dedication paid off, though, and he was rewarded with a job at his local course before turning professional in 1935. In his first event he fired two tee shots out of bounds. The starters were about to disqualify him from taking any further part, but his third attempt surged down the fairway and landed on the green. He ended up finishing eighth.

Snead won his first major in 1942 at the PGA Championship, an achievement repeated in 1949 and 1951. He won a hat-trick of Masters titles, starting in 1949, then in 1952 and finally in 1954. His only other major win came at the British Open in 1946, even though he loathed the St Andrews course. He won his final tournament before retirement when he was 53. He was honoured by the PGA Tour in 1998, four years before his death.

Born: 27 May 1912   **Died:** 23 May 2002

Place of birth: Virginia, USA

Major championships: Masters: 1949, 1952, 1954;
British Open: 1946; PGA Championship: 1942, 1949, 1951

Awards and honours: Member, World Golf Hall of Fame;
Recipient, PGA Tour Lifetime Achievement Award; 3-time PGA Tour
money leader; 4-time PGA Tour Vardon Trophy winner; 8-time
member, US Ryder Cup team; 3-time captain, US Ryder Cup team

Tiger Slam

Woods Collects his Fourth Consecutive Major

2001 When Tiger Woods won the Masters in 2001 he claimed yet another piece of history, for victory at Augusta made him the first person to hold all four of the major titles at the same time. The previous season had seen Woods on amazing form. At the 2000 US Open at Pebble Beach he won by an incredible 12 strokes – just one of nine records he either broke or equalled. Then, at St Andrews, he landed the Open title in emphatic style. He won the tournament by an incredible eight shots to finish with a total score of 19 under par. At Valhalla in Louisville he won again, this time at the PGA Championship. However, he was run a little closer by Bob May, who lost in a three-hole playoff. That win put him level with Ben Hogan, who had been the last and only other person to win three professional majors in one season, back in 1953.

When Woods arrived at Augusta the following year, people were speaking of a 'grand slam'. However, the old guard, such as Arnold Palmer, insisted that title should only be used if a golfer won all four titles in the same year. Nevertheless, Woods beat David Duval by two shots to win his fourth successive major, marking was has now become known as the 'Tiger Slam'.

Tiger Woods

Born: 30 December 1975

Place of birth: California, USA

Major championships: Masters: 1997, 2001, 2002, 2005; US Open: 2000, 2002; British Open: 2000, 2005, 2006; PGA Championship: 1999, 2000, 2006

Awards and honours: (years too many to mention!): PGA Tour Money Winner; PGA Tour Player of the Year; Vardon Trophy; Byron Nelson Award; Mark H. McCormack Award

Yanks are Spanked

Europe's Record Win in the Ryder Cup

2004 Europe firmly stamped its mark in Ryder Cup history in 2004 with a record 181/2 - 91/2 win over the USA. Over the three days, the European team ripped up the form book and defied the Official Golf World Rankings to retain the trophy at Oakland Hills Country Club in California.

Bernhard Langer's team were always in command and went into the final day's singles match with a controlling 11-5 advantage. They only needed three and a half points to retain the trophy.

Sergio Garcia was first to make his mark, by overturning Phil Mickelson's advantage to win three and two. Darren Clarke chipped in with half a point in his match with Davis Love, before Lee Westwood put Europe on the cusp of victory after beating Kenny Perry.

It was fitting that the honour of winning the cup would fall upon Colin Montgomerie. The 41-year-old had been suffering from a number of personal problems, which had dominated the pre-match headlines. However, all that was forgotten as he sank the winning putt on the eighteenth green. Monty was all square with David Toms after 15 holes, but birdied the next to go in front. He kept his nerve to the end and holed his putt before bursting into floods of tears.

Opposite: Colin Montgomerie plays a shot on the
fairway during the final day of the Ryder Cup in 2004.

Where Were the Germans?

Great Britain Claims Olympic Hockey Gold

1988 When Great Britain lined up against West Germany in the 1988 Olympic hockey final in Seoul, few expected anything resembling the England football team's World Cup final win over West Germany in 1966. The British team had not beaten their opponents for 30 years and had lost 2-1 to them in the group stages. But not only did their subsequent 3-1 win provide a defining moment in British hockey, it was also famous for its commentary. When Britain scored their third goal, BBC commentator Barry Davies could not contain his excitement: 'Where were the Germans?' he asked after Imran Sherwani had scored his second goal to put Great Britain 3-0 up. 'Frankly,' he added, 'who cares?'

Millions heard Davies's commentary at home as the sport briefly captured the nation's imagination; after England's football team had flopped at the European Championships in Germany earlier that year, hockey provided some welcome relief.

In between Sherwani's goals, Sean Kerly had scored his fifteenth goal in 14 Olympic matches (he had scored a dramatic hat-trick in a 3-2 semi-final win over Australia) and established himself as British hockey's first household name. Hockey's moment in the sun may have been brief, but even in 2006 Kerly says people approach him in the street to talk about the 1988 Olympic final.

Opposite: Great Britain's Steve Batchelor is seen with the ball racing towards the West German defence.

Elizabeth Anders

ODU Coach Inspires 'The Streak'

1990s Elizabeth Anders was a starring member of the American 1984 Olympic Games hockey team, captaining the side that claimed a bronze medal. Once retired, Anders made a noteworthy contribution to the sport from the sidelines, as the head coach of the Old Dominion University field hockey team, before coaching the USA women's national team.

In 1990, Anders and her team began what has become known as 'The Streak'. With a 4-2 win over Temple in 1990, ODU went on to win 66 consecutive games over three years, including three national titles. Anders has guided her teams through undefeated seasons in 1984 (23-0), 1991 (26-0) and 1995 (25-0).

With nine National Collegiate Athletic Association (NCAA) Division I championships, and a 390-55-7 record over a 19-year tenure, Anders is the most successful coach in college field hockey history. Twice named National Coach of the Year by the National Field Hockey Coaches Association and nine times CAA (Colonial Athletic Association) Coach of the Year, Anders was inducted into the United States Field Hockey Association Hall of Fame in 1989, and into the Pennsylvania Sports Hall of Fame in 1998.

Elizabeth Anders

Born: 13 November 1951

Place of birth: Pennsylvania, USA

Olympic medals: Bronze 1984

Awards and honours: USFHA Hall of Fame: 1989;
Pennsylvania Sports Hall of Fame: 1998; National Coach of
the Year: 1998, 2000; 9-time CAA Coach of the Year

Opposite: The American and Australian hockey teams
battle it out at the 1984 Olympic Games.

Dutch Master

De Nooijer Becomes Hockey's Top Man

1996 Teun Floris de Nooijer rarely turns up on lists of the world's best sportsmen, but there are few players as dominant in any team sport around the world. The Dutchman can lay claim to being the greatest hockey player of all time in 2006 after being named World Hockey Player of the Year for a record third time.

Making his debut in a friendly against New Zealand in 1994, his pace and creativity have been central to a Netherlands team that has dominated men's hockey for a decade, after winning the Olympic final in 1996. They won it again in 2000, with a penalties win after a 3-3 draw with South Korea, and just missed out in Athens in 2004, when they lost 2-1 to Australia in the final. In 2006, they claimed a record-equalling eighth Champions Trophy victory, and a sixth for de Nooijer.

Teun Floris de Nooijer

Born: 22 March 1976

Place of birth: Noord-Holland, The Netherlands

Olympic medals: Gold 1996, Gold 2000, Silver 2004

Awards and honours: World Hockey Player of the Year: 2003, 2005, 2006

Rod Laver's Grand Slams

The Awesome Aussie Wins All Four

1962 The godfather of tennis, Rod Laver, set the blueprint for domination that Pete Sampras and Roger Federer would seek to follow in later years. The wiry Australian held the world No. 1 spot for an astonishing six years but, impressive as that was, a clean sweep of all four Grand Slam tournaments in a calendar year will for ever be regarded as his greatest achievement.

In 1962 Laver swept all before him, becoming the first male since Don Budge in 1938 to land all four majors in a single year. The flame-haired Australian left-hander made light of his slight frame to form a complete game, which revolved around his awkward serve and deft touch at the net.

Far from being just a serve-volleyer, however, Laver was one of the leading innovators in the early 1960s – developing wristy ground-strokes, hit with vicious topspin off either flank. In his all-conquering year, Laver found little to challenge his supremacy at Wimbledon, where he dropped just one set, while his victories in Australia and at the US Open were equally, if not more, convincing.

At the French Open, however, Laver demonstrated the ferocious competitiveness and durability synonymous with all great champions. He came through three successive five-setters on the way to the first of two Grand Slam clean sweeps. Remarkably, he repeated the feat as a professional in 1969.

Rod Laver

Born: 9 August 1938

Place of birth: Rockhampton, Australia

Turned Pro: 1962

Plays: Left-handed

Opposite: Queen Elizabeth II awards Rod Laver the Men's Singles Title at Wimbledon in 1962.

Gonzales v Pasarell

The Marathon Match

1969 Pancho Gonzales may well have been considered one of the most talented players of his generation, yet for all his achievements in the game, the fiery American (of Mexican parents) will for ever be primarily associated with his marathon match against flamboyant fellow countryman Charlie Pasarell.

The match – which took place before the advent of tiebreaks – is the longest in Wimbledon history and lasted a staggering five hours and 12 minutes, incorporating 112 games spread over two days.

Gonzales, a US Open champion 20 years earlier, defied his senior status (he was 41 at the time) to triumph over his younger adversary in five sets: 22-24, 1-6, 16-14, 6-3, 11-9. The match was tinged with controversy, when the famously combustible Gonzales hurled abuse in the direction of the umpire for refusing to suspend play due to perceived bad light. Gonzales returned in the morning with the crowd against him and two sets down, but rallied to level the match and win back the crowd's affection with some stunning stroke play.

Clearly troubled by his collapse, Pasarell tossed away seven match points in the deciding set, as Gonzales twice recovered from 0-40 to complete his stunning comeback. Despite his exertions, Gonzales won through the next two rounds before falling to 1975 Wimbledon champion Arthur Ashe.

Pancho Gonzales

Born: 9 May 1928   **Died:** 3 July 1995

Place of birth: California, USA

Turned Pro: 1949

Plays: Right-handed

Opposite: Charlie Pasarell reaches for the ball during the marathon match.

Virginia Wade Wins Wimbledon

English Queen of SW19

1977 Virginia Wade was by a distance the most successful British female tennis player of her era, but many assumed she was some way past her best by the time she broke her Wimbledon duck in fairytale circumstances.

Born in Bournemouth, Wade spent her formative years in South Africa before she returned to England at the age of 15. It would be a while, though, before she made a significant breakthrough.

Wade claimed her first Grand Slam title in 1968 when she won the US Open and the Australian title in 1972, but she was considered to be on the wane by the time Wimbledon celebrated its centenary in 1977. This was Wade's sixteenth attempt at cracking the Wimbledon conundrum and few thought it possible she would find a suitable answer. However, after she overturned defending champion Chris Evert in a tense three-set semi-final, opinion began to change.

Wade's opponent in the final was the attacking Dutch player Betty Stove, but a packed Centre Court crowd was behind her, including the Queen, who was celebrating her Silver Jubilee.

Despite dropping a tight first set, the home favourite claimed the second set before raising her game to take the decider 6-1 and complete one of the most memorable days in British sporting history.

Virginia Wade

Born: 10 July 1945

Place of birth: Dorset, England

Turned Pro: 1968

Plays: Right-handed

McEnroe Ends Borg's Reign

SuperMac is Bjorn Again

1981 John McEnroe and Bjorn Borg were vastly contrasting characters, but their differing styles and demeanours made for one of the most captivating sporting duels of the twentieth century. The nerveless Swede had swept all before him on grass, notching up five successive Wimbledon titles, and was widely expected to add a sixth crown against McEnroe, who he had defeated in a thrilling final a year earlier.

After a semi-final win over Jimmy Connors, Borg had not been defeated at Wimbledon in 41 matches, while McEnroe – seeded two – had not been taken beyond four sets in reaching the final. The scene was set for an enthralling encounter, and the chalk-and-cheese duo certainly delivered in front of a captivated audience.

The indefatigable Borg ground out the first set 6-4 in typically robotic fashion. Lesser competitors than the spiky American would have crumbled, but McEnroe, always at his best when up against it, bounced back to take the next two sets in closely fought tiebreaks. Deflated by conceding the lead, Borg had no answer to the American's awkward left-handed service in the fourth set and fell to his first defeat at SW19 in five years. It was very much the end of an era, as Borg won just one more Grand Slam title before retiring.

Opposite: John McEnroe lunges across the court in an attempt to return Borg's drop shot.

Noah Wins the French Open

French Fancy

1983 Yannick Noah was rightly regarded as one of the most colourful, flamboyant and stylish tennis players of his era. His talents were never really reflected by his haul of just one Grand Slam title, memorable though that single success was.

The notoriously impatient Parisian public had waited 37 years for one of their own to taste success on the red dirt of Roland Garros, and with a number of high-profile clay tournaments under his belt, Noah, the son of a former Cameroon international footballer, was seen as their great hope.

In 1983 the dreadlocked star had already claimed victory in Madrid and Hamburg, two of the major events of the clay court season, so hopes were naturally high that he would end the French wait for a home-grown champion – and he did not disappoint.

Noah, who flattered to deceive in Grand Slam tournaments both prior to this success and after, dropped just one set over the two weeks as he found the consistency that eluded him so often before and after. He lowered the colours of defending champion Mats Wilander in straight sets in the final in front of a partisan home crowd, and in the process he became the first black male to win a Grand Slam singles event since Arthur Ashe eight years earlier.

Yannick Noah

Born: 18 May 1960

Place of birth: Ardennes, France

Turned Pro: 1977

Plays: Right-handed

Teenage Kicks

Becker Wins His First Wimbledon Title

1985 Boris Becker shattered a whole host of records on his way to becoming Wimbledon champion in 1985. He became the first German to hold aloft the famous trophy, but perhaps more impressively and significantly, at 17 years and seven months old, he was the youngest male winner of a Grand Slam tournament in history – a record that survived until eclipsed by American Michael Chang.

Becker's attacking style, powerful serve and dexterity at the net endeared him to the Centre Court crowd, which would often gasp at the sight of the athletic German throwing himself across the hallowed lawn to retrieve seemingly lost causes. Becker's all-action style was too much for his senior opponents, who found it hard to respond to his frenetic tempo and booming serve.

He dominated the final against the experienced Kevin Curren, the ginger German dropping only a second-set tiebreak on the way to a comprehensive 6-3, 6-7, 7-6, 6-4 win. Unlike the fleeting success of many teenage tennis stars, this was to be no flash in the pan for Becker. He returned a year later to successfully defend his crown against Ivan Lendl and claimed a hat-trick of triumphs in 1989 against Stefan Edberg, against whom he had lost in the previous year's final.

Boris Becker

Born: 22 November 1967

Place of birth: Leimen, Germany

Turned Pro: 1984

Plays: Right-handed

Opposite: Becker in the thrid-round match against Joakim Nystrom.

Spain Reigns Supreme

Sanchez-Vicario Wins the French Open

1989 Diminutive Spaniard Arantxa Sanchez-Vicario rocked the tennis world at 17 years old by becoming the youngest winner of the women's singles title at the French Open. Nicknamed the 'Barcelona Bumblebee' for her willingness to chase down lost causes, her busy, hustling style often unsettled her more composed and illustrious opponents.

Sanchez-Vicario came from good tennis stock: her two elder brothers, Emilio and Javier, were both successful professionals on the male touring circuit, but neither made the same impression as their younger sibling – especially at Roland Garros in 1989.

At the time, Steffi Graf was far and away the dominant force in women's tennis. She was the darling of the Parisian crowd, having won consecutive titles prior to the 1989 final, and in 1998 she became the first tennis player – male or female – to win the 'Golden Slam', which incorporated all four majors and the Olympic gold.

In the final itself, too young to be daunted by reputations, Sanchez-Vicario relentlessly attacked Graf's weak backhand to great success. The young novice, appearing in her first showcase final, took the first set on a tie-break and was not deterred when Graf levelled the match 6-4 in the second.

The Bumblebee maintained her composure to close the match 7-5 in the decider, to enter the record books.

Arantxa Sanchez-Vicario

Born: 18 December 1971

Place of birth: Barcelona, Spain

Turned Pro: 1985

Plays: Right-handed

Navratilova Wins a Record Ninth

Marvellous Martina

1990 With 167 titles under her belt by the time her career finally came to an end, Martina Navratilova could be forgiven for struggling to pick out a highlight. Yet if she was asked to choose a particular landmark success, she would no doubt be quick to point to her record-breaking ninth Wimbledon singles title.

The Czech-born star held the Wimbledon title between 1982 and 1987, having previously raised the famous shield on two earlier occasions in the late 1970s. A graceful mover, supreme competitor and unrivalled volleyer, it had seemed that her talents would not be rewarded with a record-breaking ninth title.

That was until 1990 when, at 33, she somehow defied her advancing years to reach the final against Zina Garrison, conqueror of Navratilova's arch-rival Steffi Graf in the last four. But that hard-fought win seemed to take the wind out of Garrison's sails as she let the size of the occasion get to her. That was something Navratilova seized upon with typical ruthless efficiency, to finish the match in straight sets 6-4, 6-1 in record time.

Though this was to be her last Grand Slam success, Navratilova came agonizingly close to a tenth Wimbledon singles title four years later, when she was edged out in three sets by Conchita Martinez.

Martina Navratilova

Born: 18 October 1956
Place of birth: Revnice, Czechoslovakia
Turned Pro: 1973
Plays: Left-handed

Pistol's Shot Rings Out

Sampras Powers his Way to a First US Open

1990 The most dominant tennis player of his generation, Pete Sampras is the model of consistency that all those who follow him, including the sublime Roger Federer, seek to emulate.

'Pistol' Pete possessed the most potent serve ever seen on a tennis court; one which, allied to an equally prolific forehand, catapulted the American to an as-yet unequalled 14 Grand Slam titles, though the French Open always eluded him.

Sampras secured the first of his major triumphs on home soil at Flushing Meadow, a victory that sparked the end of one era and heralded the dawn of another. Sampras concluded Ivan Lendl's bid for a ninth straight US Open final appearance before eliminating boyhood idol John McEnroe in the semi-final.

The final itself sparked the commencement of one of the sport's most intense rivalries. Sampras outwitted contemporary Andre Agassi in straight sets to become the youngest ever male winner of the US Open, at 19 years and 28 days.

Agassi went on to triumph in the French Open at Roland Garros, but Sampras had his number when they played each other; winning 20 of their 34 clashes.

Pete Sampras
Born: 12 August 1971
Place of birth: Washington DC, USA
Turned Pro: 1988
Plays: Right-handed

Andre Agassi

American Hero

1990s Andre Agassi went through nearly as many image reconstructions as Madonna during his illustrious career. Yet despite his often outlandish, rock-star appearance, there was usually a substance to match a style that few players could equal.

Though more recognizable in his preferred luminous garb, it was in conventional white at Wimbledon that Agassi first began to fulfil his abundant potential, winning one of the most memorable finals of the modern era in a tense five-set encounter against Goran Ivanisevic. Despite that landmark success, the boy from Las Vegas had to wait another two years to add to his Grand Slam collection, as Pete Sampras usually held the upper hand in a rivalry that spanned a decade.

An Australian Open and Olympic gold were to follow for Agassi, as the trademark long hair was replaced by a more aerodynamic shaven head, yet the change of image actually heralded the worst period of his career.

The recurrence of a wrist injury saw him play only 24 matches in 1997, and his ranking slipped to 141. He also suffered emotionally in the wake of a high-profile divorce from actress Brooke Shields. Never a quitter, though, Agassi returned stronger than ever, despite his advancing years, to end his career as one of only five men to have captured all four Grand Slams in a total haul of eight. Always gracious in the face of victory or defeat, Agassi, now married to Steffi Graf, retired in 2006 and will be sorely missed.

Andre Agassi

Born: 29 April 1970

Place of birth: Las Vegas, Nevada

Turned Pro: 1986

Plays: Right-handed

Opposite: Agassi during the 1992 match that saw him beat Ivanisevic.

Monica Seles is Stabbed

Horror on Court

1993 Monica Seles was the emerging challenger to Steffi Graf's dominance of the women's game in the early 1990s, and was on the verge of eclipsing her German counterpart. She already had nine Grand Slam titles to her credit before she was stabbed on court by a spectator, in an incident that rocked the sporting world and dealt her career a blow from which she never truly recovered.

The incident occurred during a routine quarter-final match against Magdalena Maleeva in Hamburg (for the record Seles was leading 6-4, 4-3). She had taken her seat at the change of ends when Günter Parche, an unemployed German labourer, ran from the stands to the edge of the court, leaned over the three-foot barrier, and plunged a 10-inch kitchen knife between her shoulder blades.

Seles was left with a deep knife wound and untold emotional scarring. She did not return to competitive action for over two years. To her immense credit, she won the Australian Open for a fourth time in 1996, defeating Anke Huber in an emotional final, but in truth she understandably failed to reach the heights she hit in the earlier part of the decade.

For his part, Parche was charged with attempted murder, but was convicted for the lesser crime of causing grievous bodily harm, an offence for which he received only a two-year suspended sentence.

'Just yesterday, I was the undeniable number one player in the world. Now everything has changed. I am no longer the strong person I had been twenty-four hours previously.'

Monica Seles recalls how she felt after the stabbing

Opposite: Before the horror: Seles hurls the ball during the quarter finals of the French Open in 1990.

Federer Reigns in UK and USA

Rampant Roger Wins Wimbledon and the US Open

2000s For Tiger Woods in golf read Roger Federer in tennis. The Swiss ace totally dominated his sport at the start of the twenty-first century – to the extent that many experts hailed him as the greatest of all time, despite his relatively tender years.

The 'Fed Express' claimed his fourth straight Wimbledon title in 2006, defeating emerging Spanish tyro Rafael Nadal, before claiming a hat-trick of consecutive US Open crowns with a four-set victory against home favourite Andy Roddick a few months later. Such was the elegance and beauty of Federer's game that few begrudged him his almost unprecedented success.

The French Open crown still eluded the world No. 1 at that stage, but his domination of the grass and hard-court scene set him apart from the rest. His deadly accurate serve, command at the net and devastating ground-strokes – off either flank – made him close to unbeatable on grass. And four straight Wimbledon titles clearly proved this.

Federer was equally impregnable on the hard courts of Flushing Meadow as Roddick, Rafael Nadal, Andre Agassi, Marat Safin and a host of others found to their cost.

Roger Federer

Born: 8 August 1981

Place of birth: Basel, Switzerland

Turned Pro: 1998

Plays: Right-handed

Opposite: Federer kisses the cherished Wimbledon trophy after his fourth consecuitve win, 2006.

Venus and Serena Williams

Sibling Rivalry

2000s While the Williams sisters may not be universally popular characters, nobody can dispute that Venus and Serena did as much as anybody to change the perception of the women's game.

Coached from a young age by their extrovert father Richard, the sisters dominated the women's tour in the late 1990s and early 2000s, exhibiting power and athleticism that had rarely – if ever – been seen before on the women's circuit. The siblings quickly won 12 Grand Slam titles between them, Venus with five and Serena seven. The marginally younger sister Serena also held the distinction of owning all four Grand Slam titles at the same time in 2003, a feat nicknamed the 'Serena Slam'. Despite the disappointing matches they often played against each other, they formed a potent doubles partnership, claiming Olympic gold in Sydney as well as a clutch of Grand Slam titles.

Their star began to wane, however, in their mid-twenties. Injury to Serena and Venus's questionable motivation led to a dip in collective standards, although Venus did return to land a second Wimbledon crown in 2005. With the success of the durable but comparatively lightweight Belgian duo Justine Henin-Hardenne and Kim Clijsters, a fresh challenge may well ignite their careers again.

Opposite: Venus and Serena Williams playing on the same side of the net for a doubles semi-final in 2000.

Global Potters Unite

The First Professional World Championship

1927 The birth of snooker is credited to British army officers stationed in India in the late nineteenth century. However, it was not until much later that the first professional snooker World Championship was held. The billiards champion Joe Davis, OBE, helped establish the event, which first took place in Birmingham in 1927.

Albert Cope made the 1927 tournament's highest break of 60 – which would today be considered exceptionally modest – but it was Davis who stole the limelight. The Derbyshire-born player beat Tom Dennis 20-10 in the final, and received a grand prize of £6 10s (about £200 in today's terms).

Davis's games drew large crowds, and he was one of the most popular sportsmen of his era, winning every snooker World Championship until 1946, when he eventually retired from the event. His classic cue action is still replicated by most of today's players. Little wonder, therefore, that he is considered the father of modern-day snooker, a sport that continues to grow in popularity.

Opposite: The progenitor of modern snooker, Joe Davis, cueing up a shot.

Ray Reardon

Dracula on Cue

1970s Ray Reardon dominated snooker in the 1970s, winning six World Championships during that decade. Nicknamed 'Dracula', the former policeman was born in Wales in 1932, but did not turn professional until the age of 35.

Reardon was a fast learner, however, and won his first World Championship within three years, beating John Pulman in the 1970 final. That victory heralded the arrival of a snooker great. When the ranking system was introduced in 1976 he was the first ever No. 1, a position he retained until 1980–81.

'Dracula' did not lose his top spot for long, however, recapturing it after his 1982 Professional Players Tournament win at the age of 50. With this he became the first player to recapture the No. 1 spot.

Arguably the sport's best tactician, Reardon was also an incredible potter. His determination to regain his position of highest world ranking is indicative of his greatest quality – his mental strength, a characteristic he seemed able to switch on at will.

Nowadays Reardon acts as mentor to Ronnie O'Sullivan. But he will always be remembered for his six world titles, and will go down in history as one of snooker's greatest players.

Ray Reardon

Born: 8 October 1932

Place of birth: Tredegar, Wales

Nickname: Dracula

Turned professional: 1967

Steve Davis

Snooker Gets Interesting

1980s In the late 1970s a new breed of player, typified by Steve Davis, started to emerge on the snooker scene. Dedication, rather than talent alone, became a prerequisite for the champions of the future.

Davis was born in London in 1957 and turned professional in 1978. He made his World Championship debut a year later in an 11-13 defeat to Dennis Taylor – the first of many historic clashes between these two great players of the era.

Davis's arrival on the big stage was confirmed in 1981, when an 18-12 victory in the World Championship final over Doug Mountjoy began a relentless domination of snooker throughout the decade. 'The Nugget', as he became known, appeared in seven of the next eight finals.

Davis has compiled more than 300 competitive centuries during his career, but most notable was the first televised maximum break of 147, in the Lada Classic tournament against John Spencer in 1982.

As of 2006, Davis has won a record 73 professional titles, 28 of them in ranking events. His record of six world titles in the modern era has been bettered only by Stephen Hendry, and no player has yet matched his tally of six UK titles.

Steve Davis

Born: 22 August 1957

Place of birth: London, England

Nickname: The Nugget

Turned professional: 1978

Jimmy White

Caught in a Whirlwind

1980s Jimmy White is considered by many to be the best player never to have won the World Championship. Having lost in six of the competition's finals, The Whirlwind's flamboyant and determined approach has made him one of snooker's most popular figures.

Arguably his best chance to win the title came in 1994 against his nemesis Stephen Hendry. Level at 17-17 in the final frame in the final game, White was leading by 37 points to 24 when he missed the black on its spot. Hendry went on to clinch the frame and the match, leaving White to consider what might have been for his fifth consecutive World Championship final.

His direct and exciting approach, combined with his notorious tendency to lose concentration at key moments, added to White's popularity, but he has overwhelmingly endeared himself to fans and players alike for his graciousness in defeat. Despite his record, there can be no doubting his genuine talent. The fact that he has won almost every tournament in the game apart from the World Championship, reached No. 2 in the world rankings, and made it to six world finals, is evidence of the fact that to this day there are few to match him.

Jimmy White
Born: 2 May 1962
Place of birth: London, England
Nickname: The Whirlwind
Turned professional: 1980

Grinding to Success

Cliff Thorburn Wins the World Championships

1980 Cliff 'The Grinder' Thorburn became the first overseas player to win the snooker World Championships when he beat Alex Higgins 18-16 in the 1980 final. Born in Canada in 1948, his slow and deliberate approach made for an interesting clash against the flamboyant Northern Irishman, Alex 'The Hurricane' Higgins.

Having lost in the 1977 world final to John Spencer, Thorburn was not about to let the opportunity to grab the trophy pass him by again. Wearing down the charismatic Higgins, the man from British Columbia slowly but surely edged his way to glory in a tightly fought contest.

The result took Thorburn to No. 2 in the rankings, and only a few years later he was back in the Crucible showpiece again. This time he faced Steve Davis in the 1983 World Championship final but, with Davis at his peak, 'the Grinder' suffered as a consequence and he went down 18-6.

Nonetheless, the man from Canada – a country not renowned for its snooker players – was a major contender in every tournament he entered in the early 1980s. Certainly no one will forget his maximum break of 147 at the Crucible in 1973, nor his defining moment of glory in the 1980 world final.

Cliff Thorburn

Born: 16 January 1948

Place of birth: British Columbia, Canada

Nickname: The Grinder

Turned professional: 1972

Irish Eyes are Smiling

Taylor Claims a Dramatic World Championship

1985 The 1985 World Snooker Championship final is regarded by many as the most exciting game of snooker ever seen. Spanning two April days in 1985, the match featured Northern Irishman Dennis Taylor – appearing in his second final – against Steve Davis, the defending world champion.

The total match time of 11 hours 50 minutes was the longest ever recorded for a 35-frame game, and it went all the way to the very last ball of the very last frame. The final frame itself lasted 68 minutes, as each player had three attempts at clinching the title, before Davis overcut the black to leave the man from County Tyrone with a fairly straightforward pot to claim victory.

With snooker at the peak of its popularity, the climax of the final was watched by a UK television audience of 18.5 million people – at the time a record audience for any sporting event in the UK. As the country collectively held its breath, Taylor eventually managed to hold his nerve and emerge victorious, collecting his first World Championship title in the process.

It was a wonderful effort from the popular Irishman, who had been 8-0 down at the start of the match before beginning his remarkable fight back.

Opposite: Dennis Taylor looks to the World Snooker Championship trophy for inspiration during the final.

Stephen Hendry

Scottish Sensation

1990s Stephen 'The Ice Man' Hendry is undoubtedly one of the best players ever to pick up a snooker cue. By his own admission he is not the most naturally talented snooker player ever to grace the game, but few could argue that there has ever been a better all-round match player.

With more titles, more century breaks, and more prize money than any other player, the Scotsman is in a league of his own. Since his first World Championship final victory in 1990, at the tender age of 21, Hendry has gone on to break record after record. With several million pounds in prize money, the Scotsman's hunger for the sport has not diminished.

Although the pace at which Hendry bulldozes through competitions has relented in recent years, the 1990s certainly belonged to the man from Auchterarder. In that decade alone he won no fewer than seven World Championship titles – a modern-day record – and countless other major victories. His domination and presence were such that many opponents were beaten before they got to the table.

Even as he approaches veteran status, it would be an error to write off this snooker great from adding yet more World Championship titles to his already enormous trophy cabinet.

Stephen Hendry

Born: 13 January 1969
Place of birth: Edinburgh, Scotland
Nicknames: The Ice Man, The Golden Boy, The Maestro, Rolls Royce of Snooker
Turned professional: 1985

Ken Doherty

Dublin's Cue King

1990s Irishman Ken Doherty lifted the World Championship trophy in 1997 – and thus became only the second man from outside the United Kingdom to claim the title (the other was Canadian Cliff Thorburn).

Beating the seemingly invincible Stephen Hendry in the final, at a time when the Scot was at the peak of his powers, 'Krafty Ken' entered the record books the hard way. His victory, though, was comprehensive as he clinched the title by 18 frames to 12.

Doherty remains one of the most successful players ever, and has earned several million pounds in prize money. Admired among his fellow professionals and the fans for having one of the best all-round games, his honest, Never Say Die attitude has been the catalyst for many a famous comeback, and has made him the scourge of his opponents.

With several ranking tournament successes to date, the Irishman can also boast being the only snooker player to have been World Professional champion and World Amateur champion. The man from Dublin lifted the amateur trophy in 1989, and less than a decade later he had achieved ultimate success in the game.

Ken Doherty

Born: 17 September 1969

Place of birth: Dublin, Ireland

Nicknames: The Darlin' of Dublin, Krafty Ken, Ken-do

Turned professional: 1990

Rocket Ronnie

O'Sullivan's Five Fastest Maximum 147 Breaks

1997 Snooker players and enthusiasts alike agree that Ronnie O'Sullivan is one of the most naturally gifted players the sport has ever seen. Reputed to have made a century break at the tender age of just 10, his prodigious talent has never been in doubt.

Sometimes in his career, O'Sullivan has been accused of being temperamental and even reckless, but he is often sublime. A perfectionist, with the ability to take shots with both his left and right hand, even frequently alternating between the two within the same frame, he has made the maximum break of 147 on no fewer than six occasions on live television. Indeed, five of his six maximum breaks make up the list of the five fastest on record. His fastest came against Mick Price in the World Championship on 21 April 1997, when the aptly named 'Rocket' Ronnie completed the clearance in a staggering five minutes and 20 seconds.

But there is much more to his game than just speed, as is evidenced by the multitude of titles he has collected in his career. Few people would bet against him continuing to add to his list of honours, nor beating his own record time for a maximum 147 clearance.

Ronnie O'Sullivan

Born: 5 December 1975

Place of birth: Essex, England

Nickname: The Rocket

Turned professional: 1992

Snooker's First Streaker

Too Much Pink

2002 Although the art of streaking is not uncommon in the world of sport, it had remained largely virgin territory in snooker. However, all that changed in 2002 when a World Championship first-round match between Paul Hunter and Quinten Hann was rudely interrupted.

The streaker was later identified as unemployed Andrew Slater from Doncaster. Somehow managing to shed his clothes while seated in the audience without alerting anybody's attention, the 36-year-old invaded the game in all his glory – other than for a Sven-Göran Eriksson mask which he used to cover his face.

Although certainly startled by the event, the players bravely played on once the streaker had been removed by officials. Hunter's eventual defeat to Hann by 10 frames to nine was unquestionably overshadowed by the man from Doncaster, who was responsible for this momentous, if not-so-sporting event, which will certainly live on in the memory.

Opposite: Two years later a similar streaking incident occurred at The Crucible during the 2004 Embassy World Snooker Championship match between Ronnie O'Sullivan and Graeme Dott.

John Higgins

Scottish Master

2005

The high point of John Higgins' glittering snooker career to date was his World Championship title, which he won in 1998, seeing off Ken Doherty with a final break of 118.

And it is his fabulous break-building ability that earned him great plaudits in the final of the 2005 Grand Prix, when Higgins became the first player to make four consecutive century breaks in a ranking tournament, scoring 103, 104, 138 and 128 against Ronnie O'Sullivan. In the process, he scored a record 494 points without reply from his opponent. It was a mesmerizing run of form that helped the Scotsman claim the title by nine frames to two.

Higgins burst on to the snooker scene in the 1994–95 season, becoming the first teenager to win three ranking events in one season. Since then the former world No. 1 has gone on to break record after record, including becoming the first ever player to make 14 centuries in a professional tournament.

His fantastic technique and mastery in break-building have made him one of the most successful players in snooker history, well capable of replicating performances such as his 2005 Grand Prix tournament victory.

John Higgins

Born: 18 May 1975

Place of birth: North Lanarkshire, Scotland

Nickname: The Wizard of Wishaw

Turned Professional: 1992

Eric Bristow

Crafty Cockney

1980s Eric Bristow emerged from the darts scene in the late 1970s, during a period when television began to show increased interest in the sport.

Bristow not only had supreme talent but was also possessed of an imposing personality and confidence in his own ability. These factors rapidly made him a big name within the sport. His confidence, however, often turned to cockiness and arrogance, and he invariably irritated opponents before and during matches with his gamesmanship.

But it was this very gamesmanship – and his undoubted talent in the 1980s – that helped turn darts into a worldwide spectator sport, just as he began to dominate the oche.

The Crafty Cockney became the most successful and consistent darts player of the decade, reigning as No. 1 in the world rankings from January 1980 until 1987. From his first World Championship title in 1980, when he beat Bobby George in the final, the Londoner never looked back. He won a further four BDO (British Darts Organisation) world titles, and was also runner-up five times between 1982 and 1990. As one of the most celebrated darts players of all time, Bristow became the first person from the sport to receive an MBE in 1989.

Eric Bristow

Born: 27 April 1957

Place of birth: London, England

Nickname: The Crafty Cockney

Current world ranking: 371

John Lowe's Nine-Dart Finish

The Perfect Game

1984 John Lowe achieved the ultimate feat in darts on 13 October 1984. During the quarter-finals of the World Matchplay Championships against Keith Deller, Old Stoneface managed a nine-dart finish and therefore a perfect game.

This was the first time the sport's equivalent of a hole-in-one in golf or a 147 break in snooker had ever been accomplished by any player in a televised game. After two 180s, he stepped up to the oche and hit a treble 17, a treble 18 and a double 18 to complete the momentous occasion.

As well as a healthy dose of prestige, Lowe also collected a cool £100,000 for this landmark achievement, before going on to clinch the tournament itself by beating Cliff Lazarenko in the final.

Despite the fact that the perfect game has since been achieved again on television, and although John Lowe went on to win a record 15 World Open titles in his career, it is his nine-dart finish for which he is most fondly remembered as one of the all-time greats.

John Lowe

Born: 21 July 1945

Place of birth: Derbyshire, England

Nickname: Old Stoneface

Current world ranking: 120

Phil Taylor

Powering On

1990s

Phil 'The Power' Taylor has an unprecedented overall list of honours, and is one of the greatest darts players of all time.

The Power burst on to the darts scene in the late 1980s after being discovered playing in the pubs of Stoke-on-Trent by the legendary Eric Bristow. Sponsoring him in the early stages of his career, Bristow was sure he had found a diamond in the rough.

History has proved him right – not that it took Taylor long to repay the faith shown in him. By 1990 he had won the BDO World Championship, ironically by beating his mentor Bristow in the final.

With so many successes, it is difficult to isolate a single highlight, but Taylor himself regards the 1992 World Championship final success against Mike Gregory as one of his best. It was an epic encounter that went right down to a tiebreak leg in the final set of the match. Taylor showed his mental strength to claim the victory – a trait he has demonstrated consistently in a sport that he virtually dominated for two decades in the 1990s and 2000s.

Phil Taylor

Born: 13 August 1960

Place of birth: Stoke-on-Trent, England

Nickname: The Power

Current world ranking: 1

Opposite: Phil Taylor with his trophy after winning the Embassy World Darts Championship in 2000.

Raymond van Barneveld

Dutch Dynamo

2005 Raymond van Barneveld was crowned BDO World Champion for the fourth time in 2005 when he beat Martin Adams 6-2. As the most successful Dutch darts player ever, he has virtually single-handedly helped turn darts in Holland into a popular spectator sport.

His first BDO World Championship title came in 1998, when he beat Welshman Richie Burnett, against whom he had lost in the 1995 final. Following that victory, van Barneveld was a dominating and imposing member of the British Darts Organisation for years. Indeed, the former postman would have equalled Eric Bristow's record of five BDO world titles, but lost in the 2006 final to his compatriot Jelle Klaasen 7-5.

Then, in February 2006, van Barneveld announced his move from the BDO to the rival Professional Darts Corporation, setting up mouth-watering clashes against some of the sport's biggest names, none more so than against Phil 'The Power' Taylor.

In March 2006, in a Premier League match in Bournemouth, van Barneveld hit his first televised nine-dart finish on the way to beating Peter Manley 8-3. It was a testament to the exciting and raw talent that only a four-time BDO world champion could possess.

Raymond van Barneveld

Born: 20 April 1967

Place of birth: The Hague, The Netherlands

Nicknames: Barney, The Man

Current world ranking: 2

No Wobbles From Jelle

Klaasen Becomes the Youngest World Champion

2006 Jelle 'The Young Matador' Klaasen sent shockwaves through the darts world when he defeated defending champion Raymond van Barneveld in the 2006 World Darts championship. Ironically, van Barneveld has done much to stir up interest in the sport of darts in Holland and helped inspire his young dethroner to turn professional.

Barney, looking to equal Eric Bristow's record of five BDO world titles, was a huge favourite going into the clash. Indeed, young Jelle had been priced at 100-1 to win the event before it started. However, alarm bells must have rung out in van Barneveld's head given that his young opponent had defeated the top seed Mervyn King en route to the final. The young Dutchman showed composure beyond his years at the oche and refused to be overawed by his compatriot.

After winning a crucial eleventh set, the young pretender retained his cool and, undeterred by the pressure, became the youngest ever darts world champion at the age of 21 by recording a famous 7-5 victory over one of the game's greats.

Jelle Klaasen

Born: 17 October 1984

Place of birth: Alphen, Netherlands

Nickname: The Young Matador

Current world ranking: 19

Opposite: Klaasen throws a dart on his way to record-breaking victory in the final against Barneveld.

ATHLETICS & GYMNASTICS

Since the times of the ancient Greeks, men and women have competed to determine who is the fastest and the strongest, who can jump the furthest or the highest, or hurl an object the furthest distance.

In this section we explore how athletics and gymnastics have seen sportsmen and women push their bodies to the limits and test how far humans can be physically pushed in all manner of disciplines, on apparatus, track and field. The modern Olympics started in 1896 and were the first Games since Roman emperor Theodosius I banned the Ancient Olympic Games in AD 393. Since then, numerous athletes and gymnasts have become heroes and heroines as they have broken records, set new markers to challenge the next wave of hopefuls, and kept the Olympic spirit of competition alive.

Spyridon Louis

Greek Legend Lives On

1896 Spyridon Louis was a Greek water-seller and shepherd who won the first Olympic marathon in 1896, at the first modern Olympic Games. The marathon was inspired by the legend of Pheidippides, the soldier who had run from Marathon to Athens to announce the Athenian victory in the Battle of Marathon in 490 BC.

Given that the first modern Olympic Games were held in Athens, when Louis entered the Panathenaic Stadium to complete his final lap in the lead, the young Greek was received with rapturous applause by an audience desperate to have a compatriot take the gold medal for an event that was steeped in Greek history.

Completing the 40 km (25 mile) race in two hours and 58 minutes, Louis was the hero of the Games. Defeating the other 16 competitors, the 24-year-old had written himself into the history books, finishing more than seven minutes ahead of his closest challenger. For achieving this historic feat, the Greek king offered young Louis any prize he desired – and he eventually requested a donkey and cart for his water-carrying business. The Olympic champion then returned to his village of Maroussi, never to compete again.

Spyridon Louis

Born: 12 January 1873 **Died:** 26 March 1940
Place of birth: Athens, Greece
Event: Marathon
Olympic medals: Gold 1896

Early Olympic Scandal

Jim Thorpe is Stripped of His Medals

1913 Jim Thorpe was stripped of his 1912 Olympic gold medals in the pentathlon and the decathlon for violating the amateur-status rules. The Olympic committee took the decision in 1913, when they discovered that Thorpe had taken part in semi professional baseball while a student at Carlisle Indian Industrial School in Pennsylvania, USA.

Thorpe was just 24 when he took part in the Olympic Games in Sweden, yet he blew away the competition with his strength, speed and versatility. King Gustav V had presented Thorpe with his gold medals for both accomplishments, and in doing so had famously declared that Thorpe was the greatest athlete in the world. Yet less than a year later he was denied his medals and had his name removed from the history books. Having left the drama of the Olympics behind him, Thorpe went on to become a professional baseball player and later a professional American Football player – leaving no doubt that he was a rare sporting talent.

Thorpe died in 1953, but was posthumously re-awarded his gold medals and had his name written back into the records in 1983, when the Olympic Committee relaxed its rule on amateur status, and hence officially accepted Thorpe as an Olympic legend.

Jim Thorpe

Born: 28 May 1887   **Died:** 28 March 1953

Place of birth: Oklahoma, USA

Events: Pentathlon and Decathlon

Olympic medals: 2 Gold 1912

Paavo Nurmi

The Flying Finn

1924 Paavo Nurmi was the best middle- and long-distance runner of the 1920s, breaking record after record. Winning a total of nine gold and three silver Olympic medals in his illustrious career, his crowning glory came in the 1924 Paris Olympic Games, where he won five golds.

Nurmi, from Finland, was ahead of his time, training with a dedication and intensity that other athletes simply could not match. Nicknamed the 'Flying Finn', he would famously run with a stopwatch in his hand, desperate to push himself to the limit.

Having won gold medals in the 1,500 metres, the 5,000 metres and the cross-country individual and team races, Nurmi collected his fifth and final Paris gold medal in the 3,000 metres team race, beating off competition from the Americans and the British. The Flying Finn had run seven races in six days and had won them all, achieving a miraculous feat.

Apart from his Olympic victories, he set 25 world records overall, at distances from 1,500 metres up to 20,000 metres over the space of 12 years. No wonder Nurmi is still regarded as one of the Olympic Games' greats.

Paavo Nurmi

Born: 13 June 1897   **Died:** 2 October 1973

Place of birth: Turku, Finland

Events: 10,000 m; 8,000 m cross country; 5,000 m; 5,000 m cross country; 3,000 m; 3,000 m steeple chase; 1,500 m

Olympic medals: 3 Gold 1920, 5 Gold 1924, Gold 1928, Silver 1920, 2 Silver 1928

Jesse Owens' Olympics

Sprinting Into History

1936 Jesse Owens was born in 1913 in Alabama to an impoverished family struggling to make ends meet at the height of racial segregation. Overcoming all these adversities, the African-American Owens developed into a national hero and a legendary Olympian, becoming the first American to win four gold medals at an individual Olympics.

Taking part in Nazi Germany's 1936 Olympics – which many believe were an attempt by Adolf Hitler to prove his theory of the supremacy of the Aryan race – Owens stunned the world with his triumphant sprinting displays.

Having shown a raw and prodigious talent as a young student, Owens realized his potential and became a cult figure at the Berlin games. The 23-year-old won gold in the 100 metres, 200 metres, long jump and the 4 x 100 metres relay, setting Olympic records in all but one of those events. Shamefully, despite his success on the track, because of the colour of his skin he was not offered any endorsement deals. For a while he was reduced to running for hire, racing against anything from motorcycles to horses.

In 1976 Owens was awarded the Medal of Freedom, the highest honour a civilian of the United States can receive in recognition of his role as a civic leader and his fantastic athletic achievements.

Jesse Owens

Born: 12 September 1913   **Died:** 31 March 1980

Place of birth: Alabama, USA

Events: 100 m, 200 m, 4 x 100 m relay and long jump

Olympic medals: 4 Gold 1936

Opposite: Owens in the foreground at the start of the 100 metres in 1936.

Babe Zaharias

First Female Superstar

1930s Babe Zaharias was born Mildred Didrikson on 26 June 1911. Considered to be the greatest all-round female athlete of all time, she was nicknamed 'Babe', after Babe Ruth, having hit five home runs in one baseball game.

Despite mastering tennis, diving, bowling, being an All American basketball player and becoming well known for her golfing achievements in the 1950s, it was in track and field in the 1930s that Zaharias made her name.

First coming to prominence at the 1932 AAU (Amateur Athletic Union) Championships, when she won the team title despite being the only member on her team, the 21-year-old went on to compete in the 1932 Los Angeles Olympics. She was only allowed to compete in three disciplines, although she had qualified for all five women's track and field events. Nevertheless, she won the javelin and the 80 metre hurdles, and pushed the high jump winner all the way, collecting two gold medals and one silver.

After her success in the Olympics, Babe turned her hand to golf and became the greatest women's player in that sport too. As a professional, she won the US Women's Open in 1948, 1950 and 1954, after which cancer cut short what was an incredible sporting career.

Babe Zaharias

Born: 26 June 1914   **Died:** 27 September 1956

Place of birth: Texas, USA

Events: Javelin, 80 m Hurdles, High Jump

Olympic medals: 2 Gold 1932, Silver 1932

Dutch Flyer

Fanny Blankers-Koen Takes London by Storm

1948 Although she had made her Olympic debut in the 1936 Berlin Games, Dutch athlete Fanny Blankers-Koen's career was interrupted until 1948 as a result of the Second World War. By then she was 30 years old and a mother of two, so despite being Holland's best female athlete, she was written off as a medal challenger before the competition had even begun.

Nonetheless Fanny Koen, who had married her coach Jan Blankers, became the first woman ever to win four gold medals at an Olympic Games, for the 100 metres, 200 metres, 80 metre hurdles and by running the anchor leg on the winning 4 x 100 metres relay team. Ironically, the 'Flying Housewife' suffered badly from homesickness at the beginning of the Games and had only been convinced to stay on by her husband and mentor. Fortunately she did, and went on to achieve unrivalled Olympic success.

Many have argued she would have won even more medals had she not been limited to entering only three individual events – after all, she was a natural and versatile athlete who had set 16 world records at eight different events.

Fanny Blankers-Koen

Born: 26 April 1918   **Died:** 25 January 2004

Place of birth: Lage Vuursche, Denmark

Events: 100 m, 200 m, 4 x 100m relay, 80 m Hurdles

Olympic medals: 4 Gold 1948

Jim Peters

Marathon Man

1953 Jim Peters, nicknamed 'Marathon Man', set new world records for the marathon four times in the 1950s. His greatest accomplishment was completing the gruelling event in under 2 hours and 20 minutes when, on 13 June 1953, he achieved a time of 2 hours 18 minutes and 40 seconds in the Polytechnic Marathon between Windsor and Chiswick.

Pushing himself further than any other athlete, his dedication and commitment to his profession meant that Peters dominated the marathon circuit in the early 1950s. Indeed, only four months after Peters had smashed the 2 hour 20 minute barrier, he broke his own world record yet again, this time by six seconds.

Sadly Peters' achievements in setting world records in the 1950s may well be overshadowed by his performance in the 1954 Commonwealth Games in Vancouver. On a swelteringly hot day, the world record holder entered the stadium to complete his final lap of the marathon but, severely dehydrated, he was forced to retire from the event, after collapsing 200 yards from the finishing line. While this iconic image is one that has lived on in the memory, though, it is for the races he won and the records he broke that he should truly be remembered.

Opposite: Jim Peters in 1954 striding through the marathon from Windsor to London to claim victory.

Bannister's Dream Mile

Four-Minute Marvel

1954 Roger Bannister made history when he became the first man to run a mile in under four minutes. At a meet at Iffley Road track in Oxford on 6 May 1954, he broke the previous world record of 4 minutes 1 second set by the Swede Gunder Hägg almost nine years earlier. To the delight of the 3,000-strong crowd that had gathered to see the meet between the British AAA (Amateur Athletic Association) and Oxford University, the 25-year-old Bannister completed the dream mile with a time of 3 minutes and 59 seconds.

The Oxford medical student had broken a psychological and physical barrier thanks to the assistance of his friends Chris Brasher and Christopher Chataway, who had acted as pacemakers. Taking the lead with a burst of energy 200 yards from the finish, Bannister collapsed over the line, and in doing so changed the perception of human limitations and potential athletic achievement.

With his intensity and dedication, combined with innovative training techniques that enabled him to increase his speed, he had managed to capture the imagination of the world. And by becoming the first man to do the sub-four-minute mile, Bannister had completed an incredible sporting achievement.

Opposite: Roger Bannister expresses relief as he approaches the finishing line, having just run a mile in under four minutes.

Abebe Bikila

African King

1960 Abebe Bikila became a household name when he won the gold medal for the marathon in the 1960 Rome Olympics. Coincidentally, Bikila was born in Ethiopia on 7 August 1932, the same day that the Argentinian legend Juan Carlos Zabala won the gold medal for the marathon in the Los Angeles Olympics.

Bikila, who was taking part in his first Olympics in Rome, made his move for victory with less than a mile to go. Pulling away from the Moroccan Rhadi Ben Abdesselem, the 28-year-old became an overnight sensation, setting a world record of 2 hours 15 minutes and 16.2 seconds, beating the record set by Sergey Popov that had stood for years. But, most amazingly of all, he did all this without wearing shoes!

Four years later, at the Tokyo Games, this sporting great went on to become the first man to win the Olympic marathon twice. Bikila's achievement was equally great this time round – although this time he wore running shoes, he had had his appendix removed only weeks before the competition began. Not that this seemed to affect him in the slightest. In an incredible testament to the man's amazing mental strength and courage, he went on to smash the world record by over a minute and a half.

Abebe Bikila

Born: 7 August 1932
Place of birth: Mout, Ethiopia
Event: Marathon
Olympic medals: Gold 1960, Gold 1964

Wilma Rudolph

No Place Like Rome

1960 Wilma Rudolph will always be remembered fondly for the three gold medals she won in the Rome 1960 Olympics, but it is for overcoming a series of obstacles in her life en route to achieving that success that she is truly remarkable.

Rudolph was born in 1940 and at a very young age was diagnosed with polio. Struck down with the debilitating disease, doctors told her she would never walk again. However, supported by her family, the young Rudolph made a miraculous recovery and went on to compete in the 1956 Olympics as a 16-year-old, winning a bronze medal in the 4 x 100 metres relay.

Her crowning glory, however, came four years later when she became the first American woman ever to win three Olympic gold medals. Despite having sprained her ankle during the competition, Rudolph claimed gold in the 100 metres, 200 metres and 4 x 100 metres relay, setting the world record in the 100 metre sprint.

Despite retiring at just 22, Rudolph's impact on track and field was great, and she remains a role model for young athletes today, embodying the principle that with hard work, determination and belief you can achieve anything.

Wilma Rudolph

Born: 23 June 1940

Place of birth: Tennessee, USA

Events: 100 m, 200 m, 4 x 100 m relay

Olympic medals: Bronze 1956, 3 Gold 1960

Opposite: Wilma Rudolph wears a headscarf as protection against the rain as she wins the 100 yards during a meeting between the British Empire and Commonwealth and the United States Olympic team.

Peter Snell

Kiwi Comes to the Fore

1962 Peter Snell came to worldwide attention in the 1960 Rome Olympics by winning gold in the 800 metres final. He had beaten the Belgian world record holder Roger Moens, who was heavily fancied, and in doing so the 21-year-old from New Zealand exploded on to the track and field scene, heralding an era of record breaking middle distance running.

A protégé of the great New Zealand athletics coach Arthur Lydiard, Snell achieved great success in the 1960s. A particularly special year for him was 1962. In January he broke the world mile record in front of a huge audience at Cook's Gardens Stadium in Wanganui with a time of 3 minutes 54 seconds, and later the same week he went on to set the world record in the 800 metres.

With Commonwealth gold medals and championship successes, Snell went on to win two more gold medals at the 1964 Olympics. He coped with the pressure of going to the Tokyo Games as favourite, completing the unique double of 800 metres and 1,500 metres gold medals. Despite retiring at a young age, his records outlasted his athletic career and he remains one of the greatest middle-distance runners of all time.

Peter Snell

Born: 17 December 1938

Place of Birth: Opunake, New Zealand

Events: 800 m; 1,500 m; 1 mile

Olympic medals: Gold 1960, 2 Gold 1964

Opposite: Peter Snell breaks the world mile record in 1962.

Bob Beamon Leaps Into History

Long, Long Jump

1968 Bob Beamon sent shockwaves around the world in the 1968 Olympics when he smashed the existing world record in long jump by over half a metre. Setting what is still the Games record, he jumped a mammoth 8.90 m (29 ft 2½ in). Indeed, the 22-year-old's jump was so long that the measuring device slid off its rail before it reached Beamon's point of impact, and officials had to use an old-fashioned steel tape to measure out the distance. Eagerly awaiting the official distance, the New Yorker fell to his knees, overcome by emotion when the result was finally announced.

Few would have believed such a jump was possible. Indeed, since the turn of the twentieth century the largest increase in the long jump was 0.15 m. Beamon's gold medal mark bettered the existing record by a huge 0.55 m (1⅘ ft). Although Bob never jumped this distance again, his spectacular leap in Mexico City that day made him the first person ever to reach both 28 and 29 feet. His jump, which went on to survive as a world record for over 20 years, remains one of the great Olympic moments.

Bob Beamon

Born: 29 August 1946
Place of birth: New York, USA
Event: Long Jump
Olympic medals: Gold 1968

Dick Fosbury Introduces the Flop

Rewriting the Style Guide

1968 Dick Fosbury revolutionized the high jump when he presented his new and unique style to the world on his international debut in the 1968 Olympic Games.

Using a back-first technique, now known as the Fosbury Flop, his method was to sprint diagonally towards the bar, then curve and leap backwards over it. At the time, it was traditional for high jumpers to take off with their inside foot and swing their outside foot up and over the bar. Taking off from his outside foot, Fosbury would twist his body so that he went over the bar head-first with his back to it. Many experts were initially critical of this unconventional technique, yet the audience in Mexico City took to the American immediately. Galvanized by the support and with the use of the Flop, Fosbury went on to win the gold medal and break the Olympic record with a height of 2.24 m (7⅓ ft).

The Fosbury Flop is the technique of choice for most professional high jumpers competing today, a great credit to the innovative genius of this Olympic gold medallist who refused to be tied down by conventional methods.

Dick Fosbury

Born: 6 March 1947

Place of birth: Oregon, USA

Events: High Jump

Olympic medals: Gold 1968

Opposite: Dick Fosbury uses his new techinque to break the Olympic record in 1968.

Brilliant Bruce

Jenner Wins the Olympic Decathlon

1976 One of the most remarkable athletes of the last century, the word 'impossible' simply did not exist in Bruce Jenner's vocabulary. He earned a football scholarship during his university days, but a cruel knee injury robbed him of a chance to play in the NFL. Such a blow would have been enough to deter most people from a sporting career – but not Jenner. A switch to the decathlon, the most rigorous and demanding of all the athletic disciplines, seemed an overly adventurous move, but mentored by track coach L.D. Weldon, he found almost instant success.

By the time of the 1976 Montreal Olympics, Jenner was considered the finest athlete of his era. He duly destroyed a high-class Olympic field, setting a new world record of 8,618 points in the process and claiming the coveted James E. Sullivan award as the top amateur athlete in the United States.

Jenner went on to become one of America's most famous faces, fronting breakfast-cereal advertising campaigns and appearing in several television sitcoms, before settling on a career as a motivational coach.

It will be for his prowess as an athlete who inspired modern American decathletes Dan O'Brien and Brendan Pappas that he will be most fondly remembered, however.

Bruce Jenner

Born: 28 October 1949

Place of birth: New York, USA

Events: Decathlon

Olympic medals: Gold 1976

Pietro Mennea

Sprinter Does Top Italian Job

1979 Pietro Mennea is regarded as one of the greatest sprinters of all time, having held the 200 metres world record for almost 17 years. Competing at the highest levels in athletics for well over a decade, the Italian – who earned himself the nickname 'The Arrow of the South' – combined his unique and natural sprinting talent with dedication and hard work.

Mennea claimed a bronze medal in the 200 metres on his Olympic debut in the 1972 Munich Games aged just 20, finishing behind Valeri Borzov and Larry Black in the final. Spurred on by what he considered a disappointment at Munich, Mennea went on to dominate the event in the 1970s. Gold medals in the European Championships of 1974 and 1978 preceded an Olympic gold medal in Moscow in 1980, where he narrowly beat Scotsman Alan Wells in the final.

But Mennea's lasting impact on athletics was to set an incredible world record in the 200 metres in 1979. Running at high altitude in Mexico City, he posted a time of 19.72 seconds, a mark that was not beaten until Michael Johnson in 1996, a mammoth 17 years later. No wonder then that Mennea is still regarded as an Italian national hero.

Pietro Mennea

Born: 28 June 1952

Place of birth: Barletta, Italy

Events: 200 m, 4 x 400 m

Olympic medals: Bronze 1972, Gold 1980, Bronze 1980

Opposite: Pietro Mennea races to 200-m gold at the Moscow Olympic Games in 1980.

Ovett beats Coe...Coe beats Ovett

Record-Breaking Rivalry

1980 The two stellar talents of Britain's golden age of middle-distance running shared one of the most bitter rivalries the sport has ever known, providing a truly enthralling spectacle. Their duel, which had simmered throughout the latter part of the 1970s, came to a head at the 1980 Olympics in Moscow.

Steve Ovett arrived in Russia as the favourite to take the 1,500 metres title, having set a new world record for the mile and equalled Sebastian Coe's world record in the 1,500 metres in the space of a month. He was also unbeaten over his favoured distance for three years. Coe, meanwhile, was the major force at 800 metres.

The Moscow Olympics marked only the second time the pair had met at a major championship and there was endless debate as to who would emerge as the undisputed middle-distance king. As it was, the honour was shared – but in surprising circumstances.

In the 800 metres final, Ovett trailed by a distance at the bell, but pushed his way through the crowd to second place. Thirty metres into the home straight, he dramatically forced his way into the lead and held off Coe to win by three metres.

In the 1,500 metres, which took place a week later, Coe – who was expected to triumph over the shorter distance – gained revenge as he too came from behind to win, with a crestfallen Ovett settling for bronze.

Opposite: Steve Ovett wins the 800 m leaving a disappointed Sebastian Coe to take second place.

Daley Express

Thompson Defies Injury to Win the Gold

1983 Never far from controversy, Daley Thompson may have had a habit of rubbing people up the wrong way with his outspoken manner and showmanship, but he can certainly lay claim to being the greatest British athlete of all time.

By the time of the 1983 World Championships Daley was by some way the dominant force in the decathlon, having comprehensively gained the upper hand in his rivalry with German Jürgen Hingsen. The two traded records but it was Daley who remained unbeaten in all competitions between 1979 and 1987. Persistent back and knee injuries had threatened to undermine Thompson's supremacy at the inaugural World Championships in 1983. His participation in Helsinki had been touch-and-go, as he had missed over three months of training, but he decided at the last minute that a chance to get one over on his great rival was too great to resist.

Thompson got off to a typically fast start in the 100 metres, exceeded expectations in the shot-put and cleared an impressive 5.10 m (16⅔ ft) in the pole vault. Hingsen and fellow German Siggi Wentz were still very much in the picture for gold, however, and it took a superhuman effort from a less than fully fit Thompson to withstand their challenge. He produced one of his finest javelin throws to head into the gruelling 1,500 metres with a clear advantage over Hingsen. Despite his lack of preparation, Thompson clung on with typical grit to become Britain's first world champion.

Daley Thompson

Born: 30 July 1958

Place of birth: London, England

Event: Decathlon

Olympic medals: Gold 1980, Gold 1984

Czech Great

Kratochvilova Breaks the 800 Metre Record

1983 Czech athlete Jarmila Kratochvilova was one of the more distinctive sportswomen of her era, but she was noteworthy for far more than her muscular physique. Back in 1983, the Eastern Bloc countries were making significant strides towards the domination of women's athletics, and Kratochvilova was soon on the embodiment of the type of athlete they were intent on producing. She utterly dominated her 800 metres final in a fashion never seen before or since, accelerating with 300 metres to go and clearing on the top bend to win in 1 minute 54.68 seconds from Lyubov Gurina and Yekaterina Podkopayeva. More than two decades later, this time remains the fastest recorded in a World Championships final. At that time it was the third fastest 800 metres by a woman in history.

To greater astonishment, a day later, seemingly invigorated rather than sapped by her record-breaking exploits, Kratochvilova took the 400 metres title in an incredible 47.99 seconds. Not only was that a world record, it has still not been matched at a World Championships.

Jarmila Kratochvilova

Born: 26 January 1951

Place of birth: Czechoslovakia

Events: 400 m, 4 x 400 m, 800 m

Olympic medals: Silver 1980

Carl Lewis Equals Jesse Owens

Golden Boy

1984 The word 'great' is often overused in sporting parlance, but when referring to American athlete Carl Lewis, there are few more fitting adjectives. Although he never truly endeared himself to the American public, few could argue that with 17 World and Olympic gold medals on display in his personal trophy cabinet – a tally never likely to be matched – he was the greatest of all time.

In a career with so many highs, it is almost impossible to separate the various outstanding achievements, but his pursuit of equalling Jesse Owens' clean sweep at the 1984 Olympics was particularly sweet. By the time the Los Angeles Games came around Lewis's fame had transcended the sporting arena, but so thorough he in his preparation that nothing was ever likely to deter him from his goal.

Lewis started his quest successfully by going sub-10 seconds to land the 100 metres and doubled up in the 200 metres. Sandwiched in between was a comfortable victory in the long jump – an event in which he was later to break Bob Beamon's long-standing world record. The final leg of his staggering achievement came in anchoring the sprint relay team to a new world record.

Not only had Lewis equalled Owens's feat but he had found the fame and fortune he had always craved, raising the profile of track and field in the process.

Carl Lewis

Born: 1 July 1961

Place of birth: Alabama, USA

Events: 100 m, 200 m, 4 x 100 m, Long Jump

Olympic medals: 4 Gold 1984, 2 Gold 1988, Silver 1988, 2 Gold 1992, Gold 1996

Florence Griffith-Joyner

Go Go Flo-Jo

1988 The Summer Olympics of 1988 belonged to Florence Griffith-Joyner. Flo-Jo, as she was affectionately nicknamed, was one of the most colourful athletes in the sport, certainly most recognizable as a consequence of her outrageously styled nails.

Though Griffith-Joyner was something of an entertainer, she was more pertinently the greatest female sprinter of all time, and the Seoul Olympics provided confirmation of her unrivalled brilliance. She was an overwhelming favourite for the titles in the sprint events, having already given note of her prowess by claiming two silver medals at the World Championships the previous year.

In the Olympic 100 metres final she ran 10.54 seconds, beating her nearest rival Evelyn Ashford by three tenths of a second. She went on to match that achievement in the 200 metres, setting a new world record of 21.34 seconds, winning by a massive four tenths.

There has always been a suspicion that Flo-Jo may have been assisted in her record-breaking feats by performance-enhancing stimulants. That scepticism grew as a result of her shockingly premature death at the age of just 38 in 1998. However, post-mortem reports suggested that she had suffocated in her pillow during a severe epileptic seizure. Though there will always be doubters, the autopsy did at least allow her stunning achievements to be recognized in the light they deserve.

Florence Griffith-Joyner

Born: 21 December 1959   **Died:** 21 September 1998

Place of birth: California, USA

Events: 100m, 200m, 4 x 100m, 4 x 400m

Olympic medals: Silver 1984, 3 Gold 1988, Silver 1988

Fermin Reigns In Spain

Cacho's Golden Run Ends an Olympic Drought

1992 Fermin Cacho will never go down as one of the great middle-distance runners, but in defeating a high-calibre field at his home Olympics, he provided one of the most abiding memories of Barcelona 1992.

Cacho was a consistent performer, and he excelled in the indoor arena, highlighted by his performances in 1990. Cacho finished second in the 1,500 metres at the European Indoor Championships in Glasgow but, exposed to the elements, he could manage only eleventh place in the same event at the European Championships in Split. With that sort of inconsistent form behind him – and a further unspectacular campaign in the lead-up to the Barcelona Games – there was only a handful of wildly optimistic and patriotic souls who were predicting that their man could overturn the form book against his major rival, Algeria's Noureddine Morceli. Cacho's best result prior to the Olympic final that year had been a mediocre fifth place in a mile race at the Bislet Games in Oslo.

However, come the moment of truth, Cacho was inspired and ignited by the passionate home support. Boosted by the strangely pedestrian pace set by the African contingent, Cacho placed himself expertly to exploit the slow tempo and launched his bid for glory in the home straight. The Spaniard held off his nemesis in gripping circumstances to claim gold and send him and the Olympic Stadium into a fit of ecstasy.

Fermin Cacho

Born: 16 February 1969
Place of Birth: Agreda, Spain
Event: 1,500 m
Olympic Medals: Gold 1992, Silver 1996

Dieter the Destroyer

Baumann Wins the 5,000 Metre Olympic Gold

1992 Dieter Baumann was regarded as the 'nearly' man of middle-distance running during the early part of the 1990s, but it was felt that his notoriously strong finishing kick would always help him to land Olympic glory one day.

The commencement of the European indoor season in the Olympic year of 1992 suggested his fortunes might change in Catalonia later that year. The German narrowly failed to break the European indoor record in the 3,000 metres and looked to be in exceptional form, but with a posse of talented Kenyans to beat at the Olympics, his task looked an unenviable one.

Baumann comfortably eased through his heats to reach the 5,000 metres final, but a mercilessly fast initial pace threatened to undermine his bid for glory. Thankfully from the German's perspective, the tempo slowed, allowing Baumann back into contention. However, he got boxed in amongst four African runners in the back straight of the last lap, and was only able to get clear coming into the home straight. From there, Baumann launched his famous finishing kick to devastating effect. He went on to sprint past his four adversaries and claim an unlikely, but thoroughly deserved, gold medal.

Opposite: An elated Dieter Baumann crosses the finishing line of the 5000 metre race at the 1992 Olympic games in Barcelona.

Christie's Grand Slam

Linford Christie Makes Sprint History

1993 Linford Christie was the first genuine world-class British sprinter since Alan Wells in the late 1970s and early 1980s. His early career, however, gave little hint to what was to follow as he developed into Britain's sprint king and one of the world's fastest men. A young Christie failed to make the Great Britain team for the 1984 Olympics in Los Angeles, and it was not until he buckled down under the tutelage of coach Ron Roddan that he began to show signs of getting the most from his impressive physique.

The Londoner was a shock winner of the 100 metres at the European Championships in 1986 and followed that up with a silver medal at the Commonwealth Games. Christie made up for his rejection in 1984 by claiming the bronze medal in Seoul four years later, benefiting from Ben Johnson's expulsion for steroid abuse.

But with Carl Lewis still the outstanding talent in world sport, let alone athletics, Christie had to wait several years before he was able to supersede the great American. His finest hour came in 1992 in Barcelona, when he claimed Olympic gold, beating Namibia's Frankie Fredricks into second place. That success heralded the start of a period of wins that may never be matched by a European sprinter.

Christie followed up his Olympic success with glory at the World Championships in Stuttgart, in the process becoming the first man in history to hold the World, Olympic, European and Commonwealth titles.

Linford Christie

Born: 2 April 1960
Place of birth: Saint Andrew, Jamaica
Events: 100 m, 200 m, 4 x 100 m
Olympic medals: 2 Silver 1988, Gold 1992

Opposite: Christie's moment of victory in the 100 m at Barcelona, 1992.

Leap of Faith in Gothenburg

Jonathan Edwards Destroys the World Record

1995 Jonathan Edwards enjoyed a golden period in the mid-1990s, putting one of the more obscure events in the sport well and truly on the map. The triple jump was seen by many a detractor as the quirky relative of the long jump, but Edwards's speed and grace through the air had people hopping, skipping and jumping throughout Britain.

In the months preceding the World Championships in Gothenburg, Edwards had produced the first leap over 18 m (60 ft) and beat the world record. He would, however, save his best for the grand stage.

With his first jump he broke his own world record, with a leap of 18.16 m (59½ ft) – it was the first jump beyond 18 m with a legal wind in history. Still – unimaginably – better was to come with his second jump, a scarcely believable 18.29 m (60 ft), a record that may never be broken.

Edwards ended 1995 unbeaten in 14 events and claimed the BBC Sports Personality of the Year award. Since then he has become an ambassador for the sport as a whole, but he will always be synonymous with that historic day in Gothenburg.

Jonathan Edwards

Born: 10 May 1966

Place of birth: London, England

Event: Triple Jump

Olympic medals: Silver 1996, Gold 200

Johnson the Unstoppable

Michael Johnson's Stunning Sprint Double

1996 Michael Johnson achieved more than many thought humanly possible during his glittering career – even before the 1996 Olympics in Atlanta. However, by the conclusion of those games, Johnson had pushed the boundaries of what was considered feasible to a new level.

Although equally dominant over his rivals at 200 metres and 400 metres, it was believed impossible to complete the double due to scheduling complications. If Johnson got a buzz from anything, though, it was from proving people wrong. He claimed the first leg of his outrageous double by the proverbial country mile. Already a two-time world 400 metre champion, the man with the famously upright running stance added Olympic gold to his collection, beating Britain's Roger Black by over a second. As impressive as that feat was, however, what followed was so staggering that live viewers doubted it was really happening.

Johnson had already shattered a 200 metres world record that had stood for 17 years when he ran a time of 19.66 seconds at the American trials, but in the Olympic final he ran 19.33 seconds to rip up the history books for a second time in the space of a few months. The Texan's time for the opening 100 metres was recorded at 10.12 seconds as he reached a top speed of 15.5 km/h (25 mph) and improved the record time for the 200 metres by its biggest ever margin. More than a decade later, nobody has even approached Johnson's time. Put simply, it was the greatest run of all time.

Michael Johnson

Born: 13 September 1967

Place of birth: Texas, USA

Events: 200 m, 400 m, 4 x 400 m

Olympic medals: Gold 1992, 2 Gold 1996, 2 Gold 2000

Opposite: Breaking the 200 m record in 19.33 seconds.

Middle-Distance Master Kipketer

Coe's 800 Metre World Record Goes

1997 Athletes always insist that medals count for more than records, but when you have held a record – and one as prestigious and long-standing as the 800 metres world best – it is only natural to feel some disappointment when it is finally beaten.

Britain's Sebastian Coe had held the accolade of being the fastest man over the two-lap distance for some 16 years, before the exceptional Kenyan-born Wilson Kipketer eventually surpassed him.

Kipketer controversially changed his nationality after studying for a degree in Denmark. He first ran in the colours of his adopted nation in the international arena at the 1995 World Championships, and claimed the gold medal.

Though he dominated his sport for nearly a decade, he never claimed the Olympic gold he so richly deserved but, in 1997, he broke a record that would have meant nearly as much to him. He tied Coe's world record (1.41.73) at a meeting in Stockholm and went on to break it twice in that same year – firstly in Zurich in a time of 1.41.24, and then again in 1.41.11 in Cologne. Though his record still stands, his failure to taste victory at an Olympic Games – mainly due to the Olympic Committee banning him in 1996 due to his change of nationality – still rankles.

Wilson Kipketer

Born: 12 December 1972

Place of birth: Kapchemoyiwo, Kenya

Event: 800 m

Olympic medals: Silver 2000, Bronze 2004

Head to Head

Bailey or Johnson: The Great Debate

1997 Technology aside, athletics could hardly be regarded as the most innovative of sports, with the majority of events having been conceived centuries ago. However, back in the summer of 1997, with the ever-bullish Michael Johnson billing himself as the self-styled 'fastest man in the world', Canadian 100 metres world record holder Donovan Bailey challenged his American rival to put his money where his notorious and considerably sized mouth was.

The build-up to the race was highly publicized, with Johnson firing some less-than-complimentary remarks in his rival's direction. Johnson criticized Bailey for calling the American public ignorant when the world champion had been using American coaches and facilities, also claiming he had no respect for his competitor. Bailey preferred to keep a lower profile, concentrating on the task in hand – that of protecting his official title of the world's fastest man.

The race was run over a 75 metre curving track with a 75 metre straight so as to suit both athletes. As it was, however, the unique track, specially designed for the occasion, had little influence on proceedings. Johnson pulled up with injured quadriceps leaving Donovan to scoop the hefty prize money on offer – and, more importantly, the bragging rights.

Opposite: Bailey (right) and Johnson sprint through the turn in their head-to-head race, several metres before Johnson was to pull up early.

The Symbol of Sydney

Cathy Freeman Wins the 400 Metres

2000 Cathy Freeman was far more than just an athlete. As an Australian Aborigine she was, and remains, an ambassador for her people, while as an athlete she had few equals. Fiercely protective and proud of her heritage, Freeman had courted controversy at the 1994 Commonwealth Games in Victoria when, while celebrating her 400 metres success, she waved both an Australian and Aboriginal flag. However, by the time her home Olympics came around six years later, the nation was united behind her crusade to become an Olympic gold medallist at the age of 27.

Freeman brought a packed Stadium Australia to its feet with a rousing run the whole nation had been waiting for. After lighting the Olympic flame to start the Games, Freeman became the first Aborigine to win a gold medal in athletics, annihilating a highly competitive field of top-class female athletes, providing a moment of great symbolism for the 'new Australia'. Although Olympic rules forbid athletes from waving the flags of non-nations, the committee was lenient enough to allow Freeman her moment of unique celebration as she toasted one of the most emotional victories the Olympics has ever seen.

Cathy Freeman

Born: 16 February 1973

Place of birth: Queensland, Australia

Event: 400 m

Olympic medals: Silver 1996, Gold 2000

Double Delight

Kelly Holmes Wins Two Olympic Golds

2004 Kelly Holmes was no stranger to adversity. Throughout her career she was plagued by injury and bouts of clinical depression. By the time the Athens Olympics came around in 2004, Holmes had finally shrugged off her persistent troubles but it was widely assumed that she was too rusty to compete with the very best, which included her training partner Maria Mutola.

Originally Holmes, a former army officer, had planned to take part only in the 1,500 metres, but a victory in the build-up to the Games over Jolanda Ceplak convinced her to try her hand at the 800 metres too. It proved to be the wisest choice of her career, although she delayed her decision until a week before the start of the Athens event.

Despite giving such short notice of her involvement, always a shrewd tactician, Holmes ran the perfect 800 metres race, taking the lead from her training partner off the final bend to claim an emotional win. Better was to follow in her preferred 1,500 metres event, where again she ignored the fast starts made by others, sticking to her measured game plan – a tactic that paid off in spectacular style.

In landing the middle-distance double, Holmes not only gained the tangible reward she had long deserved but, in doing so, captured the British public's affection and provided memories that will last a lifetime.

Kelly Holmes

Born: 19 April 1970
Place of birth: Kent, England
Events: 800 m, 1500 m
Olympic medals: Bronze 2000, 2 Gold 2004

Opposite: An emotional Kelly Holmes secures her second gold.

Olga Korbut

Gymnastics' Teen Queen

1970s The image of a young unknown Belarusian clutching a bouquet of flowers and weeping after winning a gold medal at the 1972 Olympics will always be fondly remembered by the gymnastics world and beyond. Without the influence of Olga Korbut, women's gymnastics might not have grown to the heights it has today.

Before the Olympics in Munich, gymnastics was very much dominated by older women until the 17-year-old Korbut touched the hearts of millions with her daring tricks and originality in the field. She opened the sport to younger, smaller, more agile gymnasts – performing back flips while standing on the high bar and back tucks on the beam. Korbut became the talk of the Olympics, winning three gold medals and a silver. After winning her first gold in the beam routine, Korbut burst into tears, prompting a supporter to run on to the floor to give her a bouquet of flowers. Her Olympic success earned her many prestigious awards in the sporting world, as she was named top athlete of the year in America and claimed the same award from the BBC. She returned for the Montreal Olympics in 1976 to win another gold and an additional silver medal.

Korbut was not only a great gymnast but also an icon in her native Belarus, where she helped ease the tensions of the Cold War with her sporting prowess. Korbut's achievements saw her become the first female gymnast to be entered into the Gymnastics Hall of Fame.

Olga Korbut

Born: 16 May 1955
Place of birth: Hrodna, Belarus
Events: Team competition, Balance beam, Floor
exercise, Uneven bars
Olympic medals: 3 Gold 1972, Silver 1972, Gold
1976, Silver 1976

GYMNASTICS

The Perfect Ten

Nadia Comaneci Scores Top Marks

1976 Romanian-born Nadia Comaneci went into the 1976 Montreal Olympics as an unknown 14-year-old. She left the gymnastic arena as a history-maker. Comaneci became the first gymnast in Olympic history to record a perfect score of 10.00 – a feat she repeated six more times during the Championships. She remains a record-breaker to the present day – holding the record for being the youngest all-round champion.

Comaneci picked up her first perfect score in the team competition during her bars routine, wowing both judges and spectators. In all, she took home five medals from Montreal. Her three gold medals came in the balance beam and uneven bars, with her first place in the all-around event making her the first Romanian to pick up a gold in that particular discipline. She took a silver medal in the team competition and picked up bronze in the floor exercise.

On her return to Romania, her success led her to be named a 'Hero of Socialist Labour' – the youngest Romanian to be given such a prestigious title under the power of President Nicolae Ceausescu.

Nadia Comaneci

Born: 12 November 1961

Place of birth: Onesti, Romania

Events: Team competition, All-around, Uneven bars, Balance beam, Floor exercise

Olympic medals: 3 Gold 1976, 1 Silver 1976, 1 Bronze 1976, 2 Gold 1980, 2 Silver 1980

Mary Lou Retton

America's Angel

1984 The domination of Eastern Bloc nations in the gymnastics arena in the early 1980s was as total as it gets – but this was before the emergence of the diminutive American starlet Mary Lou Retton.

Inspired by the exploits of Nadia Comăneci – one of the most famous Olympians of all time – Retton embarked on a mission to break the monopoly of the Russian and Romanian gymnasts. Coached by Comaneci's former mentors Bela and Martha Karolyi, Retton found almost instant success, claiming the American Cup and Japan's prestigious Chunichi Cup in 1983. After a second successive American Cup, as well as the American National and Olympic trials a year later, Retton suffered a cruel knee injury that threatened her participation in the 1984 Olympics. With typical guts and determination, however, the Texan battled back to ensure she would take her place alongside her rivals at the Los Angeles Games.

In the competition – which was boycotted by all the Eastern European nations except Romania – Retton became embroiled in a tit-for-tat battle with Ecaterina Szabó for the all-round title. Trailing Szabó with two events to go, Retton scored perfect 10s on floor exercise and vault to win the competition by just 0.050. She was the first American female to do so – adding to the four other medals she won at the 1984 games.

Mary Lou Retton

Born: 24 January 1968

Place of birth: West Virginia, USA

Events: All-around, Team competition, Vault, Uneven bars, Floor exercise

Olympic medals: Gold 1984, 2 Silver 1984, 2 Bronze 1984

Aleksei Nemov

The 'Nearly' Man Comes Good

1990s

The enigmatic Russian gymnast Aleksei Nemov may have been one of the most frustrating Olympians of recent times, but without question he was also one of the most talented.

Nemov, who gained the desirable nickname of 'Sexy Aleksei', was equally capable of producing performances of stunning imagination and gravity defying brilliance as he was at turning out sloppy, unfocused routines. Despite his Jekyll and Hyde nature, it was his unrivalled showmanship and willingness to please the crowd that won him admirers the world over – often during his routines he would pause and wave to the crowds.

On several occasions, though, mental aberrations have prevented him from adding to the numerous titles he has won. At the 1995 European Championships, for example, he needed a score of just 8.75 to take gold, but messed up two major release moves, crashed into the bar on another and dropped out of the medal positions.

Nemov finally began to gain the reward his talent deserved at the 1996 Olympic Games, where he won six medals in total and gold in the vault and team events. It was in Sydney four years later, however, that he claimed the coveted gold medal in the all-around competition, despite suffering recurring shoulder injuries and flagging levels of motivation.

Opposite: Aleksei Nemov is pictured holding a strength move at the Olympic Games in Atlanta, 1996.

Svetlana Khorkina

Khorkina Raises the Bar

1990s Svetlana Khorkina is the most successful Russian female gymnast since the break-up of the former Soviet Union, as recognizable for her distinctive moves as for her striking beauty.

Khorkina was unusually tall for a gymnast and was discouraged from a career in her chosen field as a youngster, but ironically it was her size that helped her to design the innovative manoeuvres and routines for which she became famous. Khorkina has an unrivalled six moves named after her in the Artistic Gymnastics Code of Points, and was at her best on the uneven bars, where she was able to put her wiry frame to best use. Indeed, she claimed the gold medal in that event at the 1996 Olympic Games, and retained the title four years later in Sydney. In addition, she earned four silvers and a bronze in other disciplines at those two Games.

Although undoubtedly supremely talented, Khorkina was not without her diva tendencies. At the Sydney Olympic Games, having fallen during one routine, she refused to go back and attempt her vaults in the all-around event after it was discovered that her apparatus had been set to the incorrect height. Away from the sporting arena, accusations of delusions of grandeur were enflamed by her decision to pose nude for the Russian *Playboy* magazine, and she also claimed to want to embark on an acting career.

It was for her prowess on the uneven bars, however, that she will best be remembered. A double Olympic gold medal in the same discipline takes some doing, but it was a feat she achieved in style.

Svetlana Khorkina

Born: 19 January 1979

Place of birth: Belgorod, Russia

Events: Uneven bars, Team competition, Floor exercise, All-around

Olympic Medals: Gold 1996, Silver 1996, Gold 2000, 2 Silver 2000, Silver 2004, Bronze 2004

Beth Tweddle's Golden Year

Beth is Britain's Best

2006 Tweddle became the first British gymnast ever to win a gold medal at the European Championships – following her scintillating display on the uneven bars in April 2006. Six months later, she went one better when she became Britain's first-ever gymnastics world champion, also in the uneven bars event, with a score of 16.200 in Aarhus, Denmark. The Liverpool-based gymnast ended the year on a high by winning the event at the World Cup Final in Brazil before claiming silver in the floor final.

Tweddle began gymnastics at the age of seven and under the experienced coach Amanda Curbishley at the City of Liverpool Gymnastics Club, she won the first of six British National Championships in 2001. In 2004 Tweddle shot to fame when she won silver medals on the uneven bars at the European Championships and the World Cup. She competed on the Great Britain team at the Olympics in Athens, but just missed out on qualifying for the bars final. Meanwhile, her floor routine was copied and used in the Athens 2004 Playstation game.

A year later, at the 2005 World Artistic Gymnastics Championships, she earned her second world medal – another bars bronze – and finished fourth in the all-around competition.

Opposite: A scintillating display: Beth Tweddle leaping between the uneven bars in April 2006.

RACING & SPEED SPORTS

Man's need for speed has produced some of the most thrilling competition in the history of sport. From cycling to Formula One, the combination of man and machine pushing the boundaries of safety in the pursuit of glory has riveted spectators across the globe.

Cycling's Tour de France has to be one of the most punishing events in sport today – a severe test of endurance over mountains and through towns in a bid to claim the coveted yellow jersey. Formula One, meanwhile, truly deserves its place at the pinnacle of motor racing. From the pioneering Juan Manuel Fangio to the legendary consistency of Michael Schumacher, F1 is still a petrolhead's dream sport. Horse racing pre-dates the invention of the car and remains a thriving sport, as jockeys show immense courage to hurtle around courses and, in the case of National Hunt racing, jump mountainous fences at breakneck speed – all the while knowing that a fall could be the end of their career, or worse should they fall under a chasing pack.

The Birth of Motor Racing

First For the French

1895 Although the petrol-driven car was invented in Germany, it was the French who flew the flag when it came to motor racing. Indeed, the very first motor race was held in France in 1895 between Paris and Bordeaux.

Sponsored by the French newspaper *Le Petit Journal*, a trial run comprising 21 cars had been held the year before between Paris and Rouen. The success of this 80 mile round trip was the inspiration for the creation of a committee of Parisian newspaper publishers, formed with the sole aim of promoting the use of the motor car. It was this very same committee that organized the first real race from Paris to Bordeaux and back in 1895.

After a staggering 48 hours and 48 minutes the race was eventually won by Émile Levassor, who had driven virtually non-stop. Unfortunately his car had only two seats instead of the required four and, as a consequence, he was denied the prize money of 31,000 Francs. Despite being stripped of the title, Levassor's achievement is recognized by a statue overlooking the finishing line at Porte Maillot in Paris, which marks the birthplace of a popular and lucrative sport.

Opposite: Émile Levassor approaches the finish line in his two-seater during the first ever motor race.

French Grand Prix

Christian Soldiers On

1914 Christian Lautenschlager rose to fame as a Grand Prix motor-racing champion in the early twentieth century. Having trained as a mechanic in Stuttgart with the German company Daimler (later to become Mercedes-Benz) at the turn of the century, he worked his way up to the position of test driver for the company's race cars, and eventually he became their official driver.

His most famous Grand Prix victory by far came in 1914 when he took part in what is still considered one of the sport's most famous meetings. Thirty-seven cars made by 13 manufacturers from six different countries battled it out for success in Lyon in July 1914. Lautenschlager emerged victorious after seven gruelling hours, leading the way for a Mercedes 1-2-3. In doing so, they had managed to fight off the challenge of the heavily fancied Frenchman Georges Boillot, who had won the race the previous two years.

With Europe on the verge of war, the event had been used as propaganda to display the technological power of the individual countries taking part. As a result, the German victory was met with displeasure by the French public, who refused to applaud Lautenschlager, despite his undoubted achievement.

Opposite: Lautenschlager speeds to victory on the Lyon cicuit of the 1914 Grand Prix.

Tazio Nuvolari

Italian Hero

1935 Tazio 'The Flying Mantuan' Nuvolari was a fearless motorcycle and car racing driver who amassed huge popularity in the early twentieth century. The fourth son of an Italian farmer, Nuvolari was introduced to motor racing as a boy by his uncle. His passion, courage and love for speed made him an absolute natural. He famously took part in a motorcycle race days after breaking his legs in the Monza Grand Prix – and amazingly went on to win it!

His greatest and most impressive performance, however, came in the German Grand Prix at Nürburgring in 1935. Driving an Alfa Romeo P3, the Italian's chances of winning were written off against the might of the four Auto Union Tipo Bs and the five Mercedes-Benz W25s. Dogged to the last, Nuvolari chased and harried the lead Mercedes until the German driver's burst tyre enabled the Flying Mantuan to cruise to the finish line for the greatest win of his career.

To the horror of the onlooking Nazi party officials, Nuvolari – racing in the Alfa Romeo – had beaten the best the German manufacturers and drivers had to offer, and what is more, he had done it in their own back yard.

'The greatest driver of the past, the present, and the future.'

Ferdinand Porsche on Nuvolari's greatness.

Moss Claims the Mille Miglia

A Stirling Effort

1955 Stirling Moss is generally regarded as the best driver never to win the world title. A pioneer in the British Formula One racing scene, he came second in the Drivers' Championship four times in a row between 1955 and 1958.

Although the Englishman competed at the highest level for well over a decade and won 16 Grand Prix, one of his greatest victories came in the Italian open-road endurance race 'Mille Miglia' in 1955. Driving for roughly 1,600 km (1,000 miles) from Brescia to Rome and back, Moss won the event in a record time of 10 hours and 8 minutes, finishing almost half an hour ahead of teammate Juan Manuel Fangio, who took second place. Assisted by his extremely able navigator, journalist Denis Jenkinson, Moss had driven his Mercedes-Benz 300 SLR with courage and guile. Jenkinson's extensive course notes enabled Moss to outwit and outpace drivers with local knowledge of the route.

The win cemented Moss's position as a skilful long-distance high-speed driver and, despite his failure to claim the biggest Formula One honour, he is still regarded as one of the most talented British drivers in motor-racing history.

Stirling Moss

Born: 17 September 1929

Place of birth: London, England

Teams: Mercedes-Benz, Maserati, Vanwall, Rob Walker Cooper, Lotus

First win: 1955 British Grand Prix

Le Mans Disaster

Tragedy on the Track

1955 Le Mans was the scene of the worst disaster in the history of motor racing when, on 11 June 1955, a car flipped over and hit spectators in the stands, killing more than 80 people and injuring hundreds of others.

The event being held was the popular '24 Hours of Le Mans', which is regarded as the world's most famous sports-car endurance race, held annually at Circuit de la Sarthe near Le Mans in France. The crash was caused when Lance Macklin's Austin Healey was forced to pull out sharply to avoid Mike Hawthorn, who was making a pit stop in his Jaguar. Sadly, the advancing Pierre Levegh did not have enough time to react to the drama unfolding in front of him and he slammed into the back of Macklin's car. Levegh was killed instantly as his Mercedes-Benz 300 SLR was catapulted into the air before crashing down on the stands. As the emergency services eventually brought the fire under control, the true extent of the horror and devastation was revealed.

Following the Le Mans crash, Mercedes withdrew from racing for over 30 years, as a mark of respect for the lives lost in the horrific tragedy.

Opposite: The wreckage of Pierre Levegh's Mercedes after the 'Le Mans Disaster' race.

He's the Juan

Fangio Comes From Behind at the Ring

1957 Juan Manuel Fangio is considered by many to be the greatest driver of all time. In seven full Formula One seasons he was world champion five times and runner-up twice. This remarkable record was achieved racing with four different teams.

Known simply as 'The Maestro', Fangio dominated the Formula One scene in the 1950s and did it all with a style and modesty that belied his remarkable talent. In 51 Grand Prix he started in pole position 29 times, won 24 of them, and set 23 fastest laps.

One of Fangio's most memorable wins came at the German Grand Prix at Nürburgring in 1957. In what is still considered one of the greatest drives in Formula One history, the Maestro recovered from a botched pit stop, in which he lost over a minute, to overtake two Ferraris and lift his fifth world championship title. Fittingly, Nürburgring was his last Grand Prix victory. The legendary Argentinian driver retired the following year, but he left a permanent mark on motor racing. Coming from behind in a less powerful Maserati to clinch the win in Germany, he displayed the sort of courage and skill that marks him out among Formula One drivers to this very day.

Juan Manuel Fangio

Born: 24 June 1911   **Died:** 17 July 1995

Place of birth: Balcarce, Argentina

Teams: Alfa Romeo, Maserati, Mercedes-Benz, Ferrari

First win: 1950 Monaco Grand Prix

Opposite: Fangio in his Maserati 250F during the 1957 Formula One Italian Grand Prix, where he finished in second place.

Jack Brabham

Aussie Action Man

1950s–60s

Jack Brabham remains the only driver to win the World Drivers' Championship in a car he had designed and built himself.

After a spell as an aircraft engineer in the Australian Air Force during the Second World War, Brabham started building a racing car for a friend, before being persuaded to give racing a try himself. In his own car, Brabham achieved considerable success in New Zealand. He made his Formula One debut in 1955 for the Cooper team at Aintree, after he had been cajoled into moving to England to further his racing career.

Eager to set up his own team, and while still working for Cooper, he built his own car. On its only outing, at Silverstone in 1956, the engine blew up, and he was forced to retire from the race. He returned to Cooper and the relationship blossomed in 1958, but it was not until 1959 that Brabham started to win races. He took first position in Monte Carlo and then again on his return to Aintree. These two victories helped him to his first Drivers' Championship title. A second title followed the next year, when Brabham won five of the eight races.

He left Cooper in 1961 to start his own team. The Brabham outfit did not win a race until 1963, and Brabham himself had to wait until 1966 to win in his own car, when he claimed victory at Reims – but he then added another three wins and a second place to claim the Drivers' Championship for a third time. Brabham finally decided to retire from driving in 1970, despite winning the opening race of the Formula One season at Kyalami.

Jack Brabham

Born: 2 April 1926

Place of birth: Sydney, Australia

Teams: Rob Walker Cooper, Brabham

First win: 1959 Monaco Grand Prix

Opposite: Brabham after winning the 1960 Bitish Grand Prix.

John Surtees

A Man for All Seasons

1950s–60s No man is ever likely to emulate John Surtees' feat of winning world championships on two wheels as well as four. The passion for motor racing was in his genes – his father Jack was a world championship sidecar racer and was taking John as his passenger by the time he was 14. Encouraged by his father, Surtees dominated the 500 cc class for eight years, as well as becoming 350 cc world champion.

Surtees tested in racing cars with Aston Martin and Vanwall in 1959, and raced in Formula Junior in a Cooper in 1960, winning first time out. He was soon snapped up by Lotus and the step up to Formula One did not faze him; in his second Grand Prix, at Silverstone, he came second behind world champion Jack Brabham.

Lotus wanted him full-time in 1961, but Surtees was not happy about the way the team went about terminating current driver Innes Ireland's contract, so he signed for the inferior Yeoman Credit Cooper instead. After a frustrating season, Surtees moved to Lola but again his talent went to waste as the car repeatedly let him down. In 1963 he joined a struggling Ferrari team.

In his three seasons with the team, 'Big John' – as the adoring Italian fans referred to him – helped turn its fortunes around. He was on the podium three times in 1963 – including a win in Germany – and after podium finishes in the six races he completed in 1964, he was crowned world champion, becoming the first man to win the title both on a motorcycle and in a car.

John Surtees

Born: 11 February 1934

Place of birth: Surrey, England

Teams: Norton, MV Agusta

First win: 1955 250cc Ulster Grand Prix

Ken Tyrell

Top Team Player

1960s–70s

Ken Tyrell was the owner and creator of the Tyrell Racing Organisation. An amateur racer, he decided to form his own team when he realized he would never have what it takes to be a top driver.

In 1964, Tyrell signed a rookie by the name of Jackie Stewart, and thus began one of the most successful partnerships in Formula One history, in which Stewart won three world championships – in 1969, 1971 and 1973. He went on to help Tyrell win the Constructors' Championship in 1971, and come runner-up in the Constructors' Championships of 1972 and 1973.

Despite employing natural talents such as Jody Scheckter, Ronnie Peterson and Patrick Depailler, Stewart's retirement in 1973 coincided with a decline in the fortunes of the Tyrell racing team, which struggled to recapture its former glory as the 1970s drew to a close. Nonetheless, the loyalty and respect that Tyrell showed his drivers throughout his long and illustrious career in the sport not only made him a popular man, but also brought him and the Tyrell team a total of 33 race victories in Formula One. The 1960s and 1970s were a fruitful and lucrative period for this affable and respected giant of motor racing.

Opposite: Ken Tyrrell trackside noting down lap times.

Jackie Stewart

Scotland's Bravest

1960s–70s

Jackie Stewart grew up in Dumbarton and worked in his father's garage before following his elder brother into a career in motor racing. Against his parents' wishes, he agreed to a test drive at a local track for one of his father's customers. Stewart gave a stunning display — even overtaking the legendary Bruce McLaren.

Formula One boss Ken Tyrell was a spectator that day and he offered Stewart the chance to join his Formula Three team. Stewart turned down that offer, and instead joined the BRM team.

In the 1965 season he won his first Grand Prix in Italy before finishing third in the Drivers' Championship. Technical problems meant that Stewart was unable to build on his blistering debut as he suffered two frustrating seasons at BRM.

In 1968 he finally joined Tyrell and finished as runner-up in the championship. The following season he went one better and won his first world crown. With the reliability of Tyrell behind him, Stewart was a regular on the podium. He won the championship again in 1971 before completing a hat-trick of wins in 1973.

Stewart was at his peak, having won five of the 15 races that season, finishing second twice and third three times, so it came as a surprise when he decided to stop racing. Stewart's decision to quit Formula One at the top was caused by the deaths of fellow drivers and close friends Jim Clark and François Cevert in racing accidents.

Jackie Stewart

Born: 11 June 1939
Place of birth: West Dunbartonshire, Scotland
Teams: BRM, Matra, March, Tyrell
First win: 1965 Italian Grand Prix

Mario Andretti

Super Mario

1960s–70s

The Andretti family emigrated to America from Italy following the Second World War, and Mario was soon to be found racing cars around the dirt track that backed on to his new home. By 1964 he was racing Indy Cars. In his first race, Andretti finished eleventh. The following season he finished in third place at the 1965 Indianapolis 500, which won him the Rookie of the Year award, and won the series championship. After two more successful years and a stint of drag racing, Andretti turned his attention to Formula One. He took to the new formula like a duck to water, qualifying in pole position in his first race with Lotus.

He secured his first Formula One win in 1971, driving for Ferrari at Kyalami, but did not join full-time until 1975 – with the Parnelli team. A disappointing season followed, and the following season saw him back with Lotus.

In 1978 Andretti fulfilled his childhood dream when he won the Drivers' Championship, winning six Grand Prix. The years that followed did not deliver a great deal of success, however, and in 1981 he decided to quit Formula One.

His retirement was short-lived, when he answered a call from Ferrari in 1982. It was a fitting end to Andretti's Formula One career, as he was asked to replace the injured Didier Pironi and race for the Italian team at their home track in Monza. Much to the admiration of the Italian fans, he finished third. Andretti was asked back to race at Las Vegas in the final Grand Prix of the season but suffered suspension problems that ended his race and ultimately his Formula One career.

Mario Andretti

Born: 28 February 1940

Place of birth: Montona d'Istria, Italy

Teams: Lotus, STP Corporation, Ferrari, Parnelli, Alfa Romeo, Williams

First win: 1965 Indy Car Championship

Niki Lauda

Scarred But Not Scared

1970s Austrian Niki Lauda was a three-time world champion who overcame adversity to reach the pinnacle of success.

Lauda began his Formula One career with the struggling March team in 1971, before switching to BRM after two seasons. Although he only managed to win two championship points in his final year with BRM, Lauda caught the eye of Ferrari, whom he joined in 1974, winning his first Grand Prix that season and taking nine pole positions.

Lauda claimed his first Drivers' Championship title the next season, winning five of the 14 races. It appeared he would land back-to-back titles in 1976, but he then suffered a horrific crash at the Nürburgring and was left scarred for life after his car exploded in a ball of flames. Many spectators feared the Austrian had died in the sickening crash, but Lauda showed remarkable courage, and returned to racing only six weeks later. It was a truly heroic decision that showed his dedication to the sport.

Having missed out in 1976, Lauda returned the following year to win his second title, dominating the season. The Austrian joined the Brabham team in 1978, but after two seasons plagued by unreliability, Lauda quit the sport, with the intention of starting up his own airline. However, the airline business did not provide Lauda with the same buzz as racing in Formula One and he returned in 1982 with McLaren. He remained there until the end of his career. He won one more Drivers' Championship, in 1984, to complete his hat-trick.

Niki Lauda

Born: 22 February 1949

Place of birth: Vienna, Austria

Teams: March, BRM, Ferrari, Brabham, McLaren

First win: 1974 Spanish Grand Prix

Opposite: Lauda at the 1983 European Grand Prix.

Prost Pips Mansell and Piquet

The Professor Teaches a Lesson

1986 Alain Prost was a four-time world champion Formula One driver who exploded on to the motor-racing scene, finishing in the points on his Formula One debut at the age of 25. The smooth, self-assured Frenchman went on to become a dominant and imperious figure in the sport throughout the 1980s and early 1990s.

Having been crowned world champion for the first time in 1985, Prost went on to retain his title the following year in spectacular fashion. In what is regarded as a classic, 'Professor Prost' – as he was fondly referred to – won the Australian Grand Prix of 1986 at Adelaide on the very last race of the season, and in doing so took his second world Drivers' Championship title.

In fact, it had appeared, right up to the latter stages of the race, that Prost and his McLaren would finish third in the championship, behind the Williamses of Nelson Piquet and Nigel Mansell. However, in a dramatic twist, Mansell, who only needed to come third to win the title, blew a tyre while leading, and the Williams team called Piquet in for a pit stop to change tyres as a safety precaution. As a result, Prost was able to cruise to victory and retain the world championship.

Alain Prost

Born: 24 February 1955

Place of birth: Loire Valley, France

Teams: McLaren, Renault, Ferrari and Williams

First win: 1981 French Grand Prix

Opposite: Prost in a McLaren MP4/2B at the 1985 Brazilian Gran Prix, which he went on to win.

Nigel Mansell

Great British Champion

1980s–90s

Nigel Mansell was a fearless driver who claimed honours in both Formula One and Indy Car. After an early career in Karts and Formula Ford, Mansell's talent was recognized by Lotus boss Colin Chapman, who handed him his Formula One debut in 1980.

After five steady but unspectacular years at Lotus, a switch to Williams culminated in three successful seasons, including his first Grand Prix win in 1985. In the following two seasons Mansell narrowly missed out on the Drivers' Championship. In 1986, challenging Alain Prost for the title, he suffered a tyre failure at almost 200 mph while leading the final race in Australia. Then in 1987 he found himself battling teammate Nelson Piquet for the crown – until he broke his back at Suzuka, ruling him out of the final two races.

He switched to Ferrari in 1989, where his tenacity earned him the respect of the Italian fans, who fondly named him 'Il Leone' – 'The Lion'. After two seasons, however, he was lured back to Williams – a move that coincided with his best form. In 1991 he reached a total of 72 points, before finally claiming the Drivers' Championship in superb style in 1992 – winning an amazing nine out of 16 racesand starting from pole position in no fewer than 14 races.

The next season Mansell moved to the USA and won the Indy Car series in his first season. Two brief but unsuccessful stints with Williams and McLaren followed, but he was unable to relive his former glories.

Nigel Mansell

Born: 8 August 1953

Place of birth: Worcestershire, England

Teams: Lotus, Williams, Ferrari, McLaren

First win: 1985 European Grand Prix

Opposite: Mansell on his way to victory in the 1992 Portuguese Grand Prix.

Awesome Ayrton

Senna's Stunning Win at Donington

1993 The iconic three-time world champion Ayrton Senna is remembered as one of the greatest Formula One drivers of all time. His untimely and tragic death in the 1994 San Marino Grand Prix ended what could have been the finest motor racing career of all time.

Despite a number of impressive victories, Senna's stunning 1993 European Grand Prix win at Donington Park is without doubt one that motor-racing enthusiasts will never forget. Driving for McLaren, the Brazilian began the race placed fourth on the grid. Having been pushed down to fifth place after the first corner, this sublime and masterful driver managed to overtake Karl Wendlinger, Michael Schumacher, Damon Hill and Alain Prost – all by the end of the first lap.

The very wet conditions at Donington added to the excitement that day, and when Senna eventually won the race, finishing a whole lap ahead of Prost, he had done so by defeating the technologically far superior Williams cars. Overcoming the weather, technology and his starting place on the grid, the 'Rain Master' confirmed at Donington that he was without question one of Formula One's greats.

Ayrton Senna

Born: 21 March 1960   **Died:** 1 May 1994

Place of birth: São Paulo, Brazil

Teams: Toleman Hart, Lotus, McLaren, Honda, Williams

First win: 1985 Portuguese Grand Prix

Opposite: Ayrton Senna preparing for the race at Donington Park.

Mika Hakkinen

Flying Finn

1990s–2000s

The ice-cool Mika Hakkinen dominated Formula One in the late 1990s, winning the Drivers' Championship in 1998 and 1999. His calculated driving was enough to at least delay Michael Schumacher's dominance.

After a remarkable junior career, Hakkinen moved to Formula One in 1991, winning a seat with Lotus. After two years he made the move to McLaren, but was limited to the role of test driver for Ayrton Senna and Michael Andretti. Fortunately for Hakkinen, Andretti did not adapt well from Indy Car to Formula One and quickly returned to America.

Hakkinen began the 1995 season well, but the Australian Grand Prix almost finished tragically. A tyre failure during free practice resulted in him crashing heavily into the wall, putting the Finn into a coma. He was saved only due to an emergency tracheotomy performed by the side of the track. A determined Hakkinen recovered in super-quick time, climbnig back into the car the following season. He finally tasted Formula One victory at Jerez in 1997. He wanted more, though, and the following year he certainly got it, winning eight of the 16 races over the season to win his first Drivers' Championship. He repeated the achievement the following year, despite making some uncharacteristic errors. The next few seasons saw Michael Schumacher revitalize Ferrari's fortunes, and not even Hakkinen's Mercedes-powered McLaren could keep him in contention for the title. Although still winning Grand Prix, Hakkinen announced his retirement from Formula One in 2002.

Mika Hakkinen

Born: 28 September 1968

Place of birth: Vantaa, Finland

Teams: Lotus, McLaren

First win: 1997 European Grand Prix

Opposite: On the way to victory in the 2001 British Grand Prix.

Jacques Villeneuve

Like Father, Like Son

1990s–2000s Jacques Villeneuve was always desperate to be a racing driver and follow in the footsteps of his illustrious father Gilles. This was in spite of Villeneuve Senior's tragic death in a practice session at Zolder in Holland, when Jacques was only 11. The young Villeneuve displayed natural talent behind the wheel and, after a successful early career in Europe, he moved to Indy Cars in 1994. In his second full season he took the title in superb style, catching the attention of a number of Formula One teams.

The Canadian joined Williams in 1996 and immediately showed his ability by grabbing pole position on his debut at Melbourne. He went on to finish runner-up to Damon Hill in the Drivers' Championship. The following year was Villeneuve's career highlight, as he snatched the Formula One title from Michael Schumacher in dramatic style in the very last race of the season – a feat that had eluded his famous father.

After a disappointing 1998, Villeneuve moved to BAR-Honda in 1999, but the new team's car proved wholly unreliable. It took 12 races for the former world champion to register a finish, after being plagued by gearbox and hydraulic problems. Four more years at BAR produced little improvement, although Villeneuve displayed his ability by guiding the under-performing car to two third places in the 2001 season. Unsuccessful spells at Renault and Sauber followed, and he was unable to reach the heights of his early career.

Jacques Villeneuve

Born: 9 April 1971
Place of birth: Quebec, Canada
Teams: Williams, BAR, Renault and BMW Sauber
First win: 1996 European Grand Prix

Opposite: Raising the trophy for the 1996 British Grand Prix.

Michael Schumacher

A Modern-Day Legend

1990s–2000s

Michael Schumacher is without question one of the most dominant drivers in Formula One history. His career started early, as he began racing karts at the tender age of five, and he became German and European Senior Kart champion in 1987. The following year he moved up to Formula Ford, and then Formula Three in 1989.

The next season he won the German Formula Three championship in 1990, before making his Formula One debut with Jordan in 1990. However, Schumacher was immediately given a place in the Benetton team, and by the end of the 1995 season he had claimed back-to-back world titles.

He joined the struggling Ferrari in 1996 and suffered a dip in fortunes. In 1999, while in contention for the Drivers' Championship, he suffered a broken leg at the British Grand Prix at Silverstone, which ended his challenge for the season. However, the German came storming back in trademark fashion and then won the world championship an incredible five times in a row for Ferrari between 2000 and 2004, overtaking Alain Prost's all-time record of 51 Grand Prix wins, and surpassing Juan Fangio's total of five world championship wins along the way. With his final championship victory in 2005, he became the only driver to win the world title seven times – gaining victory at the Canadian Grand Prix in 2004.

In his last two years in Formula One he was thrown into a duel with Fernando Alonso, who ultimately triumphed by becoming the sport's youngest double world champion in 2006 at the age of 24. After being pipped to the title by Alonso in 2006, Schumacher retired from the sport with an amazing total of 91 Grand Prix victories.

Michael Schumacher

Born: 3 January 1969

Place of birth: Hürth Hermülheim, Germany

Teams: Jordan, Benetton, Ferrari

First win: 1992 Belgian Grand Prix

Fernando Alonso

El Nano

2000s Fernando Alonso is the Spanish Formula One driving sensation who destroyed Michael Schumacher's stranglehold over the sport. Alonso became the youngest winner of a Grand Prix in the history of Formula One with his victory at the 2003 Hungarian Grand Prix. Aged just 22 years and 10 days, he had emphatically announced his arrival on the big stage.

Although his prodigious talent had been well known to racing enthusiasts for a long time, Alonso finally became a household name when he lifted the Drivers' Championship title for the first time in 2005. Finishing third in the Brazilian Grand Prix, he had clinched the title aged just 24 years and 59 days. In doing so he became the youngest Formula One champion of all time, breaking Emerson Fittipaldi's record by a year and a half.

By winning the title, the former Renault and Minardi driver had also made history by preventing Schumacher from winning his sixth consecutive title and proving that perhaps the German was human after all. The Spaniard proved he was no flash in the pan when he won his second Drivers' Championship title the following season, in October 2006.

Fernando Alonso

Born: 29 July 1981

Place of birth: Asturias, Spain

Teams: Minardi, Renault, McLaren

First win: 2003 Hungarian Grand Prix

Opposite: Fernando Alonso speeds down the track ahead of Michael Schumacher during the Shanghai Grand Prix, 2006.

James Forman 'Tod' Sloan

The Sloan Ranger

1900 Born in Indiana, USA, James Forman 'Tod' Sloan was to play a massive role in the early years of British horse racing. After winning everything he could in America, he turned his attentions to England. It was Sloan who popularized the forward seat style of riding, or the 'monkey crouch' as the British called it, when he began riding there in 1897. Initially laughed at, his style revolutionized the sport worldwide.

Such were Sloan's abilities that in 1897 he won 37 per cent of all his races, and upped this to an astonishing 46 per cent in 1898. Racing at Newmarket on 30 September 1898, he rode five consecutive winners. The prestigious Epsom Derby was a race that Sloan always felt he would have won, had it not been for a terrible tragedy. In the 1899 race, his horse Holocauste looked well placed, but suddenly collapsed to the ground with a shattered leg.

Sloan's fall from grace was as spectacular as his rise had been. He was informed by the Jockey Club that he 'need not apply for a licence' for the 1901 season due to unspecified 'conduct prejudicial to the best interests of the sport'. There were allegations of jealousy and anti-Americanism in the US press. These were no doubt justified but it seems that the primary motivation was that they just did not like him. Whatever the cause, the racing ban was upheld in America, too, and his career was effectively over.

James Forman Sloan

Born: 10 August 1874   **Died:** 21 December 1933

Place of birth: Indiana, USA

Wins and honours: One Thousand Guineas 1899,

Ascot Gold Cup 1900

Emily Davison – Derby Martyr

Rebel With a Cause

1913 The 1913 Derby, which took place on 4 June, is not remembered for its sporting significance but for the death of Emily Davison, who gave her life for the Suffragette cause.

Davison was a key member of the Women's Social and Political Union, which was fighting for the right for women in England to vote in elections. She attended the Derby where King George V had a horse called Anmer running in the race, ridden by Herbert Jones. As the horses rounded Tattenham Corner, Anmer was third from last. Davison crawled underneath the barrier and threw herself in front of the horse. Anmer went over and Jones came off. Davison took the full force of a sprinting racehorse to her upper body. Jones stayed where he fell until all the riders had gone past, and was then carried off the course by stretcher and taken to the ambulance room at the back of the grandstand. His injuries included a fractured rib, a bruised face and slight concussion. Anmer, meanwhile, got to his feet and completed the race minus his jockey. *The Times* newspaper next day reported that the horse had suffered bruised shins.

Emily Davison, however, was not so fortunate. She was taken to Epsom Cottage Hospital, but she never regained consciousness – it is believed that her heart was damaged in the impact – and she died on 8 June from substantial internal injuries.

Opposite: Emily Davison lays trampled after throwing herself in front of the galloping horse Anmer.

Sir Gordon's Coronation

Richards Rides a Derby Winner at Last

1953 Sir Gordon Richards was certainly the finest jockey of his generation. The 26-time champion had smashed a number of records in his magnificent career. In 1932, with 269 victories, he broke the record for the greatest number of wins in a year, a record which had stood for nearly 50 years. In 1942 he won four of the five 'Classics' on horses owned by King George VI, and in 1947 he won the 2,000 Guineas by an unprecedented margin of eight lengths. Despite these huge successes, there was still one race that had always eluded him: the Derby at Epsom.

The 1953 Derby occurred during a week of great national celebration, with Richards himself also in high spirits. Elizabeth II had been crowned the Queen in Westminster Abbey, the first successful ascent of Everest had taken place, and he had become Sir Gordon Richards – the only jockey to be knighted.

In the race Sir Gordon rode Pinza, a huge horse for a flat-thoroughbred, and the pair had a terrific race. Pinza was in second position for most of the 2.4 km (1.5 miles), competing against the Queen's own horse Aureole, and sweeping past the Aga Khan's horse, Shikampur, into first place with just two furlongs remaining.

The long-awaited win was accompanied by thunderous cheers from the frenzied crowd, and he was promptly summoned from the winners' enclosure to be congratulated personally by the Queen. That Derby win filled the only remaining gap in Sir Gordon's glittering CV.

Opposite: Gordon Richards steaming towards the finishing line on Pinza to win the Derby.

Lester's First Derby

Lester's Teenage Triumph

1954 With Sir Gordon Richards having finally won a Derby in 1953 at the grand old age of 49, the following year's race was a victory for youth. At only 18 years old Lester Piggott had already come close to winning a Derby, finishing second riding Gay Time in 1952. He did not go into the 1954 race with a great deal of confidence, having ridden Never Say Die on a couple of previous occasions with little success. The general public must have been of the same opinion, as when Piggott went down to the start the bookies were offering him and the horse a 33-1 chance. As far as form was concerned the horse was a no-hoper, but the first classic chapter of the Lester legend was written when Piggott forced Never Say Die home ahead of Arabian Night and Darius.

The young prodigy was already on his way to becoming the housewife's choice, with many thousands backing the boy wonder – and in one ride Piggott had captured the hearts and minds of punters up and down the country.

Opposite: 1954's Epsom Derby which Lester Piggot was to gon on to win. The Queen's horse, Landau, was in the lead at this point.

The Mystery of Devon Loch

Devon and Hell

1956 Devon Loch was not favourite for the 1956 Grand National, but nevertheless the horse was well fancied by his connections, as he had already won two races earlier that year. The confidence in him seemed well placed, as their horse coped comfortably with the mammoth obstacles, his only nervous moment coming when another runner fell in front of him. Victory seemed certain as Devon Loch went clear in the home straight.

But with just 50 yards to go – and with the crowd cheering in anticipation – disaster struck. Suddenly the horse, ridden by Dick Francis, jumped into the air for no apparent reason and collapsed on to his stomach. Although he climbed to his feet immediately there was nothing Francis could do to prevent second-placed ESP from racing past and claiming an amazing victory.

Many theories have been proposed as to what happened, including that the horse had been frightened by the roar of the crowd, he stumbled on uneven ground, or the shadow of a fence spooked him and caused him to jump. The real reason will never be known, but when checked at the stable afterwards Devon Loch was found to be in good health and never showed any sign of an abnormality – indeed he went on to win twice more.

Opposite: The sequence in which Devon Loch, the Queen Mother's horse, first collapsed (top, left to right) and then clambered back to his feet (bottom, left to right).

Willie Carson

Classic Carson

1970s

Born in Stirling, Scotland, in 1942, it took Willie Carson a while to make his name in racing. So slow was his progress that he even considered quitting altogether in his early days. However, he plugged on, with the determination that became so evident in his energetic riding style. By the end of his racing career Willie Carson was one of the most famous and best-loved jockeys in the sport.

Winner of the 1979 Epsom Derby and Irish Derby on Troy, his never-say-die racing tactics have endeared him to millions of punters as well as earning him flat racing's Champions Jockey title no fewer than five times. He won the 1972 Champion Jockey title for the first time and gained his first Classic victory on High Top in the 2000 Guineas. By that time he was becoming the heir apparent to Lester Piggott's crown.

Carson's switch to Royal Trainer Major Dick Hern, in 1977, was an unqualified success when, in Jubilee year, he won the Oaks and St Leger on the Queen's great filly Dunfermline. He went on to scoop 17 Classic victories amongst his 3,828 winning rides.

Willie Carson

Born: 16 November 1942

Place of birth: Stirling, Scotland

Wins and honours: 3,828 UK wins; British Champion Jockey 1972, 1973, 1978, 1980, 1983

Opposite: Carson and his horse, Troy, are led into the unsaddling enclosure after winning the 1979 Epsom Derby.

Red Rum's Hat-Trick

Three and Easy for Red Rum

1977 Red Rum is the only horse in the history of the Grand National Steeplechase to win the race three times. He was joint-favourite with Australian top-weight Crisp for his first Grand National in 1973. During the race, Crisp moved into a clear lead when another horse fell at the Chair, but Red Rum gained slowly, and at the line he beat Crisp by three quarters of a length. The duo were 25 lengths clear of the next horse.

In 1974, Red Rum came to the National in good form and was given top weight of 12 stone 2 pounds. He was jumping perfectly at Aintree and was in front at Becher's Brook on the second time round. Then he misjudged the fifth to last fence, but recovered well. He galloped on determinedly to beat L'Escargot by seven lengths and became the first horse since Reynoldstown (1935 and 1936) to win the Grand National in successive years.

After disappointments in 1975 and 1976, when he could only manage second-place finishes, in 1977 he was fit and ready. He had been trained to peak on National day as usual, and this time he looked really good. The only worry was whether the ground would be too wet for him. It was not. He jumped with his usual perfection, and when the favourite fell at Becher's Brook the second time round, Rummie took off to build up a good lead. His jockey Tommy Stack kept increasing the pace, and Red Rum won his third Grand National by 25 lengths, the first horse ever to win three Nationals. The crowd went crazy, surrounding the winner and shouting their praise.

Opposite: The crowd bursts into a jubilant frenzy near the finishing post as Red Rum gallops by to win his third Grand National.

The Triple Crown is Affirmed

Treble Chancer

1978 America's most recent Triple Crown winner was foaled in 1975. A champion in each of his racing seasons, Affirmed was bred in Florida by Lou Wolfson and carried his colours to Horse of the Year honours in 1978 and 1979 with Laz Barrera as trainer.

Affirmed's second season was dominated by a neck-and-neck competition with Calumet colt Alydar. As a two-year-old, Affirmed lost the Great American Stakes to Alydar, beat him by a half-length in the Hopeful, and by a nose in the Belmont Futurity, but lost to him in the Champagne Stakes. Recovering from this setback, Affirmed defeated Alydar in the Laurel Futurity.

Their duel was decided conclusively in his favour when, as a three-year-old, Affirmed earned Triple Crown honours in 1978. The event also brought teen jockey Steve Cauthen to prominence.

As the leading stakes earner of 1978, Affirmed won eight consecutive races at three years old, including the Triple Crown. Affirmed was the eleventh winner of this prestigious series.

As a four-year-old, the horse won the Hollywood Gold Cup, set a track record in the Santa Anita Handicap, defeated Belmont winner Coastal in the Woodward, and won the Jockey Club Gold Cup against Spectacular Bid. He retired with record-shattering lifetime earnings of $2,393,818.

Opposite: Affirmed noses past rival horse Alydar to win the Belmont Stakes in 1978 and thereby claim the Triple Crown.

Just Champion

Bob Champion and Aldaniti Win the Grand National

1981 One of the most famous stories in Grand National history is that of Bob Champion and Aldaniti. In 1979, Champion, trainer Josh Gifford's No. 1 jockey, was diagnosed with cancer. He may have had a reputation for toughness, but he was now facing the battle of his life. Throughout his illness, he followed closely the fortunes of Aldaniti, believing passionately he could win the Grand National aboard his favourite mount. Unfortunately, the horse was also suffering medical problems, with a series of leg injuries seriously afflicting him. Despite his problems, however, Aldaniti kept fighting back. So, too, did Champion, drawing inspiration from his dream of winning the National with Aldaniti as he fought – and won – his cancer battle. And so it was on 4 April 1981 that Champion and Aldaniti started the Grand National as 10/1 second favourites, behind the magnificent Spartan Missile.

After the penultimate fence, the dream looked on, with Aldaniti clear of Spartan Missile. Jockey John Thorne kept driving the favourite on, though and, with just a furlong to go, it looked as though Aldaniti's legs had gone. But Champion picked up his whip, Aldaniti responded gamely and the fairytale was complete – the two old crocks had done it.

Opposite: Bob Champion lands safely with Aldaniti after clearing the last fence en route to winning the Grand National.

Shergar Sweeps to Victory

Shergar Wins the Irish Sweeps Derby

1981 Celebrated Irish racehorse Shergar won the Irish Sweeps Derby in 1981, but the race is best remembered not merely for his victory, but for the ease with which it was achieved.

Shergar, who was owned by Prince Karim IV and trained by Michael Stoute, had already won the Epsom Derby in his previous race. Walter Swinburn had been his partner that day, leading from the front early on to win by 10 lengths. However, it was Lester Piggott who earned a place in the saddle for the Irish Sweeps Derby.

Shergar left the field in his wake to win by four lengths, leaving commentator Peter O'Sullivan to famously exclaim: 'It's only an exercise canter!' The horse became a national hero in Ireland and went on to set a record valuation for a stallion in stud at £10 million.

Despite these achievements, though, Shergar will be best remembered for being kidnapped from the Ballymany stud in 1983. The horse was never recovered and the kidnappers, thought by the police to be the IRA, were never brought to justice.

The Shergar Cup is now run at Ascot in his honour, and is a contest between European horses and the rest of the world.

Opposite: Shergar races past a supportive crowd to claim victory of the Epsom Derby, the race prior to the Irish Sweeps Derby.

From Sinner to Winner

Lester Piggott Wins the Breeders Cup Mile

1990 Legendary British jockey Lester Piggott won the Breeders Cup Mile in 1990 at New York's Belmont Park, in what is widely considered to be one of the all-time great races. It was all the more remarkable as Piggott's triumph came just 12 days after he was released from prison following a one-year sentence for tax irregularities. Piggott, who had retired from the sport in 1985, was aged 55 at the time.

The jockey earned a ride on Royal Academy after the horse's regular partner, John Reid, was injured in a race at Longchamp. Piggott had previous success with the colt's handler, the renowned Vincent O'Brien, in the 1960s and 1970s. Royal Academy had already been successful in the July Cup at Newmarket earlier in the season, although there were doubts over his temperament after his refusal to enter the stalls for the St James's Palace Stakes at Royal Ascot.

The pair made a poor start to the race, settling towards the rear of the field with a quarter of a mile to go. Piggott, however, in time-honoured fashion, timed his charge to perfection, moving to the outside in the straight to win by a neck.

Piggott rode his last winner in 1994 and retired from the sport for good in 1995.

'Eating's going to be a whole new ball game. I may even have to buy a new pair of trousers.'

Lester Piggott excited about the prospect of eating without the worry of gaining weight.

Aintree's False Dawn

The Grand National That Never Was

1993 The Grand National in 1993 saw one of the darkest days in the sport's history. The result had to be declared void after a false start was called, even though several horses finished the race. It left bookmakers having to refund £75 million in bets placed on the race.

Trouble started seconds before the race was due to begin, when protesters were spotted on the track. Following this initial delay, two false starts were caused by horses becoming tangled in the starting tape. On the second occasion, 30 of the 39 jockeys did not realize a false start had been declared and started the race. The frantic signalling of course officials, trainers and spectators to warn the jockeys was to no avail. The recall flag was never raised, while some jockeys ignored red flags being waved at the Chair on the first lap. Eleven horses completed one lap of the gruelling two-lap race and seven finished. However, it was declared void and the race was never re-run.

Jenny Pitman, whose horse Esha Ness was the first of the seven to finish, was devastated at the outcome. 'This is no Grand National, even though I have won it,' she said.

Opposite: Esha Ness passes the finishing post first, only for the race to be declared void after two false starts.

Frankie Dettori

Seven Up For Frankie

1996 In September 1996 Frankie Dettori sealed his place in the history of racing when he completed the 'magnificent seven' of winning every race on the card at Ascot. The housewife's favourite was beamed live into the homes of millions as the BBC interrupted their *Grandstand* programme to show coverage of the historic event.

Dettori's affable exterior masks a hard-nosed desire to win that has taken him to the very top of his profession. Only the Derby has eluded the likeable Italian – his failure to master the intricacies of Epsom Downs a constant source of frustration.

As Godolphin's stable jockey, Dettori has had the privilege of riding some of the greatest horses of modern times, including the likes of Montjeu, Sharmadal and Dubawi. Dettori, a committed family man, has battled back from adversity several times in his career, not least a life-threatening injury sustained in a helicopter crash in 2000 that killed the pilot.

Accused of putting his media commitments before his racing duties, Dettori was stung by the criticism and responded by claiming the Champion Jockey title in 2004 from his great rival Kieren Fallon.

Frankie Dettori

Born: 15 December 1970

Place of birth: Milan, Italy

Wins and honours: 2,540 wins; British Champion Jockey 2004

Opposite: Dettori leaps from Scorpion after winning the Ladbrokes St Leger at Doncaster, 2005.

Death on the Mountains

Tom Simpson Dies Climbing Mont Ventoux

1967 British cyclist Tom Simpson went into the 1967 Tour de France confident he could make an impression in the world's most gruelling road race. Certainly things started well for him and he ended the first week in sixth position. However, he began to complain of a stomach upset. His deteriorating health clearly became a hindrance as he started to lose vital time on the race leaders.

As the race headed for stage 13 in Marseilles, Simpson was seen swigging brandy during the early parts of the stage in a bid to beat dehydration. On the day's main climb, at Mont Ventoux, Simpson took an early lead before being passed by eventual stage winner, Julio Jiminez, and the chasing pack.

About 2 km (1.2 miles) from the summit, Simpson suddenly started to pedal erratically across the road and then fell against the embankment. Concerned team helpers urged him to retire but Simpson insisted on returning to the road. He managed only another 500 m (1,640 ft) before falling unconscious into the arms of a helper while still holding his handlebars.

Despite several attempts to resuscitate him, Simpson died while being airlifted to a nearby hospital. In the rear pocket of his racing jersey, two tubes of amphetamines and another empty tube were found. A post-mortem found he had taken the amphetamines and alcohol, a combination that proved fatal in the hot conditions.

Opposite: British cyclist Tom Simpson struggling during stage 13, on 13 July 1967 – he was to die later that day.

LeMond Wins the Tour de France

The Comeback King

1989 Greg LeMond's cycling career was littered with astonishing twists and turns, but his historic third Tour de France victory defied any conventional wisdom or logic.

Hunting in California in the winter of 1987, his brother-in-law accidentally set off his shotgun, striking LeMond in the chest just two months before the Tour was set to begin. LeMond missed the following two Tours recovering from his injuries and undergoing operations for appendicitis and for tendonitis in his leg. The American returned in 1989 still nursing several injuries, which included having 37 shotgun pellets in his chest – some in the lining of his heart.

LeMond set only modest targets for himself on his return, aiming at a top 20 finish. Heading into the final stage, however, the traditional time trial in Paris, LeMond was second in the overall standings but still some 50 seconds behind French hero Laurent Fignon. Somehow LeMond found the energy and determination to overhaul his rival – a double Tour winner himself – to win by just eight seconds, the smallest margin in the history of the event.

Some attributed LeMond's success to the aerodynamic handlebars he used in the sprint, others labelled Fignon's performance as lethargic, while the rider himself blamed saddle sores. Either way, LeMond's achievement remains one of the most remarkable comeback stories in sporting history.

'It doesn't get any easier. You just get faster.'

Greg LeMond

Lance Armstrong

The Miracle Man of Cycling

2005 Merely finishing the Tour de France is an accomplishment in itself. Winning it seven successive times, having suffered from life-threatening cancer, is an achievement that redefined the capabilities of the human body. Lance Armstrong was not only the most successful endurance cyclist of all time, but his heart-warming story in battling back from debilitating illness has acted as an inspiration to millions of cancer sufferers across the world.

Many have debated exactly what made Armstrong such a unique sportsman, and any number of factors have been offered as explanation. He learnt to use the focus he had drawn on in beating his illness in his preparation for Le Tour, whilst the backing of his coaches and support of his US Postal team, later known as the Discovery Channel Team, who were always so well briefed from a tactical viewpoint, gave him a big advantage. Moreover, Armstrong's riding style meant he had a higher-than-normal aerobic threshold, which allowed him to race at higher speeds in lower gears – something that was exaggerated in the time-trial events.

Armstrong won his final Tour de France in 2005, but has since been dogged by a number of drug accusations. However, nothing has ever been proved and his unrelenting charity work continues to mark him out as one of the most remarkable characters the world of sport has ever known.

'Pain is temporary, it may last a minute, or an hour, or a day, or a year, but eventually it will subside and something else will take its place.'

Lance Armstrong

BOXING & STRENGTH SPORTS

One of the most basic, and perhaps oldest, forms of sport, tests of strength have been a feature of competition through the ages.

In weightlifting, sportsmen and women are revered for the show of raw power as they haul immense loads above their heads. Boxing is arguably one of the noblest, and often most brutal, forms of competition, as protagonists test themselves in a classic one-on-one situation. In mythology it is said that Apollo was the original boxer, but presumably its beginnings are more humble, as cavemen fought for food and protection. The sport has developed into a highly skilled form of combat governed by strict rules of engagement. Similarly, in the Far East, martial arts developed in sports such as Judo, Karate and Kung Fu. Here we focus on boxing since it has made far more impact as an international and professional sport.

Dempsey Wilts Willard

Manassa Mauler Takes the Belt

1919 Jess Willard took 26 rounds to win the world heavyweight title from Jack Johnson, in the last ever 45-round fight. But it took fewer than three for him to surrender it, as he was simply battered into submission by the granite fists of the man who was to become one of the most popular champions in the sport's history, the 'Manassa Mauler', Jack Dempsey.

Willard was a poor champion in terms of ability, but he did not lack courage, and this shone through in the very one-sided fight in Toledo, Ohio. Dempsey was told just seconds before the fight by his trainer Jack Kearns that he had bet his entire purse – at 10-1 – he would win in the first round.

From the bell, Dempsey tore into Willard, knocking him down seven times in the first round alone, and left the ring thinking he had won the fight after the referee, Ollie Pecord, held his hand aloft. However, he was sent back into the ring after the time keeper confirmed he had rung the bell to save Willard, no one having heard it in the confusion. Dempsey continued to pound Willard until the champion retired in his corner at the end of the third round.

Despite having not earned a penny from this fight, Dempsey went on to participate in the first million-dollar gate just two years later.

Jack Dempsey

Born: 24 June 1895   **Died:** 31 May 1983

Place of birth: Colorado, USA

Weight: Heavyweight

Wins by KO: 50

Opposite: Dempsey (right) traps Willard in a corner during the fight.

The Wild Bull Fights Back

Firpo Digs Deep Against Dempsey

1923 Jack Dempsey was so popular with fight fans that long after he retired from the ring they would still call him 'Champ'. But the road to their hearts was built on some brutal defences of his title, and none more so than the simplest that occurred when the Manassa Mauler met Argentinian Luis Angel Firpo at the Polo Grounds in New York in 1923.

What the huge South American lacked in boxing skills he more than made up in power and pluck. Their savage fight was scheduled for 15 rounds, but lasted less than two. The fans, though, were treated to more action in those three minutes and 57 seconds than in many bouts that go the distance. Dempsey set about the Wild Bull of the Pampas with such brutality that he knocked him down seven times in the first round, but this just angered Firpo who in turn smacked Dempsey clean out of the ring. Had it not been for fans pushing the champion back into the ring he would surely have lost his title.

In the next round Dempsey knocked Firpo down twice and, when the challenger failed to get up from the second, retained his title. It was the most dramatic, heavy-hitting fight between two of the most courageous fighters the world had ever seen.

Opposite: Jack Dempsey towers over his opponent Luis Firpo who languishes on the canvas.

This Times It's Personal

Joe Louis Bites Back Against Schmeling

1938 Joe Louis, the son of an Alabama cotton picker, was a credit to the sweet science both in and out of the ring. When the Brown Bomber suffered a surprise defeat to the German champion Max Schmeling in 1936, the only thing on his mind was revenge. He had to wait two years for his chance, but when it came he took it with both hands – literally.

As with the earlier Olympics, the German Chancellor, Adolf Hitler, ensured the fight had an ugly undertone, something that did not sit easily with Schmeling, who had a Jewish manager. But for Louis it was all about winning his title back and he did so with what was, at that time, the second fastest knockout in history.

Louis ferociously attacked from the bell with both fists, smacking the face of the champion with bone-jarring power and accuracy. Two sickening left hooks gave Louis his range and what followed was a sustained barrage of punishment. Louis's trombone right found Schmeling nine times without reply to send the champion to the floor for the second and final time after two minutes and four seconds. The king was back on his rightful throne.

The pair became good friends and when Louis died in 1981 Schmeling paid for his funeral.

Joe Louis (right of picture)

Born: 13 May 1914　　**Died:** 12 April 1981

Place of birth: Alabama, USA

Weight: Heavyweight

Wins by KO: 54

'(I define fear as) standing across the ring from Joe Louis and knowing he wants to go home early.'

Max Baer

Turpin Takes On Robinson

Shock Win and Gallant Defence

1951 In July 1951, Randolph Turpin shocked the world when he out-pointed the formidable Sugar Ray Robinson in London to become Britain's first black boxing world champion. The charismatic Turpin, formerly a cook in the Royal Navy, became a national hero overnight at the age of 23, but his reign as champion was short lived, as the contract for the fight stipulated a return bout within 64 days at the New York Polo Grounds.

In the first clash, Robinson went in unbeaten in 91 fights, but paid the price for taking the talented, but un-fancied, Turpin too lightly. The former champion was not expected to make the same mistake twice in their rematch in September that year.

Robinson started quickly and was soon ahead on points as his class shone through, but the plucky Turpin fought back and opened up a dangerous cut above Robinson's eye. In the tenth round, Robinson's eye was attracting the attention of the referee, and the former champion, with a new sense of urgency, took the fight to Turpin. Under a flurry of blows Turpin went down for a count of seven and Robinson followed up with some dazzling punches, forcing referee Ruby Goldstein to call a halt with eight seconds of the round remaining. Turpin's reign as world champion was the shortest in boxing history.

Opposite: Sugar Ray Robinson delivers a devastating blow to Randolph Turpin's head.

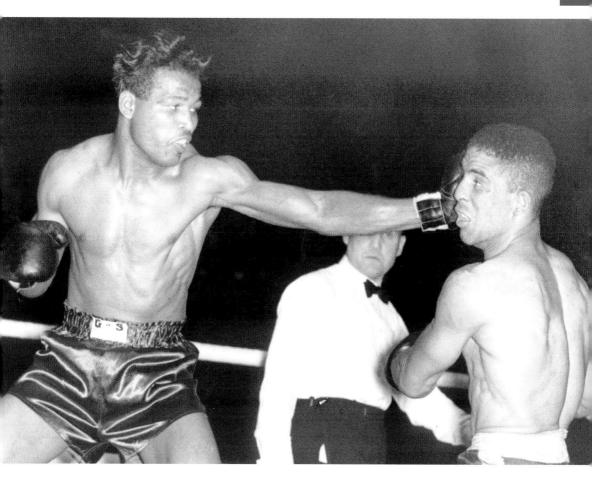

Marciano Stops Jersey Joe

Rocky Steps Up

1952 When Jersey Joe Walcott defeated Ezzard Charles in June 1952, he became the oldest ever heavyweight champion, aged 37 years and five months. But time caught up with him in the form of a hard-hitting youngster called Rocky Marciano just three months later.

Marciano was considered by many too small to be a force in the heavyweight division and, with a reach of just 67 inches, he often had to jump into opponents to connect, leaving him open to a counter-attack. This proved the case early on in his fight with Walcott, as the challenger had to recover from a first-round knock-down before wearing down the champ with his relentless, brawling style. In the thirteenth round a fearsome right was enough to put Walcott on the canvas and see the belt change hands. Walcott was not alone in not seeing the punch coming – many of the spectators missed it too.

The two met again in May 1953 in a much briefer affair, but with a similar outcome. This time Marciano took just two minutes and 25 seconds to finish the fight, one of the hardest punches of his career leaving Walcott motionless on the canvas.

Marciano went on to become the only heavyweight world champion to retire unbeaten by winning all of his 49 professional fights. Walcott, however, never fought again.

Rocky Marciano (right of picture)

Born: 1 September 1923 **Died:** 31 August 1969

Place of birth: Massachusetts, USA

Weight: Heavyweight

Wins by KO: 43

Liston Knocks Out Patterson

Boxing's Bad Guy Too Good

1962 Boxing fans love nothing more than a good-versus-evil contest, and when the likeable world heavyweight champion Floyd Patterson (saint) fought the Arkansas tearaway Sonny Liston (sinner), a classic was guaranteed.

Patterson was the golden boy of the 1952 Olympics, who went on to become the youngest ever world champion a month before his twenty-second birthday. Liston was a brutal, ferocious-punching giant, with bigger fists than any previous heavyweight, who learned to fight in a St Louis reform school and never shook off his perceived gangster links. 'In the films the good guy always wins, but this ain't no film and this is one bad guy who is not going to lose,' said Liston in the build-up.

With only one defeat in 34 – and that because of a broken jaw – Liston used his reach advantage of 13 inches to devastating effect. The writing was on the wall for the champion within a minute of the fight starting, when he was lifted clean off his feet. Two rib-bending blows, followed by a left-right combination to Patterson's head, finished the fight after just two minutes and six seconds.

Patterson fared only a little better in the rematch nine months later – lasting just 10 seconds longer.

Sonny Liston

Born: 8 May 1932   **Died:** 30 December 1970

Place of birth: Arkansas, USA

Weight: Heavyweight

Wins by KO: 39

Cooper Fells Clay

Louisville Lip is Clipped

1963 Henry Cooper, one of a pair of fighting twins with his brother George, was highly respected because of his gentlemanly behaviour, natural talent and stomach for a fight. In the biggest fight to date in his career, Cooper faced the colourful Cassius Clay at Wembley Stadium to determine who would get a crack at the world champion, Sonny Liston.

No one could promote a fight quite like Clay, who later changed his name to Muhammad Ali. The self-styled 'greatest' would whip up a frenzy over any fight he was involved in – earning him the nickname the Louisville Lip.

Cooper, cheered on by the partisan home fans, started well, and in the fourth round he knocked Clay down with 'Enry's 'Ammer', his trademark left hook, but the bell sounded before Cooper could finish off the dazed American.

In order to gain recovery time, Clay's trainer, Angelo Dundee, is said to have deliberately cut his fighter's glove in order to waste valuable seconds while a replacement pair had to be found – although the gloves were never actually changed.

Cooper's career is littered with fights in which he promised much, but ultimately lost because of his tendency to cut – and this was no different. The fight was stopped in the next round after Clay opened up Cooper's troublesome right eye. Clay later said Cooper 'had hit him so hard that his ancestors in Africa felt it'.

Opposite: Henry Cooper ready to resume the fight having just knocked Clay down in Wembley Stadium.

The Fight of the Century

Ali Faces Frazier for the First Time

1971 When Muhammad Ali and Joe Frazier met it was the fight the entire boxing world wanted to see. This was the first time that two undefeated heavyweights had been brought together in contest the title – with an expected worldwide television audience of 300 million, the promoters ramped up the hype by pitching the bout as 'The Fight of the Century'.

Ali had been out of the ring for three years because of legal wranglings with the US government over the war in Vietnam, and Frazier took the title in his absence. Ali's inactivity showed as Frazier's all-action style allowed him to dominate the first few rounds – even taunting Ali by poking his chin out at him.

The pair traded heavy blows throughout the 15 rounds, with neither fighter giving an inch. In the final round, with both men looking weary, Frazier summoned up every last ounce of energy and smacked Ali with a sledgehammer left hook that sent the former champion flying through the air and on to the canvas. Ali beat the count, but was out on his feet. The devastating power of that punch became apparent minutes later as, after the bell, Ali had to look on with his jaw ballooning as Frazier was awarded the points decision to inflict his first professional defeat.

Joe Frazier (right of picture)

Born: 12 January 1944

Place of birth: South Carolina, USA

Weight: Heavyweight

Wins by KO: 27

Gone in Two

Fired-Up Foreman Floors Frazier

1973 After Joe Frazier dismissed Muhammad Ali's heavyweight title challenge in 1971, it was always going to take someone very special to inflict the first defeat on him. After a couple of uninspiring title defences, Frazier could no longer ignore the division's rising star, George Foreman.

The giant Foreman shot to fame when he followed in Frazier's footsteps as Olympic champion, winning a gold medal in 1968. He was a hard-hitting no-nonsense fighter with a clubbing right. There were no hidden depths to Foreman, but surviving the relentless punishment, let alone stopping him, was another matter. After 37 fights undefeated as a professional, Foreman finally got his crack at the title.

The champion was a notoriously quick starter, and bounded out of his corner on the bell. Foreman, unlike every other opponent Frazier had met, stood his ground and the pair tore up the ring, toe-to-toe. Frazier's all-action blur of hooks and jabs was countered by Foreman's slow, accurate cross-shots. Something had to give – and it was Frazier's legs after yet another bone-jarring right.

As the fight wore on Frazier continued to run at his opponent with all guns blazing, only to walk into punishing, calculated blows. After six second-round knock-downs, the referee finally halted the fight, handing Foreman the title and his sixth successive second-round victory.

George Foreman (right of picture)

Born: 10 January 1949

Place of birth: Texas, USA

Weight: Heavyweight

Wins by KO: 68

The Rumble in the Jungle

African Adventure for Ali and Foreman

1974 The 'Rumble in the Jungle' between champion George Foreman and challenger Muhammad Ali was a unique event in boxing history. The brainchild of a budding boxing promoter called Don King and his business associates, the fight was scheduled to take place in a jungle clearing on the outskirts of Zaïre's (now Democratic Republic of Congo) capital, Kinshasa.

Beset by problems from the start, including a month-long delay when Foreman cut his eye eight days before the fight was due to take place, the bout was worth waiting for. In the meantime, the powerful Foreman whiled away the time perfecting his body blows with relentless pounding of the heavy bag. The charismatic Ali joked around and worked on his speed, telling all who would listen he would dance his way out of trouble.

When the fight finally took place, it did not go as everyone expected. Rather than moving, Ali adopted his now-legendary 'rope-a-dope' policy of soaking up the sickening punishment that Foreman was dishing out by backing on to the ropes and rolling with the punches. From the outside it looked like suicide, but Ali's plan became clear when Foreman began to tire. Ali had let the champion punch himself out before launching a counter-attack in the eighth round. With a perfect right hook, Ali floored Foreman to become only the second heavyweight to regain the title.

Muhammad Ali (right of picture)

Born: 17 January 1942

Place of birth: Kentucky, USA

Weight: Heavyweight

Wins by KO: 37

Hagler KOs the Hitman

Marvellous Marvin

1985 Marvellous Marvin Hagler, to which he later legally changed his name, was the ultimate blue-collar champion – a real working-class hero. The hard-hitting southpaw learned his trade the hard way and spent far too many years as the No. 1 contender without getting a shot at the title. Once champion, at the second attempt, Hagler made busy defending his title against anyone who wanted to fight him.

It was only a matter of time before boxing fans got their wish. A showdown with the most feared middleweight puncher in the world – Thomas 'The Hitman' Hearns. The bout was simply billed as 'The War', aptly so as it remains one of the most brutal, violent and thrilling eight minutes in boxing history.

From the first bell Hearns, who was expected to use his reach to pick off Hagler, stood toe-to-toe with the champion in the centre of the ring and traded powerful blows to a standing ovation from the baying crowd. Hagler looked hurt in the first round, Hearns in the second, as the two continued to use fists, elbows, heads and low blows to bring down their opponent. In this Mexican stand-off it was Hearns who blinked first, as Hagler – already with a badly cut head – saw off his opponent with a series of thudding punches in the third round.

Marvin Hagler (right of picture)

Born: 23 May 1954

Place of birth: New Jersey, USA

Weight: Middleweight

Wins by KO: 52

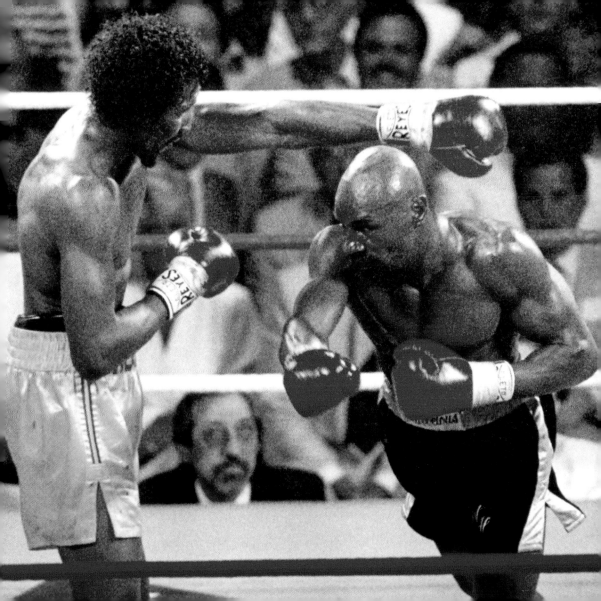

Sugar Ray's Finest Hour

Leonard Upsets the Odds to Beat Hagler

1987 Sugar Ray Leonard was style personified during the 1970s. His immaculate footwork, precise punching and methodical approach to fights proved too much for many opponents. But the five-weight champion was never a hit with the public, as he came across as too cold and calculated. Despite this, no one ever denied his talent.

Hagler's pronouncement of himself 'King of the Ring' in the 1980s proved too much for the much-maligned Leonard, who came out of retirement for this multi-million dollar showdown at Caesar's Palace, Las Vegas, on 6 April 1987.

Hagler started as the clear favourite, but Sugar Ray danced liked Fred Astaire around the ring and picked off the champion with flurries of fast, point-scoring punches, even though they lacked the power to seriously hurt his opponent.

In the ninth round, an increasingly frustrated Hagler surged forward and finally managed to land some punishing blows, but Leonard stayed on his feet and used all his experience to ride the powerful shots and earn a controversial points victory.

A bitter Hagler, who was in line for a record-equalling 13 successful defences, never fought again. He fumed: 'Leonard fought like a girl – his punches meant nothing. I fought my heart out. I kept my belt. I can't believe they took it away from me.' Ever the showman, Leonard countered: 'I had fun tonight. This is what I said I would do and I did it. It wasn't for the title. Beating Marvin Hagler was enough.'

Sugar Ray Leonard (left of picture)

Born: 17 May 1956

Place of birth: North Carolina, USA

Weight: Welterweight

Wins by KO: 25

De La Hoya Wins Six Titles

Oscar-Winning Performances

1980s Because boxing is categorized by weight divisions to ensure a fair fight, pundits annually argue over who is the best overall, pound-for-pound fighter currently operating on the planet. Oscar De La Hoya has almost rendered the argument pointless, having defeated challengers in no fewer than six different weight divisions.

De La Hoya was a successful amateur, with a career record of 223 wins – of which 163 were knockouts – and five defeats, culminating in winning gold for the USA in the Barcelona Olympics. After turning pro in 1992, De La Hoya was crowned WBO (World Boxing Organization) super featherweight champion within two years after defeating Jimmi Bredahl to stretch his unbeaten run to 16. World titles at lightweight, light welterweight, welterweight, super welterweight, light middleweight and middleweight followed as he won 38 of his 42 professional fights. In his wake, the fighters he has beaten read like a Who's Who of recent boxing history, including Troy Dorsey, Julio César Chávez, Pernell Whitaker, Arturo Gatti and Fernando Vargas. De La Hoya has set up his own stable of boxers and is moving into fight promotion, but is not ready to hang up his gloves – having agreed to meet Floyd Mayweather, who is the unified welterweight champion and pound-for-pound No. 1 in the world, in May 2007.

Oscar De La Hoya

Born: 4 February 1973

Place of birth: California, USA

Weight: Lightweight, light welterweight, welterweight, super welterweight, light middleweight, middleweight

Wins by KO: 30

Opposite: De La Hoya after defending his multiple light-middleweight titles by knocking out Yory Boy Campos, 2003.

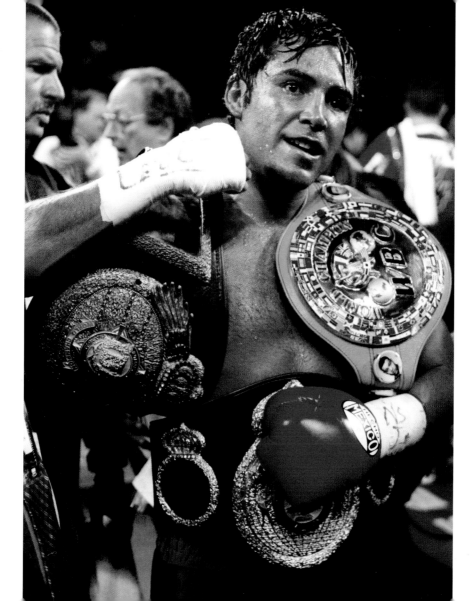

Iron Mike is shocked

Douglas Stuns Tyson – and the World

1990 It is said that bookmakers are never wrong, but on 11 February 1990 they were miles wide of the mark as James 'Buster' Douglas caused one of the biggest upsets in sporting history. His defeat of the fearsome Mike Tyson in 10 rounds ensured he became one of the most surprising world heavyweight champions in boxing history.

Rated at odds of 42/1 by some – extreme for any two-horse race – many bookmakers were refusing to give a price as it was deemed to be so one-sided. But, as every old pro knows, the danger of a heavy puncher is ever present. In context, Tyson was the most feared man on the planet. Crowned the youngest champion in history at 21 years old, Tyson had cleared out the generation of spent former champions doing the rounds, to hail a new generation of lean, tough, athletic boxers. He was an awesome fighting machine.

The signs were there early in the fight, as Douglas used his reach to stay away from the dangerous champion and picked him off with jabs. In the eighth round, Tyson floored Douglas, but the bell rang before Tyson could follow up his success.

In the tenth round, a devastating uppercut followed by two left-right combos from Douglas KOd Tyson for the first time in his boxing career and the world had a new heavyweight champion. *Sports Illustrated* magazine captured the moment perfectly with their front-cover headline, 'Rocky Lives!'

James Douglas (right of picture)

Born: 7 April 1960

Place of birth: Ohio, USA

Weight: Heavyweight

Wins by KO: 25

British Brawn

The Golden Age of Home-Grown Middleweights

1990s When a brash and brutal Nigel Benn came back from Atlantic City in 1989 after wrestling the WBO title from Doug DeWitt, it heralded a time of unparalleled success for British middleweights. There were previous champions in Alan Minter and the popular John Conteh, but never the glut that appeared at the turn of the decade.

The title was passed to the dapper Chris Eubank, the WBC (World Boxing Council) champion, in 1990 following a ninth-round knockout in one of the best fights ever seen in a British ring. Eubank went on to make a controversial defence in September 1991 against the reserved and thoughtful people's favourite, Michael Watson. In the rematch Watson collapsed after the fight was stopped in the twelfth round, and fell into a coma – starting the toughest fight of his life that he is fortunately winning.

Benn and Eubank were to meet again, but it was never likely to reach the heights of the first fantastic bout, with Benn, the 'Dark Destroyer', losing out again.

In 1994 Steve Collins was the next to burst on to the scene, with a ferocious victory over Eubank. The hard-hitting Irishman went on to defend his title successfully seven times (including a second meeting with Eubank and two fights against Benn). Their dominance was total, their bravery unequalled and their legacy lives on in Joe Calzaghe.

Opposite: Chris Eubank fires his right fist into the face of opponent Michael Watson during the September 1991 fight.

What's Going on Ear?

Tyson Takes a Bite out of Holyfield

1997 This eagerly awaited rematch turned out to be one of the most controversial moments in sporting history. Evander Holyfield had beaten Mike Tyson a year before and made history by becoming – after Muhammad Ali – only the second fighter to win the world heavyweight championship three times, with an eleventh-round knockout.

After having a fan parachute into the ring during his third title bout with Riddick Bowe, Holyfield was used to bizarre events in the ring. But what followed against Iron Mike was unheard of in boxing history. Tyson was desperate to get his boxing career – and his life for that matter – back on track. Still bearing a grudge for a perceived butt in their first fight, Tyson was enraged when the two clashed heads in a clinch during the third round and reacted by biting a lump out of Holyfield's ear before spitting it on to the canvas.

The champion reacted by screaming and flicking his right glove as if swatting a fly from his right ear. Referee Mills Lane deducted two points and told the fighters to continue. In the next clinch Tyson repeated the barbarity and was disqualified. Cue mayhem. Once calm was restored, a piece of Holyfield's ear was found lying in the ring, and it had to be surgically re-attached and repaired in the hours after the rematch. Unsurprisingly, Tyson was banned.

'I felt Holyfield was using his head illegally. I told the referee I wasn't getting any help, so I went back to the streets. I cannot defend it, but it happened.'
Mike Tyson after biting Evander Holyfield's ear.

Eugen Sandow

The Father of Modern Bodybuilding

1890s Born Frederick Mueller in Germany 1867, Sandow – widely credited as the 'father of bodybuilding' – began his road to stardom as a gymnast after running away from home. He was a competent performer but he lacked the technical ability to be a true great in the field. However, professional strongman Oscard Attila noticed that the 20 year old had something more to offer. Attila took Mueller under his wing and began to mould his protégé's gymnastic build into that of a bodybuilder. It was at this point that Mueller changed his name to Eugen Sandow.

The pair began to tour northern Europe, and in London in 1889 Sandow challenged well-known stage strongman 'Samson' to a contest. He won – and the name of Sandow began to gain credence in the world of strength sports.

In 1893 his career took another turn. Chicago showman Florenz Ziegfeld believed Sandow, still only 25, could be used as a sex symbol instead of a weightlifter. One of Ziegfeld's first decisions was to get Sandow to doff his pink tights and show a bit more skin; he also encouraged his subject to pose for a masterful series of photographs clad in only a fig leaf. Soon these innovations had made Sandow a prime attraction, and Chicago's finest clamoured to see 'the world's most perfectly developed man'.

By his death in 1925, Sandow had produced a plethora of books, magazines, exercise devices and diets. The 'modern Hercules', as he was known, pioneered much of what has made bodybuilding a profitable enterprise today.

Opposite: Eugen Sandow poses with only a fig leaf to maximize the exposure of muscle.

India's Trailblazer

Khashaba Jhadhav Claims the First Olympic Medal

1952 Khashaba Jhadhav was the first Indian to win an individual medal at the Olympics when he came third at the 1952 Helsinki Games in bantamweight wrestling. The 26-year-old lost in the semi finals but managed to regain his composure and defeat his opponent in the bronze medal play-off, putting India on the wrestling map.

Jhadhav had previously competed in the 1948 London Olympic Games but had failed to make any real impact as a flyweight. In truth, he was not expected to challenge for any medals in Helsinki either. Nevertheless, despite having stepped up a weight, he was a stronger competitor four years later and fully deserved his bronze medal.

Surprisingly, Jhadhav was not given a hero's welcome on his return to India – he was largely overlooked by a country more interested in cricket. It was only when he died in 1984 that his achievements were finally given the respect they truly deserved.

When Leander Paes won a bronze medal for tennis in the Atlanta Olympics of 1996, he became only the second Indian to win an individual medal at the Olympics. This 44-year gap only serves to further highlight Jhadhav's great accomplishment.

Opposite: An aerial view of the Helsinki stadium in which Jhadhav won his bronze medal during the 1952 Olympic games.

Tommy Kono

Awesome Olympian

1950s Tommy Kono was arguably the greatest Olympic weightlifter the world has ever seen. An American of Japanese descent, he became the only man to set world records in four different weight classes – in lightweight (148 pounds), middleweight (165 pounds), light heavyweight (181 pounds), and middle-heavyweight (198 pounds).

Kono was a key member of the United States weightlifting team as soon as his career began, precisely because his versatility enabled him to move up or down in weight without losing any strength. In fact, only two years after he began his Olympic lifting career, he had made the highest total of any lightweight lifter in the United States.

Kono won gold medals at the 1952 Olympic Games in Helsinki and the 1956 Games in Melbourne, as well as a silver medal at the 1960 Olympics in Rome. Furthermore, he was world champion every year from 1953 to 1959. He established 26 world records and seven Olympic records. And, as if that was not enough, he was crowned Mr Universe three times. Kono's achievements in weightlifting remain unparalleled. His versatility, agility and, more importantly, his raw power, enabled him to set standards that most have struggled to match since.

Tommy Kono

Born: 27 June 1930

Place of birth: California, USA

Event: Men's Weightlifting

Olympic medals: Gold 1952, Gold 1956, Silver 1960

Arnold Schwarzenegger

The Austrian Oak

1960s Before his move into acting and then politics, Arnold Schwarzenegger was a hugely successful bodybuilder. The 'Austrian Oak' started his career in Graz, Austria, with only one thing on his mind – to win the Mr Universe title.

In 1961, at the age of 15, he teamed up with the former Mr Austria, Kurt Marnul. Marnul was impressed with young Arnold's physique and asked him to train in the Athletic Union in Graz. In 1965 Schwarzenegger enlisted in the Austrian army, but he was so determined to attend a competition in Stuttgart that he went AWOL, and was subsequently jailed. However, it proved to be worth the time, as he earned his first competitive win in Stuttgart to become Junior Mr Europe.

This was just the beginning of his success, as he went on to dominate the bodybuilding scene for the next 15 years, adding the Best-Built Athlete of Europe, International Powerlifting Championship, and the amateur Mr Universe titles to his collection before he had even reached the age of 20.

The 1970s brought equal success, as he won the Mr Olympia title six times before the turn of the decade – with six consecutive wins from 1970 to 1975. After this he turned his attention to acting, and after five relatively high-grossing hits he scored his first major success starring in *The Terminator* in 1984.

Opposite: Arnold Schwarzenegger flexing his muscles during his time as a bodybuilder, prior to the take-off of his film career.

WINTER SPORTS

Winter sports provide arguably the most diverse selection of activities in the world. Commonly defined as sports that are played on snow or ice, categories include ice skating, skiing, sledding and team sports such as ice hockey and curling. Although ice skating was proposed as an event when the International Olympic Committee was established in 1894, it did not feature in competition until 1912.

When the Olympics were held in France in 1924, a separate winter sports week was held in Chamonix under the patronage of the IOC. Around 200 athletes from 16 different nations completed in 16 different events, in what was retrospectively considered to be the first Winter Olympic Games. Over the years the number of winter sports included in the Winter Olympic programme has increased. Sports such as speed skating, ski jumping and cross-country skiing have been included since the first Games, while more recent additions include biathlon and snowboarding.

Dick Button

Dick at the Double

1948 With five consecutive world championships between 1948 and 1952 and back-to-back Olympic titles as well, it is no wonder that figure-skating legend Dick Button is regarded as one of the greatest American athletes of all time. Button's CV is arguably as impressive as any sportsperson that has ever lived, and it is not based purely on what he won.

The man from Englewood, New Jersey, can also list the 1949 Sullivan award for the nation's outstanding amateur athlete – the only time it has ever been won by a skater – among his achievements, but even that is not considered his finest hour.

Never one to rest on his laurels, Button strove to develop new techniques and movements. At the 1948 Olympics, as a 19-year-old Harvard freshman, he became the first person to execute the double axel. The move earned him global fame and first place from eight of the nine judges. Of the historic jump, Button says: 'The lift was strong, the revolution certain and the landing sure.'

Four years later, Button again showed his love for risk-taking. Ignoring the fact that a safe, simple routine would win him the gold, he decided to gamble by attempting the triple-jump – a technique that had never been performed in competitive action before. Button executed it to perfection to take the gold as the judges' unanimous choice.

Dick Button

Born: 18 July 1929

Place of birth: New Jersey, USA

Event: Men's singles figure skating

Olympic medals: Gold 1948, Gold 1952

Opposite: Button on the way to winning the men's figure skating event at the Winter Olympics, 1952.

Czech Mates Celebrate

Czechoslovakia Beat Russia Twice

1969 The former Czechoslovakia's two grudge matches with Russia at the World Championships in Stockholm in 1969 remain the most politically and emotionally charged ice-hockey matches in modern history.

The first game, won by the Czechs, sparked riots and emotional scenes in Prague the following week, and will never be forgotten by those who witnessed them. Czechoslovakia, which had a fine tradition in ice hockey, ran out 2-0 winners thanks to the brilliance of Jan Suchy. He scored the first and went on to be chosen as one of the tournament's top three players. The decisive second, which came from Josef Cerny, proved to be too much for Soviet coach Anatoly Tarasov – he was taken to hospital for a cardiogram check-up after suffering chest pains.

The result had a similar effect on the Czech captain Josef Golanka, as he fainted at the end. It was Russia's first defeat in over a year, and the first time they had failed to score in a match since 1955.

To add insult to injury, this was quickly followed by a second defeat at the hands of the Czechs, this time by a 4-3 scoreline. The Soviets went on to take gold, on points scored, ahead of Sweden and the Czechs, but the two wins over their old enemies made Czechoslovakia just as ecstatic.

One of the 2,000 telegrams sent to the team read: 'Our thanks to you for the bronze medal with two diamonds. It's worth more to us than the gold.'

Opposite: Anti-Soviet sentiment followed the decision to award the Soviets the gold medal, despite Czechoslovakia's recent double victory.

Franz Wins on Home Soil

Klammer Time

1976 A hugely popular figure in Winter Olympics history, Franz Klammer is best remembered for his performance during the 1976 Games in his native Austria. Klammer, who had won eight of nine World Cup downhill races the year before, enjoyed a truly memorable race against defending Olympic downhill champion Bernhard Russi from Switzerland.

With the event in Klammer's back yard, there was huge pressure on him to succeed, and that was made even greater when the Austrian was forced to start from fifteenth place among the 15 starters.

Klammer was struggling to keep pace with Russi's time of 1:46.06, but the man dubbed 'the Austrian Astronaut', refused to give up. Spurred on by over 60,000 of his fellow countrymen, Klammer fought back, somewhat dangerously, over the last 1,000 metres to take the title from Russia by one third of a second.

Afterwards, Klammer said: 'The best moment was when Bernhard came running up to me and gave me a big hug. It was the most sincere congratulations of all.'

Klammer became so popular in Austria that when he was left off the Austrian team in 1980, the team manager had to explain the decision on national television.

Franz Klammer

Born: 3 December 1953

Place of birth: Carinthia, Austria

Event: Downhill Skiing

Olympic Medal: Gold 1976

Miracle on Ice

The USA Triumphs over the USSR

1980 The victory by the United States over the Soviet Union in the 1980 Winter Olympics ice-hockey medal round is still ranked by many as one of the greatest underdog victories of all time. The team of inexperienced American college players was given no hope of beating the USSR, arguably the best team in the world, after they had been thumped 10-3 in an exhibition match 13 days previously. Lifted by a vociferous home support in Lake Placid, New York, however, they produced one of their nation's finest ever sporting results.

The match, which was given an extra edge because of the Cold War conflict between the two nations, started at a ferocious pace with the Soviet Union taking a two-goal lead. However, Mark Johnson struck back for the home side and levelled the game at 2-2 just before the end of the second period. This prompted the Soviets to make a change, taking off legendary goalkeeper Vladislav Tretiak and replacing him with the younger, less experienced Vladimir Myshkin.

It appeared to have the desired effect for the Russians as they regained the lead. But the Americans refused to be beaten and the hero of the first period, Johnson, brought his team level again at three each. With time running out and US goalkeeper Jim Craig performing heroics, it was left to captain Mike Eruzione to land the winning goal.

The US went on to take the gold, beating Finland 4-2 in their final medal-round match, but the real fairytale, given the chasm of quality – and political hostility – between the nations was in that 4-3 victory over the USSR 48 hours earlier.

Opposite: Mark Johnson glides into a position to shoot past the Soviet goalkeeper, Vladislav Tretiak.

Torvill and Dean Take Gold

Pairs Perfection

1984 St Valentine's Day 1984 may be memorable for many British couples, but it is doubtful any will have experienced the emotions that ice-skating duo Jayne Torvill and Christopher Dean felt after their unforgettable Olympic gold-winning performance in (the then) Yugoslavia.

More than 24 million people watched on television in Britain as the pair from Nottingham scored 12 perfect sixes for their free-dance performance – a record that will remain unmatched, since a new scoring system was introduced at the 2005 European Championships.

Their four-minute routine, to the haunting tune of Ravel's 'Bolero', brought a standing ovation and flowers from the crowd of 8,500. Afterwards, a tearful Dean said: 'Tonight we reached the pinnacle. I don't remember the performance at all. It just happened. It was the most emotional performance we have ever given. What just happened out there – getting the medals – that is what we've worked so hard for, for so long.'

Torvill and Dean's Olympic gold in Sarajevo was the beginning of a special year for the pair, as they achieved record-breaking maximum points at the world figure skating championships shortly after. Their 23-year partnership came to an end in 1998.

'I found them to be delightful young people, the kind you want to help if you can.'

Singer-actor Michael Crawford mentored the pair and helped shape their 1984 routine.

The Jamaican Bobsleigh Team

Reggae Boys Get Bobbing

1988 Bizarre and unheralded concepts may have been formed with alarming regularity during the 1980s, but not many have surpassed the idea of Jamaica entering a bobsleigh team into the 1988 Calgary Winter Olympics.

The Caribbean nation, better known for soaring temperatures and unbroken sunshine, shocked the sporting world by entering the Games for the first time in their history. The tropical island team unsurprisingly finished in last place, but they did manage to command the attention of the world's media during their time in Italy.

Thankfully, despite that experience, the Jamaican team – who were the subject of the 1993 Disney film *Cool Runnings* and by now huge crowd favourites – returned to the Games in the years to come. They were rewarded at the 1994 Olympics in Lillehammer, Norway, when the four-man team finished in fourteenth place, ahead of crews from France, Italy and the United States.

Although they did not qualify for the Games in Turin in 2006, the reggae boys have improved beyond all recognition from their first appearance 18 years ago.

Opposite: The two-man Jamaican bobsleigh team hurtling down the ice at the 1988 Calgary Winter Olympics.

Björn Daehlie

Greatest Winter Olympian

1998 Even though he is one of the greatest Olympians of all time, Norwegian cross-country skier Björn Daehlie has never enjoyed the fame of Sir Steve Redgrave or Haile Gebrselassie. Daehlie, or the 'Nannestad Express' as he is known in tribute to his home town, has been world champion no fewer than nine times and is the most successful athlete in the history of the Winter Games.

The first of Daehlie's 15 Olympic races was the 30 km (19 mile) classical, in Albertville in 1992, in which he earned the silver medal behind fellow Norwegian Vegard Ulvang. The pair went on to lead their country to a clean sweep of the five events in men's cross-country. After placing fourth in the 10 km (6 mile) classical, Daehlie came from behind in the second half of the combined pursuit to win his first gold medal. He also added a second gold in the relay, crossing the finish line backwards, and he closed out the Games by winning the 50 km (31 mile) classical.

Over the course of his nine-year career, Daehlie went on to win a total of eight Olympic gold and four Olympic silver medals. His final Olympic victory was in the 50 km, at the Nagano Games in 1998. After skiing for more than two hours, in what he would later describe as the hardest race of his life, the 31-year-old crossed the finish line ahead of Sweden's Niklas Jonsson.

Björn Daehlie

Born: 19 June 1967

Place of birth: Elverum, Norway

Event: Cross-Country Skiing

Olympic medals: 3 Gold 1992, 2 Gold 1994, Silver 1992, 2 Silver 1994, Silver 1998

Opposite: Daehlie is followed by Thomas Alsgaard, who went on to beat him to the gold in the 15 km free pusuit, 1998.

SWIMMING & SAILING

Swimming and sailing are undoubtedly the most popular water sports. The earliest known swimming races can be traced to Japan in 36 BC, although competitive swimming rose in popularity in the nineteenth century. It generally consists of 17 different events using four different styles – breaststroke, backstroke, butterfly and freestyle. International swimming events are regulated by FINA (*Fédération Internationale de Natation*) and it remains a popular Olympic event.

Sailing is considered to be one of the most expensive sports in the world. Although sailboat class and event type can vary greatly, the standard practice is to race around buoys in closed water. Some endurance races, such as the Vendée Globe, which are conducted in open water, rate amongst the most dangerous sporting events. Sailboats used can range from single-person dinghies to the larger boats with crews of up to 20 people used in events such as the America's Cup.

Swim When You're Winning!

Gertrude Ederle Crosses the English Channel

1926 Up to 6 August 1926, only five men had ever managed to complete the gruelling swim across the English Channel. The thought of a female swimmer ever achieving the feat seemed to be a pipe dream – a swim physically beyond the capabilities of the female body. But on that summer morning, at 7.05 a.m., 19-year-old Olympic swimmer Gertrude Ederle took to the waters at Cap Gris-Nez in France in her bid to rewrite history.

Her guts and determination proved women were not inferior to men, and she became a real sports heroine. The American swimmer not only completed the distance, coming ashore on the English coast at 9.04 p.m., but she also managed to do it in a time of 14 hours and 31 minutes – knocking two hours and two minutes off the previous best time by Argentine Enrique Tiraboschi.

After walking up the beach in Dover, Ederle was greeted by a British immigration officer demanding her passport. But on her return to her native America she was feted with a ticker-tape parade in her home city, New York, with more than two million people lining the streets to see their new sporting heroine. Her new-found fame resulted in her playing herself in a movie called *Swim, Girl Swim* before she was officially accepted into the International Swimming Hall of Fame in 1965.

Gertrude Ederle

Born: 23 October 1906   **Died:** 30 November 2003

Place of birth: New York, USA

Events: 4 x 100 m Freestyle Relay, 100 m Freestyle, 400 m Freestyle

Olympic medals: Gold 1924, 2 Bronze 1924

Mark Spitz's Magnificent Seven

Swimming's Gold-en Boy

1972 Mark Spitz will always be remembered as one of the greatest Olympians to ever grace a swimming pool. Never short on self-confidence, the American held 10 world records before boldly predicting he would scoop six gold medals in the 1968 Summer Olympics. In the event, he picked up only two team golds, in the 4 x 100 metres and 4 x 200 metres freestyle.

However, on his return four years later for the Games in Munich, Spitz went one better than his earlier prediction – winning seven gold medals and setting a world record in each of the seven events he entered: the 100 metres and 200 metres freestyle, 100 metres and 200 metres butterfly, 4 x 100 metres freestyle, 4 x 200 metres freestyle and 4 x 100 metres medley. His record-breaking feat still stands as the best performance by an athlete at an Olympic Games.

After the Games, Spitz made the surprise decision to retire from swimming at the tender age of 22. However, he did attempt a comeback for the 1992 Olympics, aged 41, but missed out on the qualifying times for Barcelona despite swimming as fast as his record-breaking times of the 1970s.

Mark Spitz

Born: 10 February 1950

Place of birth: California, USA

Events: 4 x 100 m freestyle relay, 4 x 200 m freestyle relay, 100 m butterfly, 100 m freestyle, 200 m butterfly, 200 m freestyle, 4 x 100 m medley relay

Olympic medals: 2 Gold 1968, Silver 1968, Bronze 1968, 7 Gold 1972

Louganis Fails to Make a Splash

Greg Louganis Hits the Diving Board

1988 Not all Olympic competitors are remembered for triumphing against the odds or setting new records. Some, like American diving legend Greg Louganis, are best remembered for things they wish they had not done.

The US star was an overwhelming favourite to win the three-metre springboard event at the 1988 Olympics in Seoul, but he misjudged the ninth of his 11 dives. Attempting a reverse 2.5-somersault pike, he failed to get enough distance between himself and the board, and cracked his head open as he came down. 'I didn't realize I was that close to the board,' Louganis said later, with a hint of comic understatement.

He was treated for his head wound and went on to win two gold medals in Seoul, although the story could have had a tragic postscript after it became public in 1995 that the diver was HIV positive at the time of the accident. 'I was in a total panic that I might cause someone else harm,' he wrote in his autobiography, *Breaking the Surface*. 'I wanted to warn Dr Puffer [who treated his head injury in 1988 without wearing gloves], but I was paralysed. Everything was all so mixed up at that point: the HIV, the shock and embarrassment of hitting my head and an awful feeling that it was all over.' Thankfully, Dr Puffer was later given a clean bill of health.

Opposite: Greg Louganis begins his dive, but knocks his head on the board during his descent.

Ian Thorpe

The Human Fish

1990s–2000s

Having suffered from a chlorine allergy at an early age, forcing him to swim with his head above water, few would have imagined that Ian Thorpe would grow up to be one of the most prolific gold-medal winners in the sport's history. At his largest, 'The Thorpedo' stood way over 1.8 m (6 ft) – and with size 17 feet, he was a truly awesome physical specimen. At the age of 14, he became the youngest male ever to represent Australia; his victory in the 400 metres freestyle at the 1998 Perth World Championships made him the youngest individual male world champion. Thorpe shattered many world records, but reached his peak in time for the Sydney Olympics in 2000.

The pressure on the national hero was immense, with one of the national newspapers printing a front page with his picture underneath a headline of 'Invincible' – but Thorpe did not disappoint. He claimed Australia's first gold of the Games in the 400 metres freestyle in a new world-record time before a partisan and expectant crowd. More was to follow, as Thorpe anchored both the 100 metres and 200 metres freestyle relay teams to gold, again setting new world records in the process. In Sydney, Thorpe not only demonstrated he was a swimmer of unrivalled pedigree but also, as with all the greats, he had an immaculate sense of occasion too.

Ian Thorpe

Born: 13 October 1982

Place of birth: Milperra, Australia

Events: 400 m freestyle, 4 x 100 m freestyle relay, 4 x 200 m freestyle relay, 200 m freestyle, 400 m freestyle, 4 x 100 m medley relay, 4 x 200 m freestyle relay, 100 m freestyle

Olympic medals: 3 Gold 2000, 2 Silver 2000, 2 Gold 2004, Silver 2004, Bronze 2004

Loser Lipton

Scotland's Attempt to Win the America's Cup

1901 Sir Thomas Lipton is one of the great losers in sailing history. The Scottish tea magnate was the most persistent challenger in the history of the America's Cup, with five entries between 1899 and 1930, all on boats called *Shamrock* – a nod to his Irish heritage. His first big sail had been as a 14-year-old, when he persuaded his parents to let him sail from Scotland to New York.

After Lipton's last unsuccessful attempt on the America's Cup, the mayor of New York wrote that he was 'possibly the world's worst yacht builder but absolutely the most cheerful loser'. Harold Vanderbilt said: 'He was the most wonderful sportsman it has been our good fortune to race against.'

For Lipton's part, it mattered little that he never got his hands on 'the most elusive piece of metal in all the world' as the competition kept him 'young, eager, buoyant and hopeful'. His noble performances also captured the imagination of the American public, and he was awarded a special cup as 'the best of all losers'. His endeavours also served to make his tea brand famous across the Atlantic.

When Lipton died in October 1931, aged 81, he was said to be planning a sixth attempt at the America's Cup.

Opposite: Sir Thomas Lipton aboard one of his *Shamrock* boats that was still under construction.

Across the Atlantic in 12 Days

Best Barr None

1905

In 1905, crossing the Atlantic Ocean on board the *Atlantic* – a 56 m (185 ft) schooner – in 12 days, four hours and one minute was a record-breaking feat.

Racing for the Kaiser's Cup from New York Harbour to Lizard skipper Charlie Barr, renamed for pushing the limits, and his crew proved the best of 11 vessels in the race across the pond.

After their victory, Barr told the *New York Herald*: 'It amounts to this: I have got the best yacht afloat, next we had good leading breezes, then the crew worked nobly and you couldn't find a better set of fellows.'

In the world of yacht racing, the *Atlantic*'s record stood for a remarkable 100 years until the Rolex Transatlantic Challenge of 2005, when Robert Miller's *Maricha IV* crossed the same finish line in nine days, 15 hours, 55 minutes and 23 seconds.

While it remained the record of the century, the *Atlantic*'s time was actually beaten outside official racing by Frenchman Eric Tabarly in 1980 aboard a Trimaran in 10 days and five hours, still a notable 75 years after Charlie Barr's amazing feat.

The beloved *Atlantic* has been called the best-known schooner in the United States, as it also served in the US Navy during the First World War and in the Coastguard during the Second World War.

Opposite: *New York Harbour* by Thomas Birch, *c.* 1827–35 – the starting point from which Charlie Barr was to set sail across the Atlantic some 70 years later.

Solo Sensation

Francis Chichester Circles the Globe Alone

1967 When Francis Chichester arrived as a national hero in Plymouth on 28 May 1967, it was difficult to believe that nine years earlier he had been diagnosed with terminal lung cancer. The 65-year-old had just become the first person to sail single-handedly around the world by the clipper route, the riskiest journey with the most time spent in the perilous Southern Ocean. Just as he had staved off the most lethal form of cancer, he had conquered the seas around Cape Horn. The Devon-born sailor and aviator (he had already tried to fly around the world) had a simple reason for his risky pursuits. 'Because it intensifies life,' he said at the time.

He had left on 27 August the previous year, planning to get to his one stop in Sydney faster than the great Australian wool clippers of the nineteenth century. He succeeded in that goal, and completed the round-the-world journey in just 226 days, arriving home to a 10-gun salute from the Royal Artillery and a crowd of 250,000. Chichester was knighted in July with a sword that had belonged to Sir Francis Drake, and was honoured by having his image on a postage stamp in 1967. He finally succumbed to lung cancer in 1972.

'What I would like after four months of my own cooking is the best dinner from the best chef in the best surroundings and in the best company.'

Francis Chichester after his return from his solo round-the-world voyage.

Opposite: Francis Chichester nears Plymouth in *Gypsy Moth IV* after his mammoth journey.

Glorious Defeat

Moitessier Surrenders the Chance for Glory

1969

In 1969 Bernard Moitessier sailed in the *Sunday Times* Golden Globe Race and looked set to become the first man to sail alone non-stop around the world.

Seven months into the race the Frenchman, in his ketch called *Joshua*, held the lead but he decided to drop out as he disapproved of the event being commercialized. Instead of heading towards the finish line in Europe he changed course and headed for Polynesia. Moitessier said: 'I have no desire to return to Europe with all its false gods. They eat your liver out and suck your marrow and brutalize you.'

Moitessier's somewhat unorthodox approach ensured that Robin Knox-Johnston, the only other competitor to finish the *Sunday Times*-sponsored race, claimed the honour of the first solo voyage around the world without stopping.

Moitessier continued his own unique journey, circling the globe one and a half times before finally lowering his sails in Tahiti. In his book *The Long Way*, he describes his feat as a spiritual journey. Moitessier, who died of cancer in 1994, was also an ecologist and an environmental activist.

'What was waiting for him in Plymouth was also the other side of glory, the tumultuous crowds, the lack of respect for the individual, prying indiscretions. The rape of his realized dream; he could not accept this.'
Jean-Michel Barrault on Moitessier's decision to change course.

Opposite: It is easy to see one of the reasons why Tahiti would have been more appealing to Moitessier than returning to Europe.

Aussies Stun the USA

America Surrenders the America's Cup

1983 The 'race of the century' in the 1983 America's Cup was notable for many reasons. It was best known as the first time in the Cup's 132-year history that an American boat had not won as *Australia II* beat *Liberty* in a dramatic sudden death race. It was a major shake-up in a race that had been completely dominated by the Americans. As the skipper of *Australia II*, John Bertrand, said after the race: 'This puts yacht racing back on the map!'

But perhaps the most controversial thing about the race was the design of the boat that won it. *Australia II* had a revolutionary winged keel, which provoked a sceptical reaction when it was first unveiled by designers, and had represented a considerable risk for Australian millionaire and team backer Alan Bond.

The design risk paid off, though – *Australia II* had the shortest waterline of any 12 m (40 ft) boat and the smallest wetted surface, giving it exceptional speed through the water. That, and a talented team made up of sailors who had America's Cup experience and Olympic medals to their names, allowed the Australian boat to edge out *Liberty*, which was captained by the legendary Dennis Conner.

Stars and Stripes won back the Cup for America, but they lost it again in 1995 and showed little sign of regaining it over a decade later, with New Zealand and Switzerland claiming glory along the way.

Opposite: During the celebratory ceremony, designer Ben Lexcen, of the winning 12 metre yacht *Australia II*, holds his silver trophy high with pride.

Pride Restored

Captain Conner Wins Back the America's Cup

1987 The America's Cup regatta is known as the most famous and prestigious yachting race in the world. As he celebrated winning the 1987 America's Cup, skipper Dennis Conner told the *New York Times*: 'This is a great moment for America, a great moment for the *Stars and Stripes* team, a great moment for the *Stars and Stripes* crew, and a great moment for Dennis Conner.'

The victory restored American pride after they had lost the Cup to challenger *Australia II* in 1983. Conner and his crew aboard *Liberty* were unable to defend America's reign, which brought to an end the longest winning streak in the history of any sport.

Therefore, when Conner took on *Kookaburra III* four years later, he was determined to get the cup back and did so in fine style with a 4-0 whitewash in the best-of-seven series.

Having previously won the America's Cup in 1974 and 1980, Conner's success made it a personal hat-trick, and he went on to claim the trophy again in 1988. That was not enough, though, but he went on to lose again in 1995 to New Zealand challenger *Black Magic*.

Conner was three times US Yachtsman of the Year, and claimed a bronze medal at the 1976 Olympic Games.

Born: 16 December 1942
Place of birth: California, USA
Event: Tempest Class
Olympic medals: Bronze 1976

Opposite: Dennis Connor, right, receives a model depicting the hull of *Stars and Stripes* from Donald Trump, during a reception for the winning crew, 1987.

Dramatic Rescue

British Sailor Survives Five Days in Freezing Water

1997

The media had assumed that Tony Bullimore was dead when the 55-year-old sailor's boat *Exide Challenger* capsized 800 km (500 miles) from Antarctica during the 1996 Vendee Globe race.

In such cold waters, survival could normally be counted in minutes when wearing normal clothes. As it was the Bristol-born sailor had to wait five days for the Australian Navy to cover the 3,200 km (2,000 miles) to mount a rescue – surely too long for survival. But incredibly, when one of the Navy seamen tapped on the upturned yacht, there was a tap back. Bullimore, who had luckily been wearing his survival suit, had made a perch for himself from an upturned bunk and retrieved his emergency rations from the wrecked hull. When he was rescued, he was attempting to drill a hole in the upturned hull in order to rig up an emergency radio antenna. It was then that he heard the tap, swam under the boat and greeted a burly Chief Petty Officer with a kiss on the lips.

Bullimore lost two toes to frostbite and took months to regain feeling in his hands and feet, but lost none of his passion for sailing. Within three months, he was racing in the Round Europe Race.

Opposite: Tony Bullimore alive and well aboard the *HMAS Adelaide* with Thierry Dubois and the Australian rescue crew, 10 January 1997.

Magic MacArthur

Female Sailor Breaks Global Record

2005

When Frenchman Francis Joyon smashed the round-the-world sailing record by 20 days in 2004, he would surely never have predicted that his feat would be bettered the following year.

In February 2005, however, against all predictions, he watched Ellen MacArthur take the record and complete one of the most incredible achievements in sailing history by navigating the world in 71 days, 14 hours and 18 minutes.

MacArthur had braved icebergs in the South Atlantic, sailed over a whale and survived enormous swells in the Pacific. On her return, she became the youngest ever Dame Commander of the Order of the British Empire, following in the footsteps of Sir Francis Drake and Sir Francis Chichester, and was second to David Beckham in the BBC's Sports Personality of the Year award.

It was, quite simply, a phenomenal achievement that few had thought possible when she set off in November 2004. 'I always believed I could break the record,' she said after finishing. 'But I really didn't think I would do it at the first attempt. The whole South Atlantic was terrible and it has just been one big draining event from there onwards.'

Opposite: Ellen MacArthur celebrates her achievement as the fastest person to sail solo around the world without stopping.

Authors and Contributors

Mark Ryan (Football, Rugby) has been a sports journalist for more than 20 years, and has worked with virtually every British national newspaper. He is also a media trainer. Ryan's first book, *Tie-Break!*, charted the rise of Justine Henin-Hardenne to the very top of women's tennis.

Tony Stevens (American Football) is a sports reporter at Hayters, specializing in football.

Toby Skinner (Aussie Rules, Hockey, Gaelic Football) has written sports features for a number of national newspapers, and major magazines.

Andrew Sleight (Baseball, Basketball) is a sports journalist at Hayters, he has written books on football and rugby.

Sam Peters (Cricket) is Hayters' rugby union and cricket correspondent. He is a keen collector of, and contributor to, sports books.

Ben Hunt (Golf) is a football and golf journalist with Hayters. He has covered football matches and golf events across the world for the international press.

James Goldman (Tennis, Cricket, Athletics) has worked as a sports writer at both the Racing Post and The Sportsman covering a vast array of sports.

Chris Hughes (Snooker, Darts, Athletics) has worked for various national newspapers and websites.

Simon Vincent (Gymnastics, Swimming) has seen his work printed in numerous national newspapers. At Hayters, Simon covers Premiership football clubs Arsenal and Watford as well as a number of other sports.

James Pilliger (Motorsport, Horse Racing) has written extensively for magazines and newspapers about horse racing and sports betting.

Alan Wilson (Boxing) has covered many major sporting events in football, rugby, cricket, snooker and boxing, in his career at Hayters.

Jonathan Mckeith (Strength Sports, Winter Sports) reports on a wide range of sports from Judo to Stock Car Racing.

Marisa Meier (Sailing) is a Sports Broadcast Journalist. She was raised around the sport of sailing in Austin, Texas.

Neil Martin (contributor and sub-editor) has been a sports journalist, specializing in football, for the past ten years – during which time he has written for national and international newspapers and leading magazines. A lifelong Liverpool fan, he was in Istanbul as the Reds lifted their fifth European Cup against AC Milan in 2005.

Ian Cruise (sub-editor) has been covering football and other sports for national and international newspapers and magazines for 20 years. He has also written and contributed to several books.

Index

Page numbers in *italics* refer to picture captions

A
Ablett, Gary 130
AC Milan 74
Affirmed (racehorse) 422
Agassi, Andre 256
Ajax 42
Akron Pros 106
Aldaniti (racehorse) 424
Ali, Muhammad (formerly Cassius Clay) 456, 460
Alonso, Fernando 406
Ambrose, Curtly 184
American football
    1920s 106
    1930s 108
    1960s 110–15
    1970s 116
    1980s 118–21
    1990s 122–25
America's Cup (sailing) 508, 516, 518
Anders, Elizabeth 234
Andretti, Mario 390
Anmer (racehorse) 410
Argentina (football) 24, 52
Armstrong, Lance 438
Ascot (horse racing) 432
Ashes (cricket) 162, 166, 172, 174, 190, 192
Atherton, Michael 180
athletics
    19th century 298
    1910s 300
    1920s 302
    1930s 304–7
    1940s 308

    1950s 310–13
    1960s 314–23
    1970s 324–27
    1980s 328–37
    1990s 338–51
    2000s 352–55
Australia (cricket) 160, 162, 166, 174, 188, 190
Australia (rugby league) 92, 100
Australia (rugby union) 96, 104
Australia (sailing) 516
Australia (swimming) 506
Australian (Aussie) Rules Football 126–33
Azinger, Paul *218*

B
'Babe' Ruth *see* George Ruth
Bahr, Walter *18*
Bailey, Donovan 350
Ballesteros, Seve 214
Baltimore Colts 114
Bannister, Roger 312
Barbarians 90
Barr, Charlie 510
baseball 138–45
basketball 146–59
Batchelor, Steve *232*
Baumann, Dieter 340
Bayern Munich 64
Beamon, Bob 320
Beckenbauer, Franz 58
Becker, Boris 248
Belov, Aleksandr *150*
Benn, Nigel 470

Bikila, Abebe 314
Blankers-Koen, Fanny 308
bobsleigh 494–95
bodybuilding 474–75, 480–81
Bolton Wanderers 16
Bonds, Barry 144
Borg, Bjorn 244
Botham, Ian 174
boxing
    1910s 442
    1920s 444
    1930s 446
    1950s 448–51
    1960s 452–55
    1970s 456–61
    1980s 462–67
    1990s 468–73
Boycott, Geoff 172
Brabham, Jack 382
Bradman, Don 160
Brazil (football) 20, 40, 62
Breeders' Cup Mile (horse racing) 428
Brehme, Andreas 58
Bristow, Eric 286
British Lions (rugby union) 88
British Open (golf) 214
Buffalo All-Americans 106
Buffalo Bills 116
Bullimore, Tony 520
Busby Babes 30
Button, Dick 484

C
Cacho, Fermin 338
Calzaghe, Joe 470
Carling, Will 98

Carlton, Australia 128
Carson, Willie 418
Celtic Football Club 36
Challenge Cup Finals (rugby league) 82
Chamberlain, Wilt 146
Champion, Bob 424
Champions League/European Cup (football) 36, 38, 42, 64, 72, 74
Chicago Bulls 156, 158
Chichester, Francis 512
Christie, Linford 342
Clay, Cassius (later Muhammad Ali) 454
Coe, Sebastian 328, 348
Collingwood, Australia 128
Collins, Steve 470
Comaneci, Nadia 358
Compton, Denis 164
Conner, Dennis 518
Cooper, Henry 454
cricket
    1930s 160–63
    1940s 164
    1950s 166
    1960s 168–71
    1970s 172
    1980s 174–77
    1990s 178–85
    2000s 190–93
cross-country skiing 496–97
Cruyff, Johan 44
cycling 434–39
Czechoslovakia (ice hockey) 486

D

Daehlie, Björn 496
Dallas Cowboys 110
darts 286–95
Davis, Joe *264*
Davis, Steve 268, 274
Davison, Emily 410
Dawes, John *88*
Dawson, Len *112*
De La Hoya, Oscar 466
de Nooijer, Teun Floris 236
Dean, Christopher
    (Torvill and Dean) 492
Dempsey, Jack 442, 444
Denver Broncos *108, 120*
The Derby (horse racing)
    410, 412–15
Dettori, Frankie 432
Devon Loch (racehorse)
    416
Di Maggio, Joe 142
di Stefano, Alfredo 24
diving 504–5
Doherty, Ken 278
d'Oliveira, Basil 'Dolly'
    168
Douglas, James 'Buster'
    468
Duckham, David *86*

E

Ederle, Gertrude 500
Edrich, Bill 164
Edwards, Duncan 30
Edwards, Gareth 90
Edwards, Jonathan 344
Elway, John 120
England (cricket) 160,
    162, 166, 168, 174,
    178, 190
England (football) 18, 34,
    56, 60, 68
England (rugby union) 84,
    86, 96, 98, 104

Epsom Derby (horse
    racing) 408, 414,
    418, 426
Esha Ness (racehorse)
    430
Eubank, Chris 470
European Cup (football)
    see Champions League
European Football
    Championships (Euro)
    60, 72

F

FA Cup Finals (football)
    16, 28
Faldo, Nick 222
Fangio, Juan Manuel 380
Farmer, Graham 'Polly'
    126
Federer, Roger 260
figure skating 484–85,
    492–93
Firpo, Luis Angel 444
Five Nations Championship
    (rugby union) 78, 84
Fleck, Jack 198
Flowers, Tim *60*
football
    1920s 16
    1950s 18–31
    1960s 34–39
    1970s 40–43
    1980s 46–55
    1990s 56–65
    2000s 66–75
Foreman, George 458,
    460
Fosbury, Dick 322
France (football) 48, 66
France (rugby union) 78
Frazier, Joe 456, 458
Freeman, Cathy 352
French Open (tennis)
    246, 250

G

Gaelic football 134–35
Gascoigne, Paul 'Gazza'
    56
Germany (football) 58
    see also West Germany
Gilmour, Lee *100*
Golden Globe (sailing) 514
golf
    19th century 194
    1940s 196
    1950s 198–201
    1960s 202–203
    1970s 204–11
    1980s 212–17
    1990s 218–25
    2000s 228–31
Gonzales, Pancho 240
Gooch, Graham 178
The Grand National
    (horse racing) 416, 420,
    424, 430
Grand Prix (motor racing)
    372, 374, 380,
    394, 398
Grand Prix (snooker) 284
Grand Slams (rugby union)
    98
Grand Slams (tennis) 238
Great Britain (hockey) 232
Great Britain (rugby
    league) 100
Greece (football) 72
Green, Hubert 210
Green Bay Packers *112*
Griffith-Joyner, Florence
    'Flo-Jo' 336
gymnastics 356–67

H

Hagler, Marvin 462, 464
Hakkinen, Mika 400
Hancock, Andy 84
Hearns, Thomas 462

Hendry, Stephen 276
Heysel Stadium Disaster
    (1985) 48, 50
Hick, Graeme 176
Higgins, John 284
Hillsborough Disaster
    (1989) 54
hockey 232–37
    see also ice hockey
Hogan, Ben 198
Holmes, Kelly 354
Holyfield, Evander 472
horse racing
    1900s 408
    1910s 410
    1950s 412–17
    1970s 418–23
    1980s 424–27
    1990s 428–33
Hungary (football) 22, 26
Hunslet 82
Hutton, Len 162

I

ice hockey 486–87,
    490–91
India (cricket) 178, 182
Inter Milan 36
Irish Sweeps Derby
    (horse racing) 426
Italy (football) 46, 70

J

Jacklin, Tony 206
Jamaica (bobsleigh) 494
Jenner, Bruce 324
Jhadhav, Khashaba 476
John, Barry *88*
Johnson, Earvin 'Magic'
    152
Johnson, Mark *490*
Johnson, Michael 346,
    350
Jordan, Michael 154, 156